Palgrave Macmillan Studies in Banking and Financial Institutions

Series Editor: **Professor Philip Molyneux**

The Palgrave Macmillan Studies in Banking and Financial Institutions are international in orientation and include studies of banking within particular countries or regions, and studies of particular themes such as Corporate Banking, Risk Management, Mergers and Acquisitions, etc. The books focus on research and practice, and include up-to-date and innovative studies on contemporary topics in banking that have global impact and influence.

Titles include:

Yener Altunbaş, Blaise Gadanecz and Alper Kara
SYNDICATED LOANS
A Hybrid of Relationship Lending and Publicly Traded Debt

Yener Altunbaş, Alper Kara and Özlem Olgu
TURKISH BANKING
Banking under Political Instability and Chronic High Inflation

Elena Beccalli
IT AND EUROPEAN BANK PERFORMANCE

Paola Bongini, Stefano Chiarlone and Giovanni Ferri *(editors)*
EMERGING BANKING SYSTEMS

Santiago Carbó, Edward P.M. Gardener and Philip Molyneux
FINANCIAL EXCLUSION

Allessandro Carretta, Franco Fiordelisi and Gianluca Mattarocci *(editors)*
NEW DRIVERS OF PERFORMANCE IN A CHANGING FINANCIAL WORLD

Violaine Cousin
BANKING IN CHINA

Franco Fiordelisi and Philip Molyneux
SHAREHOLDER VALUE IN BANKING

Hans Genberg and Cho-Hoi Hui
THE BANKING CENTRE IN HONG KONG
Competition, Efficiency, Performance and Risk

Carlo Gola and Alessandro Roselli
THE UK BANKING SYSTEM AND ITS REGULATORY AND SUPERVISORY FRAMEWORK

Elisabetta Gualandri and Valeria Venturelli *(editors)*
BRIDGING THE EQUITY GAP FOR INNOVATIVE SMEs

Munawar Iqbal and Philip Molyneux
THIRTY YEARS OF ISLAMIC BANKING
History, Performance and Prospects

Kimio Kase and Tanguy Jacopin
CEOs AS LEADERS AND STRATEGY DESIGNERS
Explaining the Success of Spanish Banks

M. Mansoor Khan and M. Ishaq Bhatti
DEVELOPMENTS IN ISLAMIC BANKING
The Case of Pakistan

Mario La Torre and Gianfranco A. Vento
MICROFINANCE

Philip Molyneux and Munawar Iqbal
BANKING AND FINANCIAL SYSTEMS IN THE ARAB WORLD

Philip Molyneux and Eleuterio Vallelado *(editors)*
FRONTIERS OF BANKS IN A GLOBAL WORLD

Anastasia Nesvetailova
FRAGILE FINANCE
Debt, Speculation and Crisis in the Age of Global Credit

Dominique Rambure and Alec Nacamuli
PAYMENT SYSTEMS
From the Salt Mines to the Board Room

Catherine Schenk *(editor)*
HONG KONG SAR's MONETARY AND EXCHANGE RATE CHALLENGES
Historical Perspectives

Andrea Schertler
THE VENTURE CAPITAL INDUSTRY IN EUROPE

Alfred Slager
THE INTERNATIONALIZATION OF BANKS

Noel K. Tshiani
BUILDING CREDIBLE CENTRAL BANKS
Policy Lessons for Emerging Economies

Palgrave Macmillan Studies in Banking and Financial Institutions
Series Standing Order ISBN 978-1-4039-4872-4

You can receive future titles in this series as they are published by placing a standing order. Please contact your bookseller or, in case of difficulty, write to us at the address below with your name and address, the title of the series and the ISBN quoted above.

Customer Services Department, Macmillan Distribution Ltd, Houndmills, Basingstoke, Hampshire RG21 6XS, England

Payment Systems

From the Salt Mines to the Board Room

Dominique Rambure

and

Alec Nacamuli

palgrave
macmillan

Softcover reprint of the hardcover 1st edition 2008 978-0-230-20250-4

First published 2008 by
PALGRAVE MACMILLAN

Palgrave Macmillan in the UK is an imprint of Macmillan Publishers Limited, registered in England, company number 785998, of Houndmills, Basingstoke, Hampshire RG21 6XS.

Palgrave Macmillan in the US is a division of St Martin's Press LLC, 175 Fifth Avenue, New York, NY 10010.

Palgrave Macmillan is the global academic imprint of the above companies and has companies and representatives throughout the world.

ISBN 971-1-349-30055-6 ISBN 978-0-230-22721-7 (eBook)
DOI 10.1057/9780230227217

This book is printed on paper suitable for recycling and made from fully managed and sustained forest sources. Logging, pulping and manufacturing processes are expected to conform to the environmental regulations of the country of origin.

A catalogue record for this book is available from the British Library.

Library of Congress Cataloging-in-Publication Data
Rambure, Dominique.
Payment systems : from the salt mines to the board room / Dominique Rambure, Alec Nacamuli.
p. cm. – (Palgrave Macmillan studies in banking and financial institutions)
Includes bibliographical references and index.

1. Payment. 2. Clearinghouses (Banking). 3. Banks and banking, Central. I. Nacamuli, Alec, 1943– II. Title.
HG1692.R34 2008
332.1'78—dc22 2008026093

10 9 8 7 6 5 4 3 2 1
17 16 15 14 13 12 11 10 09 08

Transferred to Digital Printing 2010

To our families

'In the theory of money, it is curious and worth noting that its usage was first considered progress and that, once it existed, getting rid of it was considered further progress.'

Léon Walras (1834–1910) *Théorie de la circulation et de la monnaie (1900)*

Contents

Part V Banks and the Payments Business

Part VI The Future

List of Figures

List of Tables

Acknowledgements

Our thanks first to Gerard Hartsink, Chairman of the European Payments Council (EPC), who honoured us by agreeing to write the foreword to this book.

We are indebted to many colleagues, former colleagues and friends who helped us invaluably by providing information, clarifying points of detail, reviewing portions of the text, correcting errors and suggesting improvements. We are particularly grateful to Vincent Bonnier, Charles Bryant, Neil Burton, Sean Daly, Nicolas de Seze, Filipe dos Santos, Roger Gate, Eliot Heilpern, Peter Jones, Raymond Mulhern, Blanche Petre, Paul Smee, Sophie Tacchi, Masayuki (Mike) Tagai and Ruth Wandhöfer.

Above all we wish to thank our families who supported us in spite of total neglect during the final weeks of writing.

DOMINIQUE RAMBURE
ALEC NACAMULI

Foreword

Payment systems are an important building block of the economic and financial system. Every day consumers, businesses and public administrations pay or receive money for the delivery of goods and services, as compensation for work executed, for buying and selling shares or for taxes and social benefits.

Suppliers of goods and services have more and more customers in multiple markets. Consumers also spend a substantial proportion of their income outside their home country. These economic and social developments impact the requirements for our future payment systems.

The launch of the euro in 1999 made it clear that a restructuring of the payment systems in the euro area was unavoidable. An integrated economic area with a single currency required the same set of payment instruments that all consumers, businesses and public administrations could use to pay and receive euros within the euro area.

In addition to the economic and social evolution, technology is a catalyser to rethink the structure and access channels of our payment systems. Nearly all consumers have a mobile phone and a chip card to initiate payments. Businesses sell more and more services via their web portals and have installed accounting packages and ERP systems to manage their physical and financial supply chains, inventory and accounts payable and receivable.

Public authorities and banks in Europe, the US, Russia, Brazil, China and Japan are rethinking the future of payment systems within their communities and the global economy. A consensus is rapidly emerging amongst regulators, banks, enterprises and technology vendors that there are no fundamental differences any more in requirements between domestic and international payments. All stakeholders would benefit from migrating to the same standards for domestic and cross-border payments in any currency.

This book by Alec Nacamuli and Dominique Rambure is a positive and timely contribution to the dialogue on the future of payments, taking into account the requirements of users and service providers in the light of technological progress. I recommend all managers who have an interest in payment systems and the financial supply chain to take note of this contribution to the payments industry.

GERARD HARTSINK
Chair – European Payments Council
Senior Executive Vice President, Global Transaction Services, Payment and Market Infrastructures, ABN AMRO Bank

Commonly Used Abbreviations and Acronyms

ABE/EBA	see EBA
ACH	Automated Clearing House
AML	Anti Money Laundering
ARC	Accounts Receivable Cheque Conversion
ATM	Automated Teller Machine
B2B	Business to Business
B2C	Business to Consumer
B2G	Business to Government
BaFin	Bundesaufsichtsamt fuer Finanziellen Instituten (Germany)
BIC	Bank Identifier Code
BIS	Bank for International Settlements, Basel
CCP	Central Counterparty
CET	Central European time
CHIPS	Clearing House Interbank Payments System (US)
CLS	Continuous Linked Settlement
CNAPS	Chinese National Advanced Payment System
CNP	Card not Present
CPSS	Committee on Payment and Settlement Systems (BIS)
CRM	Customer Relationship Management
CSD	Central Securities Depository
CSM	Clearing and Settlement Mechanism
CTF	Counter Terrorist Finance
DNS	Deferred Net System
DSO	Days Sales Outstanding
DVP	Delivery versus Payment
EACHA	European Automated Clearing Houses Association
EBA/ABE	Euro Banking Association – Association Bancaire pour l'Euro
EBPP	Electronic Bill Presentment and Payment
EC	European Commission
ECB	European Central Bank, Frankfurt
EEA	European Economic Area
EIPP	Electronic Invoice Presentment and Payment

EMV	Europay, MasterCard, Visa standard for chip card
EPC	European Payments Council
ERP	Enterprise Resource Planning system
ESCB	European System of Central Banks
ET	Eastern Time (US)
EU	European Union
Eurosystem	European System of Central Banks
FIFO	First-in-first-out
FOP	Free of Payment
FSA	Financial Services Authority (UK)
FX	Foreign Exchange
FXYCS	Foreign Exchange Yen Clearing System (Japan)
IBAN	International Bank Account Number
ICS	International Card Schemes
ICSD	International Central Securities Depository
IRD	Image Replacement Document
ISD	Investment Services Directive
KYC	Know your Customer
MICR	Magnetic Ink Character Recognition
MiFID	Markets in Financial Instruments Directive
NFC	Near Field Communication
NSS	National Settlement Service (US)
OCC	Office of the Controller of the Currency (US)
OCR	Optical Character Recognition
OFAC	Office of Foreign Asset Control
OTC	Over The Counter
PBOC	People's Bank of China
PCI DSS	Payment Card Industry Data Security Standard
PE-ACH	Pan European Automated Clearing House
PIN	Personal Identification Number
PKI	Public Key Infrastructure
POS	Point of sale
PSD	Payment Services Directive (EU)
PSP	Payment Service Provider (within PSD)
PSU	Payment Service User (within PSD)
PVP	Pay versus Pay
RFID	Radio Frequency Identification
SCF	SEPA Cards Framework
SCF	Supply Chain Financing
SCT	SEPA Credit Transfer
SDD	SEPA Direct Debit

SEC	Securities and Exchanges Commission (US)
SECA	Single Euro Cash Area Framework
SEPA	Single Euro Payments Area
SIPS	Systemically Important Payment System
SLA	Service level agreement
SME	Small and Medium Enterprise
SOA	Service Oriented Architecture
SSI	Standard Settlement Instruction
SSS	Securities Settlement System
STO	Standing Order
STP	Straight Through Processing
T2S	TARGET2-Securities
TBA	Tokyo Bankers Association
UPIC	Universal Payment Identification Code
VAR	Value at Risk

Introduction

On Friday 24 March 2008 the Federal Reserve granted Bear Stearns, the fifth largest investment bank in the US, a credit line for an unspecified amount through JP Morgan Chase. Rumours had been circulating for several days on the bank's solvability, in other words its ability to meet its obligations towards the clearing houses and the Fed which centralizes settlement of interbank payments in the US. For the first time since World War II, the Fed was applying a disposition which had been established following the 1929 crash and announced that it was ready to refinance the major US banks up to $400 billion (half its balance sheet). In practice, it agreed to purchase illiquid assets that were weighing on the banks' balance sheets against liquid securities such as government bonds which could be rapidly negotiated to obtain the liquidity required to finalize interbank settlements. This rescue operation followed a series of concerted actions with other major central banks to halt the crisis and prevent it from spreading to other financial markets and spilling in to the global economy. On 11 March 2008, in concertation with the European Central Bank (ECB), the Bank of England, the Bank of Canada and the Swiss National Bank, the Fed made available to the US banks, asphyxiated by the monetary crisis, two credit lines, one of which was for $200 billion. On 10 January the ECB in concertation with the Fed auctioned dollar liquidities through two operations at different maturities of $10 billion each. On 12 December 2007 the same central banks had jointly offered liquidity in dollars against liquid assets such as US government bonds. On 10 August 2007 the American, European and Asian central banks injected liquidity to avoid paralysis of the money markets: $330 billion are loaned to the banks.

Interventions on a global scale for such large amounts, involving several instruments and markets (cash in many currencies and delivery of several securities such as government bonds) require speedy, efficient and reliable payment and securities settlement systems. These demand resilient and scalable infrastructures capable of rapidly transmitting information and instructions, which raise significant legal, financial, technical, regulatory and competition issues which we will attempt to examine and explain throughout this book.

'To pay' comes from the Latin 'pacare' which means 'to pacify'. It probably originated from the ancient tradition of a guilty party paying the victims of the misdeed to prevent a bloody revenge. Today we use this verb to purchase goods or services for an amount agreed to represent their perceived value, in other words 'pacify' the vendor to avoid legal proceedings! Payment systems, which ensure the circulation of money, are therefore indispensable to our lives as individuals and to the smooth functioning of the economy, allowing money to fulfil its role of accepted means of exchange.

The computer systems and telecommunication networks which constitute the technical infrastructure rely on continuously evolving technology. The liquidity necessary to ensure settlement demands instruments of varying types, amounts and maturities relying on sophisticated and liquid financial markets. The legal framework to guarantee discharge of obligation, the schemes and standards required to ensure that operations unfold safely, smoothly, rapidly and at a sustainable cost demand agreement and cooperation between the various stakeholders. Finally, regulation and oversight by authorities are mandatory to minimize risk and ensure stability. Payment and settlement systems are therefore subject to financial and technological innovation as well as consensus among human beings. Innovation is however a double-edged sword: as we learned from bitter experience from mid-2007 and up to the time of writing in early 2008, instruments created to mitigate certain risks can create others. Technological innovation can create environmental problems. But do we ever learn?

Central banks and supervisory authorities are involved in many ways. They use payment systems as a channel to implement their monetary policies and require systems enabling them to carry out rapidly their interventions and measure their impact. They are also settlement agents as sole issuer of central bank money, an asset accepted by all. Above all, they are the lenders of last resort and must therefore have at their disposal financial instruments and infrastructures enabling them to fulfil this role as quickly and reliably as possible. Finally, they have oversight over payment systems to ensure that risk is contained and that they evolve in line with financial and technical innovation.

Regulation is accelerating, often in directions that were not anticipated. The European Union and the ECB are actively pursuing the completion of the Single Market. It is in the context of providing integrated market infrastructures for the euro that we must view their sequence of services and regulation: TARGET2, SEPA and TARGET2 Securities. Banks were already subject to competition from non-financial new entrants. The European Payment Services Directive officially opens this area, in which financial institutions enjoyed a virtual monopoly, to non-financial payment service providers.

Banks were originally created to effect payments and no commercial bank can today effectively operate without offering payment services to its customers. Payments are estimated to account for up to 35 per cent of revenues and 40 per cent of costs for banks.[1] Profitability of payment services varies however from country to country and between banks in the same country depending on the payment instruments they offer, the customer segments (retail or corporate) they serve, the revenue basis (fees, interest, float) and the efficiency of their back-offices and computer systems. Pricing to end users is rarely transparent, which contributes to inertia when attempting to introduce new instruments.

A leading industry expert is fond of repeating that 'nobody wakes up in the morning thinking that he has to buy a payment'. This reminds us that a payment does not exist in isolation. It arises solely as the result of a purchase of goods or service, repayment of an obligation or the settlement of a trading operation on the financial markets. As the fees for basic payment services are forced down by regulation, competition and customer pressure and standardization is leading to commoditization, all payment service providers are seeking to develop value-added services linking the payment with the commercial transaction, information and other financial services to maintain and increase profitability.

Regulation, competition from within and from innovative new entrants, new services, consolidation: the payments and settlement business is again fascinating following a period at the end of the twentieth century when back-offices were the bank's salt mines and clearing and settlement were considered 'plumbing' and rarely discussed at Board level. This is what led us to write this book, attempting to explain the hydraulics behind the plumbing, why the salt miners are essential, as well as the business and strategic issues payments raise.

The first part of the book examines the structure of payments systems, explaining the fundamental principles, characteristics, risk and business implications of payment instruments and systems as well as their role in the economy. The second part describes the payment systems and their evolution within a historic and economic context in Europe, the US and major Asian markets. The third part looks at the settlement of foreign exchange and securities trading. The fourth part reviews what financial services do enterprises require to profitably run their business and the corporate banking services offered by banks in response. The fifth part examines the role of payments within a bank's overall strategy and the back office systems required to provide these services. Finally, the last part will attempt to forecast the direction of the payments business, how the various stakeholders will manage to maintain profitability and which are most likely to emerge as winners.

Throughout the book, we have purposely refrained from converting currency figures on account of the variations in exchange rates. A comparative table of high-value payment systems is however provided in the Appendix.

Part I
The Structure and Economics of Payment Systems

1
The Architecture of Payment Systems

Payment systems are indispensable to our lives as individuals and to the smooth functioning of the economy. They allow money to fulfil its role of accepted means of exchange when purchasing goods or services. As private persons, it is through payment systems that we receive our salaries and pay our bills. Enterprises use the same payment systems to settle invoices within the terms of their contractual relationships. Finally, financial trading activities also result in one cash leg through a payment system to purchase shares, or two for a foreign exchange deal, one in each currency.

It is difficult to trace the birth of the first payment system, but Box 1.1 at the end of this chapter describes one of the earliest.

A payment system includes private or corporate customers, financial intermediaries, generally commercial banks, and central banks, linked by telecommunication networks transmitting information between computer systems. It is important to understand the roles and responsibilities of each to reach the optimum balance between speed, efficiency, cost, security and economic safety. On the other hand, each participant is driven by its own objectives which are often contradictory. Can speed be increased without impacting costs? Can costs be reduced without creating opportunities for fraud? Each payment system reflects therefore a compromise depending on the participants, the speed of execution and level of security required and, last but not least, the risk posed by the amounts involved. These will determine the most appropriate operating mode, legal framework, security level and technology. Payment systems operate in a competitive environment and technological innovation is one of the most important drivers in the evolution of payment, chip cards being one of the most obvious examples.

This opening chapter will attempt to define and describe some fundamental concepts which will enable readers to understand the rationale behind the various payment instruments and systems described.

1 Introduction and basic concepts

'A payment system consists of a set of instruments, banking procedures and, typically, interbank funds transfer systems that ensure the circulation of money'[1] and normally requires:

- a payment instrument, for example cash, a cheque, an electronic funds transfer, a credit or debit card;
- scheme rules defining the procedures, practices and standards agreed between the payment service providers;
- a transfer mechanism; and
- a legal framework to guarantee irrevocable and unconditional finality, that is the discharge of the obligation between debtor and creditor.

It is particularly important to distinguish between the information relevant to the payment and the final transfer of value. If you settle a purchase in cash for instance, your debt is immediately extinguished. If, however, you remit a cheque, the vendor will need to clear the cheque to ensure that the drawer has sufficient funds (or credit line) on his account for the cheque to be honoured (that it will not 'bounce') which can sometimes take a few days.

The participants in a non-cash payment system include at least service providers, generally banks, which effect the payment on behalf of the debtor and remit the funds to the creditor, and a settlement agent that discharges the obligation as shown in Figure 1.1

The role of settlement agent is normally assumed by the central bank for the relevant currency, which transfers funds between accounts held with it by the commercial banks, known as 'settlement in central bank money' which guarantees unconditional and irrevocable settlement. As shown in Figure 1.1, we see that the debtor would still be liable if his bank fails even after debiting his account. He is however no longer liable if the creditor's bank fails after its account has been credited by the central bank. The time interval between the moment at which the debtor's account is debited and the funds are made available to the creditor is known as the *float*.

As the volumes of payments grew (and we are talking nowadays about tens of millions of payments daily in an advanced economy) it was

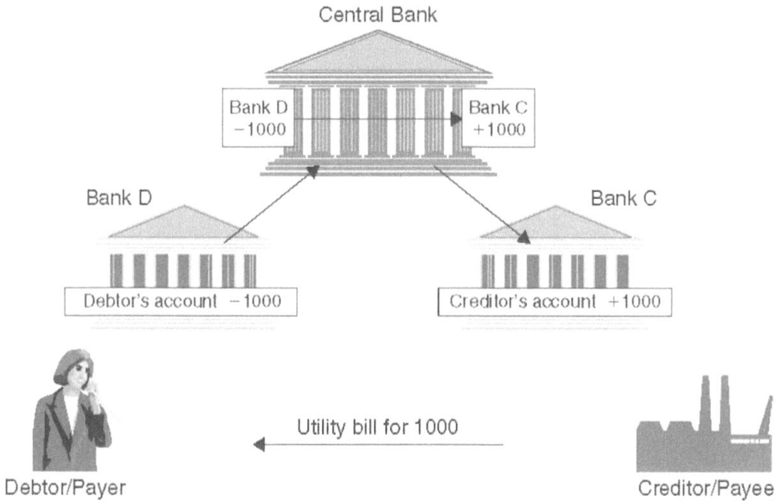

Figure 1.1 Settlement and discharge of obligation

no longer possible to settle each payment gross in central bank money as described above. It became therefore necessary to introduce Automated Clearing Houses (ACH) which perform the clearing, defined as 'the process of transmitting, reconciling and, in some cases, confirming payment orders or security transfer instructions prior to settlement, possibly including the netting of instructions and the establishment of final positions for settlement'[2] (see Figure 1.2).

Banks send batches of payments to the ACH which, after sorting and merging, sends the banks details of payments for their customers. It also calculates and transmits the net positions between the banks to the settlement agent (normally the central bank) which transfers the net amounts between the settlement accounts of the participating banks, therefore assuring final settlement for all payments in that cycle. It is therefore important to distinguish between clearing, which is a set of processes, and settlement which is an event which guarantees the discharge of the debts which takes place when the central bank transfers the funds between the accounts of the debtors' and the creditors' banks.

Clearing Houses would settle at the end of the day. As the value of payments grew, reaching trillions of dollars daily (1 trillion = 1 million millions = 10^{12}), central banks became concerned that a bank could default on its obligation at the end of the day. This *intraday (or daylight) risk* could easily generate *systemic risk* 'the risk that the failure of

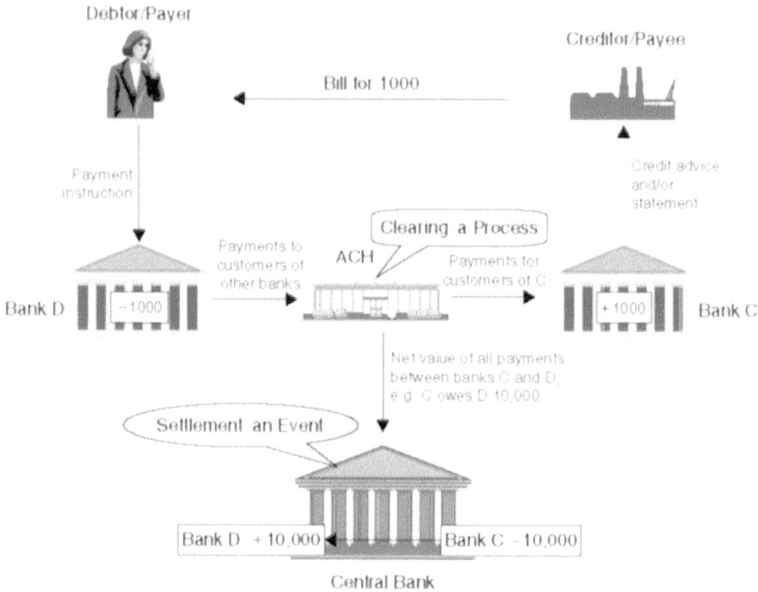

Figure 1.2 The clearing and settlement chain

one participant in a transfer system, or in financial markets generally, to meet its required obligations will cause other participants or financial institutions to be unable to meet their obligations (including settlement obligations in a transfer system) when due'.[3] Central banks imposed therefore that large value transactions had to be settled gross (without netting) as they are initiated, giving birth to Real-time Gross Settlement Systems (RTGS) which debit and credit the banks' accounts at the central bank in real-time, providing instant irrevocable finality. These systems normally process a relatively small amount of large-value payments: in the UK for instance, the CHAPS sterling RTGS system accounted in 2006 for 90 per cent of non-cash payment values (in £s) as opposed to only 0.2 per cent of the volume (number) of non-cash payments![4]

This move to RTGS for the large-value payments resulted in dramatic changes in the way banks manage their treasury and liquidity as shown in Figure 1.3.

For a net system settling end-of-day, it suffices for the bank to have enough liquidity to settle its end-of-day net position, its short positions (amounts it owes to other banks) being reduced by its long positions (amounts owed to it by other banks). In a RTGS system, the balance on

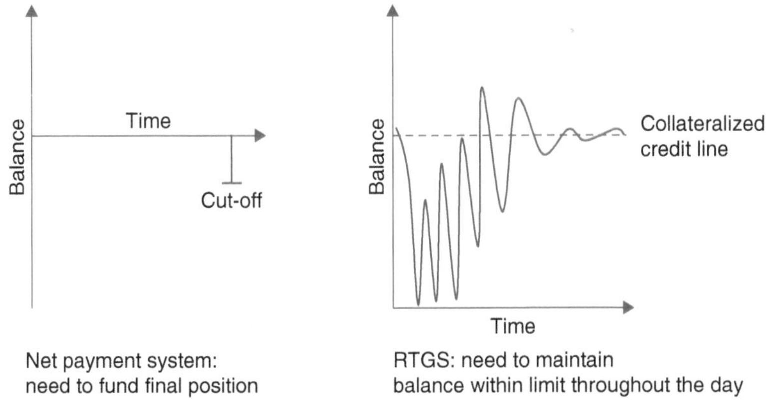

Figure 1.3 Intraday liquidity management is essential in a RTGS environment

its settlement account with the central bank will fluctuate according to the payments it sends and receives. Central banks, no longer willing to act as 'lender of last resort', will only grant credit facilities to the commercial banks against collateral, normally securities on deposit or repurchase agreements (repos), which represents an opportunity cost to the banks who cannot trade them. Payments which cannot be effected because they would breach the credit limit are queued, therefore delayed, awaiting incoming payments or a further injection of liquidity. Banks must therefore manage their liquidity carefully during the day, seeking to minimize the collateral posted to secure credit facilities. We will see in section 3.3 of this chapter how RTGS systems have evolved to optimize liquidity.

Payment systems generally operate during pre-determined opening hours; most important is the *cut-off time* beyond which payments received will not be processed and are carried over until the next working day.

2 Participants in a payment system

2.1 The banks

Banks are the compulsory intermediates between users and payment systems as they hold a license to take deposits and effect payments for which they are subjected to regulation. They maintain accounts on behalf of their customers which are debited or credited when a payment is effected or funds are received.

If a payment is effected between two accounts held by the same bank, the amount will be transferred between the debtor's and the creditor's accounts. These *intrabank* payments, known as 'on us' or 'book entry' payments, do not affect the bank's overall treasury position. If, however, the creditor's account is held by a different financial institution this *interbank* payment results in a debt between the two banks which has to be settled through correspondent accounts (accounts held by banks with each other) or a payment system, which impacts the treasury, liquidity and risk positions of both banks.

Although access to most payment systems is restricted to banks, several disintermediation factors have emerged over the past 10 years.

Legal: Deposit taking is a regulated activity subject to minimum capital requirements, deposit insurance and supervision by a national regulatory authority, for instance the Financial Services Authority (FSA) in the UK, The Federal Reserve System in the US, or the Banque de France in France. However, the banks' monopoly on payments is gradually eroding. The recently enacted Payment Services Directive (PSD) in the EU allows non-banks to offer payments services; these payment institutions will be subject to much lighter regulatory requirements (see ch. 6 sec. 2).

Functional: Non-banking payment systems operate with or without the involvement of banks. Most multinational corporations operate internal payment and netting systems for transfers between their different national subsidiaries and/or affiliated legal entities to reduce banking fees and float. They will also operate treasury and financing subsidiaries in tax-efficient locations, often with limited banking licences, for internal netting, balance optimization and often, trading in foreign exchange, debt instruments and derivatives. In the best cases, banks intervene to provide access to payment systems and/or to manage net balances.

Commercial: Several closed payment systems operate in every country, particularly stored-value prepaid cards offered by transport authorities (for instance Oyster in London, MetroCard in New York, Navigo in Paris) and mobile phone operators. Other organizations (for instance Western Union and MoneyGram) offer cross-border low value transfers, known as remittances, to migrant workers sending money to their families back home (see ch. 3 sec. 4). Store and supermarket chains, which until recently just offered store cards accepted only by their outlets, now offer credit cards co-branded with Visa or MasterCard thereby gaining universal acceptance: banks are losing out on the fees and the interest on outstanding balances. Again, it should be noted that the processes and IT systems required to operate these schemes are often subcontracted to banks or payments processors.

Technical: The internet and mobile telephony have enabled a host of parallel payment systems to flourish and disintermediate the banks. PayPal, building on the success of the on-line auction system eBay, is gaining its market share in the person-to-person (P2P) segment (see ch. 9. sec. 5). Several mobile phone operators are offering mobile payment services either independently or in cooperation with banks (see ch. 9 sec. 4). If they are not totally by-passed the banks are forced, at the very best, to share the revenues.

2.2 Membership and economics of payment systems

Membership of a clearing house or RTGS system implies meeting specific eligibility criteria as well as the implementation of procedures and IT infrastructures to comply with the operating rules and performance criteria set by the system.

Membership is often two-tiered, differentiating between *direct members* and *indirect members* – generally banks which do not meet the eligibility criteria or are unwilling to invest to comply with the technical and operational requirements. Indirect members participate by clearing and/or settling through a direct member. In this case, the direct member assumes responsibility for settling and managing the liquidity on behalf of the indirect member, activities for which direct members compete on services offered, credit lines and fees. Direct members can offer a better service to their customers: they will accept payments later, credit beneficiaries earlier and will be able to offer lower charges. Direct membership becomes a competitive advantage in addition to the benefits in terms of float and improved liquidity. These factors need to be taken into account when banks choose to join as direct or indirect members, assuming of course that they meet the eligibility criteria.

Financial eligibility criteria revolve around creditworthiness, usually capitalization and credit rating. The robustness of a payment system is directly related to that of its weakest direct member, a factor which is more important in net than in gross systems. As payment systems will inevitably include banks of varying creditworthiness, they generally offer facilities by which each bank can set limits, or caps, on other members to manage its risk towards them. An element of reciprocity can intervene in these allocations. These caps can be varied throughout the day to take into account payment volumes . . . or market rumours on a specific bank's solvability. Ultimately, a bank can reduce its cap on another bank to zero, but this drastic measure is only taken under extreme circumstances.

A related criterion is the number of payments a bank will contribute to the system. Eligibility criteria normally stipulate either a minimum number of transactions or a minimum market share in terms of value. If an indirect member's payment volumes grow, accession to direct membership will not increase the total number of payments across the system, except for the small amount which it might settle directly with its former direct member.

Each payment system sets technical and operational criteria according to the schemes it operates: messaging and file formatting standards; communication interface specifications; liquidity management; ability to respect deadlines and response times; and recovery and backup requirements in case of technical failure of the payment system itself or of the members' back-office systems. These place heavy demands in terms of investments and human resources which often cause even sizeable banks to opt for indirect membership.

Payment systems generally operate on a cost-recovery basis: revenues originating from membership fees, annual charges and transaction fees should cover operating costs and the funding of new developments. Some Clearing Houses operate on a cost-plus basis in order to generate a profit for their owners. RTGS systems operated by central banks are sometimes subsidized in the interest of risk reduction, the subsidy being euphemistically referred to as a 'public good factor'. The annual charges are usually fixed and therefore to the disadvantage of low-volume members. Transaction fees are independent of the value of the payment and generally reduce in relation to the volume of payments each member contributes to the system. In the US and particularly Europe since the advent of SEPA which allows clearing houses to offer services across borders (see ch. 6 sec. 4), competition is constantly forcing transaction fees downwards to attract new members and volumes. When a new payment system is developed, membership fees generally help fund the initial investments and launch costs. When banks seek to join an existing system, the fee should theoretically reflect the actual value of the system in operation balanced by the fact that the new member contributes payment volumes which can reduce the transaction fee and improve liquidity; these valuations are extremely complex and the pursuit of volumes to achieve economies of scale in the current competitive environment generally result in 'token' joining fees. Ultimately, the balance between these pricing components reflects the objective of the payment system owners: do they wish to expand its use or maintain it as an 'exclusive club'? Regulators however demand full transparency of pricing and participation criteria.

2.3 The settlement agent

The settlement agent manages the settlement accounts of the direct members and transfers amounts between them to achieve finality. Technically this role could be undertaken by a commercial bank or a central bank, but risk management considerations point towards the central bank which holds the monopoly for issuing legal tender: the credit and liquidity risk are theoretically nil as only the central bank can issue currency without limits or security, influenced only by macro-economic considerations such as money supply, price stability, interest or exchange rates. This has given rise to the *settlement in central bank money* doctrine which dictates that 'assets used for settlement should preferably be a claim on the central bank',[5] particularly for systemically important systems. This categorization will be explained in Chapter 4, suffice it to state at this point that all large-value systems and national ACHs are considered to be systemically important.

2.4 The central bank

As we have seen, central banks act generally as settlement agent. They also, most often, operate the large-value RTGS systems, while the private sector operates some large-value systems (for instance CHIPS in the US and the EURO1 system operated by the Euro Banking Association (EBA)) as well as virtually all low-value ACHs and card clearings. Central banks are however responsible for oversight: 'a central bank task, principally intended to promote the smooth functioning of payment systems and to protect the financial system from possible "domino effects" which may occur when one or more participants in the payment system incur credit or liquidity problems. Payment systems oversight aims at a given system (e.g. a funds transfer system) rather than individual participants'.[6] The Committee on Payment and Settlement Systems (CPSS) of the Bank for International Settlements (BIS) in Basel is the main forum where central banks cooperate internationally to issue common guidelines on oversight and managing risks in payment systems.

Although bank supervision is not always the responsibility of the central bank (for instance in the UK where it has been devolved to the FSA), it can take action against the entire banking system or individual banks. As it maintains the settlement accounts, the central bank is well positioned to monitor each bank's position in real time: balance, liquidity, number of payments queued, ability to secure funding in the money markets.

If a bank appears to be in difficulty, the central bank can secure emergency funding or, in extreme cases, suspend the bank from the payment system; this would however be a very serious decision as it could create a systemic, or 'domino' crisis which would affect the reputation of the financial marketplace. Whatever action it takes, the central bank will be open to criticism, either for intervening too late, or too early! In theory, central banks are not obligated to help a commercial bank in difficulty according to the 'moral hazard' principle; historically however, central banks have intervened in most cases to prevent a run on banks under the 'too big to fail' principle or to prevent a panic, as witnessed during the liquidity crisis since mid-2007.

Finally, central banks are also active participants in payment systems for payments between them and commercial banks and 'open market' purchase or sale of government bonds to implement their monetary policy.

2.5 The money market

The money market is an essential component of payment systems although it is not, strictly speaking, part of them. An efficient and liquid intraday (for instance repos) market, offering a variety of instruments with varied maturities, is essential for the smooth operation of a payment system as it enables the commercial banks to fund their liquidity and settlement positions. From a macro-economic viewpoint, a payment system can only function if those members of the clearing with long positions accept to lend funds to those with short positions. Some payment systems even incorporate automatic lending-borrowing facilities to facilitate settlement.

The money market would be 'perfect' if:

- all participants had access to the same information at the same time;
- no participant held a dominant share enabling it to influence liquidity and pricing (interest rates); and
- the market was sufficiently liquid.

In practice, imperfections in the market are introduced by the bilateral credit lines which limit the funds a bank is prepared to lend to another.

In addition to the interbank money market, whether directly between institutions or through brokers, the central bank can also intervene by granting credit to the commercial banks, generally end-of-day when the money market closes and dealers have squared their positions. In certain countries, this facility is known as the Discount Window, referring to the

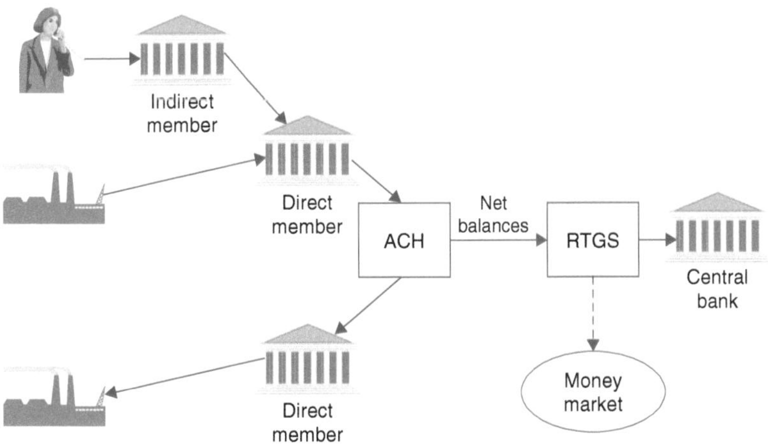

Figure 1.4 The chain of payment operations

time when banks would send representatives to a teller window at the central bank to negotiate credit facilities.

3 Payment operations

3.1 Payment initiation

The payment instrument is agreed between the payer and the beneficiary. In the case of a remote (not face-to-face) electronic payment, for instance to pay a utility bill, it could be a cheque, a credit transfer initiated by the payer or a direct debit where the beneficiary has a mandate to draw funds from the payer's account. In the case of a credit transfer, the payer will issue a payment instruction and send it to his bank. If this instruction is not in a compatible electronic form (for instance from internet banking), bank staff will input the payment details, an operation which inevitably creates the risk of transposition errors. If the payer's bank is an indirect member of the system, it will transmit the instruction to its direct member after checking the balance or credit limit of its client. The direct member then transmits the instruction to the clearing house if it is a low-value payment or to the RTGS payment system if it is a high-value payment. If this sequence of processes, see Figure 1.4, is entirely electronic with no human intervention likely to cause errors, it is known as STP (Straight Through Processing).

3.2 Clearing and ACHs

The ACH receives batches of payments from all banks which are first validated in terms of formatting and non-duplication. Some ACHs will also receive files of payments directly from corporations, for instance the payroll, which they will process subject to authorization from the account holding bank. This authorization can either be for each file, or against credit limits which the bank sets on each customer registered to use this corporate access service. Files are opened and the payments are sorted and merged into files of payments for the banks of the beneficiaries. Procedures exist to handle *returns*, payments which cannot be effected because of incorrect account numbers, closed accounts and, in the case of direct debits, insufficient funds. Some ACHs incorporate risk management procedures enabling banks to place limits on each other or imposing net debit caps on each member's overall position. Once a payment has entered the ACH, it cannot be cancelled; should this be necessary, the bank would have to ask the beneficiary's bank to initiate a reverse payment.

The ACH also calculates the net positions. These can be either bilateral between each member or multilateral (also known as net/net): the algebraic sum of the bilateral positions of each bank resulting for each into one position vis-à-vis the system: short if the bank owes money or long if it is owed funds (see Figure 1.5). Multilateral netting reduces the amounts and the number of payments each participant has to handle.

These net positions are then transmitted either to the central bank for settlement, or to the relevant RTGS system which will settle them with other high-value and systemic payments. The ACH is financially neutral as all net positions should algebraically add to zero. Clearing houses also issue reports for reconciliation and maintain audit trails and historical data for queries, investigations, billing and statistics.

These payment systems are known as Deferred Net Systems (DNS) as settlement takes place at some later time. DNS systems would generally settle end-of-day: batches were transmitted to the banks in the evening which would process them overnight and credit the beneficiaries next day if not later. Several ACHs now run multiple settlement cycles throughout the day to reduce the window of intraday risk and provide earlier availability of funds.

In the current competitive climate among ACHs, most now offer additional value-added services: back office processing for banks and corporates, queries and investigations, e-billing, mobile payments, etc.

It should be noted that some countries do not operate an ACH (for instance Australia, Germany, Ireland and Finland) in which case the

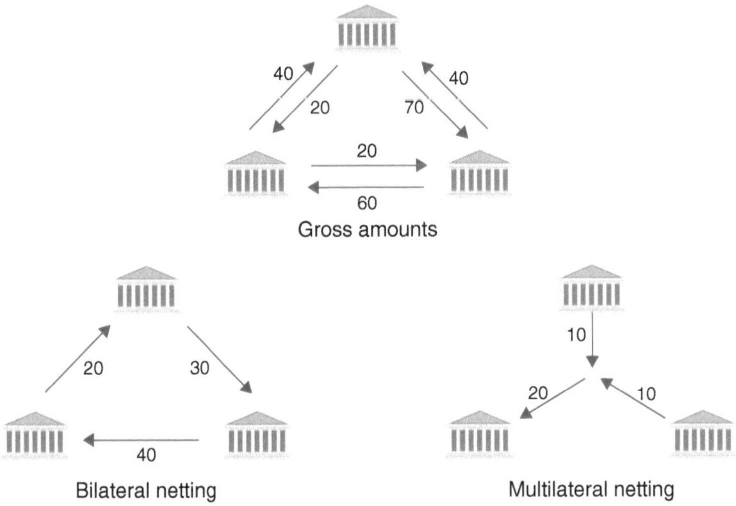

Figure 1.5 Bilateral and multilateral netting

banks exchange files of payments bilaterally, agree the net amount, and settle through the local RTGS system. The generic term Clearing and Settlement Mechanism (CSM) is therefore used to describe these operations irrespective of whether an ACH is involved or not.

3.3 RTGS systems

As briefly explained in sec. 1 of this chapter, RTGS systems, which handle a small amount of large value payments, settle payments one-by-one gross through the settlement accounts held with the central bank. Payments, after format and non-duplicate validation, are only processed if sufficient funds or credit is available at the initiating bank's settlement account. Payments which cannot be effected are queued and consequently delayed. Each bank must therefore carefully assess its liquidity requirements throughout the day:

$$\text{Liquidity} = \text{funds brought in by the bank} + \text{incoming payments} + \text{collateralized credit line negotiated with the central bank} - \text{outgoing payments.}$$

At the beginning of each day, banks will transfer funds into their settlement account and/or post the collateral required to secure the necessary credit facility. Should the queue lengthen because of insufficient incoming payments, the bank must either top-up its settlement account by transferring own funds, accessing the money market, or post additional collateral with the central bank to extend its credit line. Efficient liquidity management is essential in RTGS systems as the substantially higher cost of RTGS payments relative to ACH payments is less dependent on the processing charge than on the cost of the liquidity: interest on money market operations or the opportunity cost of immobilizing securities for collateral.

For this reason, great efforts have been deployed to implement liquidity saving features in RTGS systems:

- *Priority levels*: high level priority payments will always take precedence over lower priority payments: separate queues are maintained for each priority. The highest priority is normally reserved for payments related to operations with the central bank and the settlement of DNS payment systems, or securities clearing systems, which settle through the RTGS system (known as ancillary systems). The higher priority queue(s) are normally processed on a first-in-first-out basis (FIFO).
- *Queue management*: up until settlement, payments can be re-ordered within queues, moved between priorities or even cancelled.
- *Offsetting payments*: a lower priority payment from bank A to bank B will be delayed until a payment from bank B to bank A is presented: both payments will be submitted simultaneously so that only the difference will reduce the liquidity. RTGS systems which also include such netting facilities are known as *hybrid* payment systems.
- *Liquidity reservation*: liquidity can be set aside for high priority payments and the settlement of ancillary systems.
- *Timing of payments*: earliest and/or latest submission times can be allocated to payments, which can be changed before settlement.
- Liquidity pooling across the various subsidiaries and foreign branches of a multinational bank.

In addition, banks can limit their risk vis-à-vis other direct members by setting bilateral limits against individual banks and/or multilateral limits against groups of banks which can be changed throughout the day.

A situation may arise when the system is *gridlocked*, meaning that payments are queued because of insufficient funds on some banks' settlement accounts which, if settled, would lift the balance to allow other banks' payments to be settled. In Figure 1.6 we can see that payments are queued for banks A, B and C which, if released, would allow all to be settled. Facilities exist therefore for authorized staff at the central

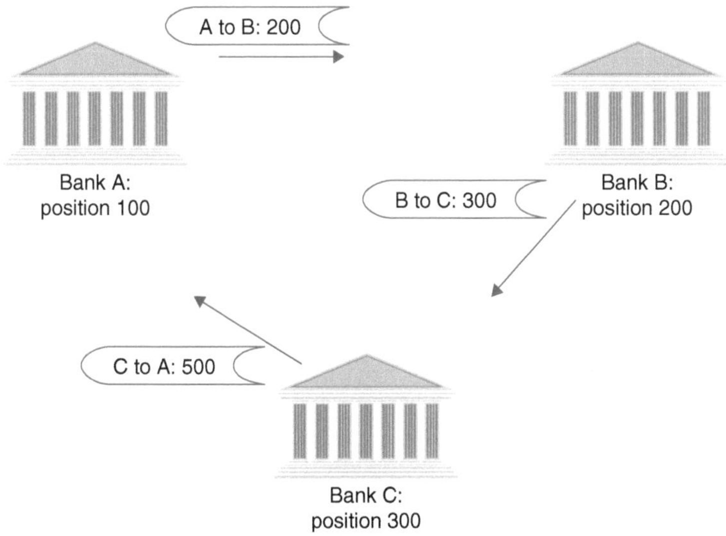

Figure 1.6 Gridlock

bank to release payments to solve the gridlock. Modern systems include automated gridlock resolution routines which allow payments to flow in most cases. Information and control facilities are also available to enable banks and the central bank to monitor balances, liquidity, limits and track progress of individual payments in real-time. RTGS systems also issue end-of-day reports for reconciliation and maintain audit trails and historical data for queries, investigations, billing and statistics.

We will see in later (ch. 6 sec. 3) how these various features operate in the euro based TARGET2 RTGS.

3.4 Communication networks

The transmission of payments and reports between customers, the banks, the ACHs, the RTGS systems and the central bank should take place over secure and resilient transmission networks. SWIFT, a bank-owned global network for financial messages and service provider (see ch. 3 sec. 2), has established itself as the preferred transmission network for large-value systems.

Several routing solutions have evolved over time in response to requirements emanating from the scheme owners, designated by the capital letter they resemble.

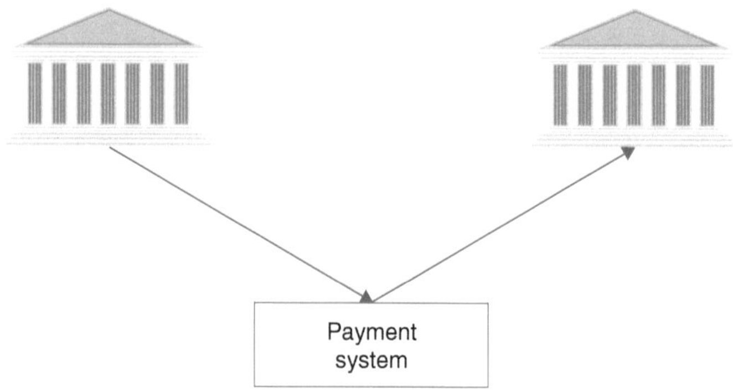

Figure 1.7 V routing

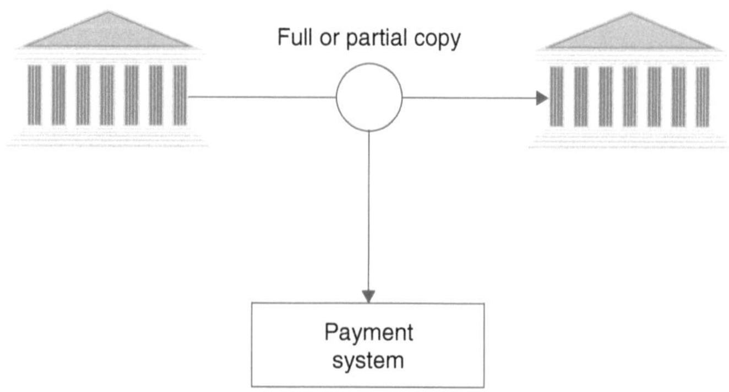

Figure 1.8 T-copy

The simplest is the V routing, whereby the payment messages are simply transmitted between the direct members and the payment system (see Figure 1.7).

In the T-copy routing, messages are sent between banks and copied to the payment system (see Figure 1.8).

The copy can either contain the full payment message, or only the information necessary for clearing and/or settlement: essentially identifiers for the payer's and beneficiary's bank and the amount; information such as the originating and beneficiary customers as well as the motive for the payment, such as an invoice reference, are not required for settlement.

The most sophisticated is the Y-copy, essentially used for RTGS systems (see Figure 1.9).

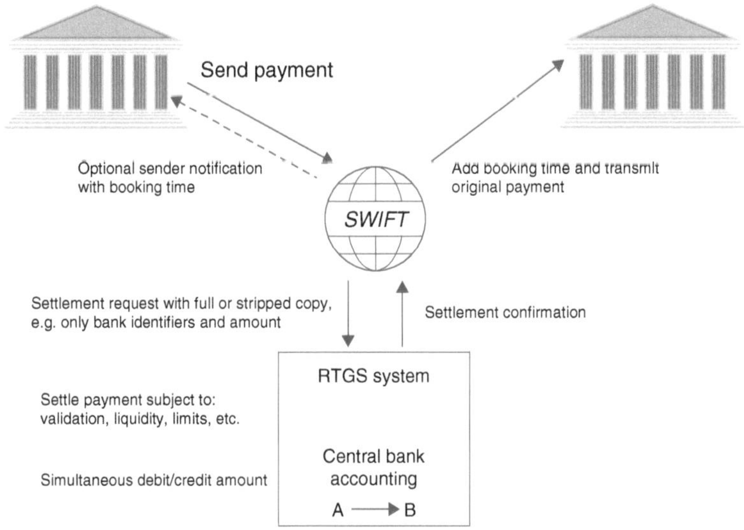

Figure 1.9 Y-copy

The message is copied to the RTGS system and held by SWIFT until settlement confirmation has been received from the RTGS system so that the receiving bank knows that the funds have been irrevocably settled.

The architectures described in this opening chapter represent the 'established order' and the paradigms prevailing until the end of the twentieth century. We will develop in subsequent chapters how these models and the payments business have evolved under global competitive pressures and regulation.

4 Standards

Standards are an important element of payment systems. They ensure that all participants can automate the process by specifying that, within a message containing payment details, each field (such as name of beneficiary, amount, etc.) can be uniquely identified and that the information is transmitted using the same format to avoid, for instance, the potential confusion created by an Englishman writing €100.60 and a Frenchman writing €100,60. Each country has developed its own standards for domestic systems while all international payments use the SWIFT standards (see ch. 3 sec. 2). The current trend is to move towards the ISO20022 standard for electronic payments, which is a methodology by which standards can be created and a framework by which standard syntaxes can be made to coexist. The adoption of the UNIFI ISO 20022 XML syntax enables interoperability between messaging standards, for instance, between those adopted for payment initiation between the bank and its customer and those for messages between banks. XML standards include a naming field (tag) and the characteristics (attributes) for each data item. The adoption of the UNIFI ISO 20022 XML syntax enables therefore interoperability between messaging standards, for instance, between those adopted for payment initiation between the bank and its customer and those for messages between banks, each application capturing the data it requires. Several payment service providers and infrastructures have developed converters between the various industry and national formats which, while easing transition, can encourage inertia.

Standards have been developed for all instruments: magnetic stripe and chip for cards, optical or magnetic character recognition as well as imaging for cheques and notes and coins for cash!

5 Efficiency criteria for payment systems

The efficiency of a payment system is generally measured by three criteria: execution time; risk; and cost.

Execution time represents a cost for the customers who do not have access to funds: this float is dependent on the interest rate and elapsed time. Risk can be quantified as the cost of the risk management procedures, such as the opportunity cost of assets immobilized by collateral requirements. Costs reflect not only the processing and infrastructure costs, but also the cost of liquidity, be it interest charges or collateral. These criteria are interdependent and are ultimately reflected in the cost, the final choice representing a trade-off: RTGS systems, for instance, minimize risk but at the cost of collateral. A high-volume retailer who operates on competition-driven margins will be more sensitive to transaction costs and might refuse to use instruments which bear high handling charges and operational overheads, such as cheques, which might wipe out the company profit. Each participant in the value chain will have its own selection criteria.

Retail customers, or individuals, are most sensitive to transaction costs, less to execution times except when needing to transfer emergency funds; the risk management costs are hidden from them.

Small and medium enterprises (SMEs) are also most sensitive to costs and execution times. Large corporations are more interested in accelerating receivables than transaction costs. This customer segment is also best positioned to negotiate fees and execution times with the banks and issue requests for competitive proposals. We will see in Part IV how the banks attempt to lock them in with cash management and other value-added services. Businesses are also, generally speaking, impervious to the risk management costs.

Commercial banks are most sensitive to the profitability of payment services: maximizing revenues and reducing overall costs. These include clearing and settlement fees, investments in infrastructure and operating expenses, as well as the cost of liquidity and collateral reflecting risk management. Certain banks specialize in payment services, seeking participation in clearing and settlement systems in several countries to accelerate execution times. They are also constantly streamlining processes and upgrading their technology to improve STP and liquidity management (see ch. 14 sec. 1). Faced with increased investments, several small and medium-sized banks are seeking to outsource their payment operations to these specialized transaction banks, which are keen to increase volumes to reduce unit processing costs through economies of scale.

Central banks are primarily concerned with risk minimization, particularly systemic risk which could destabilize the entire financial system. They have responsibility for oversight over payment systems and to promote technological innovation for risk minimization and smooth liquidity management. They also require efficient systems as a tool to implement their monetary policy, to rapidly transmit their interventions and to measure their impact.

We can see that payment systems are not neutral. They transfer funds and demand liquidity. They require heavy investments, operational discipline and resources from the commercial banks, as well as vigilance from the central banks and regulators.

Box 1.1 An international payments system during the Middle Ages: the Papacy

For security reasons, the Papacy transferred itself to Avignon, in the south of France, from 1309 to 1418. This coincided with a period of turbulence between 1378 and 1417, during which the Church was ruled by no less than four popes and anti-popes until the Council of Konstanz ended the Great Western Schism. Substantial funds and new financial collection and management systems were required to recruit mercenaries to regain the Papal States, as well as build the sumptuous

Palais des Papes. Italian popes often came from merchant and banking families and were therefore fully aware of the latest financing techniques. They would appoint a senior Church official, experienced in banking and payment networks, to manage the Papacy's finances. The Church would maintain a network of tax collectors extending to the most remote regions: Poland, Scandinavia, the Levant, etc., so funds had to be repatriated to Rome or Avignon. As physical transportation was too dangerous, the Papacy would contract with the great Italian merchant and banking families such as the Medici or the Bardi. The pontifical tax collectors would remit the taxes into the foreign branches of the bankers, who would make them available (minus a pre-agreed commission) to the Papacy in Rome or Avignon by using the funds deposited with them by the Church dignitaries and members of the Curia. They would use the funds collected locally to purchase goods, such as wool from England which was sold to the Florentine weavers for the sumptuous cloths and robes we see today in the portraits by Holbein and Titian. The bankers ensured the safe availability of funds collected remotely, the settlement and the foreign exchange, all sources of fees.

2
Payment Instruments

Buyer and Seller must first agree on a payment instrument, be it cash, cheque, card or electronic. These various instruments are the 'raw materials' of payment systems and have evolved in response to demands for ease of use, cost reduction, security and more information, as well as technological progress.

1 Characteristics of payment instruments

The choice of a payment instrument represents a compromise between the various counterparties based on consideration of the features and benefits:

- ease of use and convenience for the debtor or the creditor;
- terms, conditions and execution time: the beneficiary, in particular, wishes to know when the funds are available for him to draw upon;
- ease of automation, not only for processing the payment but also transmitting the reason for the payment, or remittance information, to facilitate reconciliation;
- costs, in terms of fees charged to the initiator and/or the beneficiary, as well as processing costs to the service providers including the cost of liquidity;
- security, expressed in terms of authenticity, confidentiality and integrity: the assurance that the declared source is the true source and that no outside party could have seen and/or changed any of the data: amount, beneficiary's name, references, etc. Another factor gaining importance with internet banking is non-repudiation: the inability for a counterparty to deny that it has taken a specific action; and

- auditability and traceability: the ability to prove that a payment has been effected and/or received, as well as facilities to track and trace the payment in case of delayed receipt or queries.

Retail customers mainly base their choice on convenience and execution times, principally the date at which their account will be debited, less so as to when the beneficiary will be credited unless for emergencies, for example, transfers to children at university having prematurely exhausted their monthly allowance!

Corporate customers are mainly concerned with fees and execution times; they are anxious to optimize their cash flow: accelerated availability of remitted funds, latest possible debiting of their account when initiating payments and minimizing idle balances. Fees and execution times are keenly negotiated between large corporations and financial institutions as we will see in Chapter 13 (sec. 4). Enterprises also favour payment instruments which maximize the accuracy of the remittance information so that they can reconcile, for instance, payments received against invoices issued.

Banks and service providers will be mainly concerned with processing costs and security. They are keen to reduce the processing costs of generic payment services to a minimum so as to devote funds and resources to value-added services and customer relations. This is achieved by maximizing STP and automating the entire chain of processes: receipt of payment instruction, validation, balance check, debit/credit accounts, transmission to clearing and settlement mechanism through to final reconciliation; any manual intervention is to be avoided as it will increase costs (see ch. 14 sec.1).

Central banks are mainly concerned with security and minimizing risks (see ch. 4). As we have seen, they are responsible for oversight and sometimes regulation and operation, but should not interfere in the competition between service providers. They should however promote efficiency and ensure that technological progress is used advantageously.

Before we examine the various payment instruments in more detail, it is worth looking at two other factors which influence the choice of instruments:

- Circumstances: face-to-face when creditor and debtor are in physical presence of each other, as opposed to remote payments when mail and/or electronic transmission must be relied upon; and

- Frequency: occasional (or one-off) payments for shopping or, for instance, professional fees, as opposed to recurring payments such as mortgage repayments, insurance premiums or utility bills.

2 Cash

Cash – notes and coins – is the oldest payment instrument since mankind progressed beyond barter. Coins are usually minted by the government (the Mint in the UK, the Hôtel des Monnaies under the Ministry of Finance in France), while notes are printed under the authority of the central bank, either by themselves – the Bank of England – and/or subcontracted to other central banks or specialist security printers such as De la Rue or Giesecke and Devriendt. Several illustrious historical figures have been in charge of issuing notes and coins, from Thomas Gresham and Isaac Newton to ... Che Guevara who was governor of the central bank after the 1959 revolution in Cuba.

Cash is linked to the concept of seigniorage: 'In a historical context, the term seigniorage was used to refer to the share, fee or tax which the seignior, or sovereign, took to cover the expenses of coinage and for profit. With the introduction of paper money, larger profits could be made because banknotes cost much less to produce than their face value. When central banks came to be monopoly suppliers of banknotes, seigniorage came to be reflected in the profits made by them and ultimately their major or only shareholder, the government. Seigniorage can be estimated by multiplying notes and coin outstanding (non-interest bearing central bank liabilities) by the long-term rate of interest on government securities (a proxy for the return on central bank assets)'.[1]

Cash has the advantage of providing instant finality and discharge of debt, but is bulky and expensive to handle in terms of transport, storage, security and counting. For this reason several countries have passed legislation to ensure that salaries, pensions and social benefits are paid by cheque and/or electronic credit transfers. The scenarios of gangster films based on attacking the payroll vans are today obsolete, but cash still accounts for the largest number of personal payments (63% in the UK, two-thirds of which being five pounds or less in 2006[2]), so hold-ups on security transport vans and their staff are still common ... no change in the scenario from attacking the Wells Fargo (the precursor of the global Californian bank) stagecoach in westerns!

Cash handling costs are estimated at €45–70 billion in the EU, or 0.4–0.6 per cent of GDP.[3] No explicit charge is made to retail customers for cash handling, but banks attempt to recover transport and handling costs from large retail outlets such as supermarket chains.

Recent anti-money laundering (AML) legislation also compels merchants to report cash payments in excess of a certain amount which varies by country.

3 Cheques

A cheque (or *check* in the US) is a signed written payment instrument drawn by the debtor (or payer) on his/her bank and presented, either face-to-face or by mail, to the creditor (or payee). The cheque is a 'pull' payment. The theoretical sequence of events should be:

- creditor presents the cheque to his/her bank (collecting bank) who verifies that amounts in figures and in letters match;
- creditor's bank sends cheque to debtor's bank (paying bank), either directly or via a clearing house;
- clearing house sorts the cheques received from the collecting banks and sends them to the paying banks;
- payer's bank verifies debtor's signature and balance (or credit line) on the account;
- payer's bank notifies creditor's bank that the cheque will be honoured and that the funds can be credited to his/her account, or that the cheque is refused for insufficient funds (commonly known as 'bounced') or suspected fraud, in which case the dishonoured cheque is *returned*; and
- payer's bank returns the cheque to the drawer with the statement of his/her account.

In cases where immediate acceptance is required, banks will issue a banker's cheque (or draft) after debiting the debtor, therefore guaranteeing good funds; these drafts can become negotiable instruments, hence their name *assegni circulari* (circulating cheques) in Italy.

This is a long, cumbersome and expensive process which has proven difficult to automate. The magnetic (MICR: magnetic ink character recognition) or optical (OCR: optical character recognition) encoding or pre-printing of the drawer's account identifiers (account number, generally accompanied by a sort code) and cheque number, allied with progress in optical recognition of the handwritten amount in figures (but not the amount in letters or the beneficiary, even less the signature) have greatly facilitated automation.

Legislation was first passed dispensing the banks from returning the cheques to the drawers, but compelling them to store them – either physically, or on microfilm or digital image. To increase acceptance by retailers, cheque guarantee cards were introduced which guaranteed the cheque up to a specified amount, subject to the creditor verifying the card number written on the reverse of the cheque, the signature and in some cases the photograph – this however only being truly effective in the case of face-to-face payments.

The next step in certain countries was cheque truncation, whereby the data is captured by the creditor's bank (who stores the cheque or its image and charges the debtor's bank for his efforts) and transmitted electronically to the debtor's bank or the clearing house – thereby omitting signature verification! Cheque imaging is also gaining wider acceptance (see ch. 7 sec. 5). Under customer pressure, banks have recently credited the beneficiary immediately (especially if the cheque is guaranteed by a cheque guarantee card), but reserve the right to recover the funds should the cheque not be honoured. The system is therefore wide-open to fraud and counterfeiting, the onus resting squarely on the debtor to verify his bank statement regularly and report any cheque debit which appears suspect: this triggers the recovery of the original cheque or its image for investigation.

The average cost of processing a cheque is estimated at 6.3 cents[4] in the US.

The number of cheque payments is declining regularly (8 per cent in the UK in 2006[5]), which means that the processing costs per item are rising as the infrastructure costs are largely fixed. Economies of scale are essential, so cheque processing is generally outsourced – in Great Britain, all banks entrust cheque processing and clearing to their jointly owned Cheque and Credit Clearing Company.

Corporations dislike cheques as they require manual handling and reconciliation is difficult, relying mainly on the drawer scribbling the invoice number and/or customer reference on the reverse! Many leading retailers and petrol chains in the UK refuse to accept cheques. Cheques remain however popular with retail customers and small businesses on account of convenience (particularly for remote occasional payments), force of habit and the float – 'the cheque is in the mail (!)'. France and the US remain the largest cheque users, while some countries (for instance Sweden, the Netherlands, and Japan for retail customers) have withdrawn cheques. Several countries however have taken measures to proactively reduce the usage of cheques by differential pricing to encourage the use of more efficient instruments.

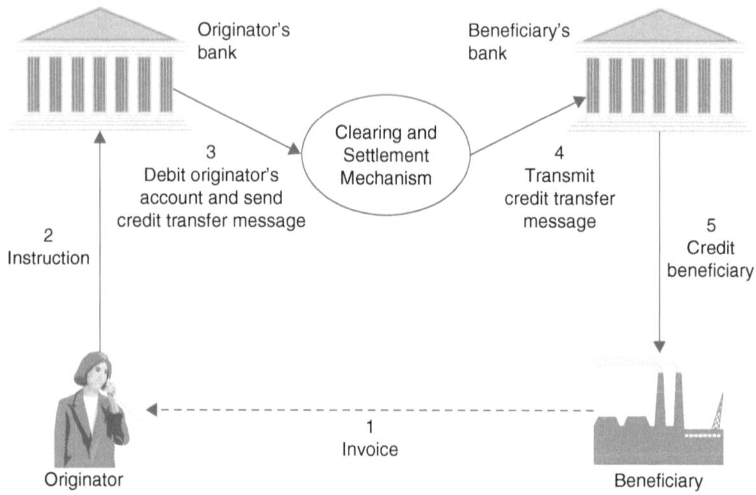

Figure 2.1 Credit transfer

4 Credit transfers

Credit transfers (or direct credits) are initiated by the debtor (or originator) who instructs his bank to debit his account; the bank verifies the instruction and availability of funds prior to transferring the information to a clearing house or directly to the beneficiary's bank which credits the latter's account after verification (see Figure 2.1). The credit transfer is a 'push' payment.

Exceptions are defined as:

- Rejects: credit transfer rejected by the originator's bank before interbank settlement for incorrect formatting, invalid account numbers or insufficient funds; the originator will be notified with the reason of the reject.
- Returns: credit transfer rejected after interbank settlement if the beneficiary cannot be credited, for instance if the account number is incorrect or has been closed; the creditor's bank will advise the originator's bank which will notify and refund him/her.

The scheme rules will define a maximum execution time following acceptance by the debtor (or originator's) bank, expressed in interbank business days.

The majority of credit transfers (payroll, corporate payments, pensions and social benefits, etc.) are initiated electronically from internet banking portals, accounting software packages or Enterprise Resource Planning systems (ERP supplied for instance by SAP or Oracle). Paper forms, optimized for optical reading, are used for transfers initiated manually. Banks will issue to each customer preprinted forms containing their name, address and account identifier, either as initiator or beneficiary. Conversely, enterprises will send with the invoice a computer-generated preprinted form with their account identifier, name and address, amount and invoice reference: the customer needs only to enter his name and account details, sign the form and send it to his bank.

The credit transfer offers therefore major advantages in terms of automated processing; reconciliation is good if the reference is provided by the creditor, less reliable if entered by the debtor. Processing costs are low as even paper forms achieve a very high (over 98 per cent) STP rate thanks to progress in optical character recognition (OCR).

For regular payments for the same amount (for instance rents), standing orders (STO) are a repetitive credit transfer whereby the debtor instructs his bank to transfer the sum at regular intervals – monthly, quarterly, annually.

For completeness sake, we should also mention the giro transfers offered by the post office banks. These were mainly established during the late nineteenth and early twentieth centuries to provide deposit and payment services to rural populations, as banks were then mainly concentrated in cities. The first was created by the Austro-Hungarian empire (the Kaiser Franz-Joseph even symbolically opened an account), followed by Switzerland, Japan, Germany, Benelux and France. Customers opened accounts from which they could initiate credit transfers, but no overdrafts or credit facilities were allowed. Transfers can also be initiated by paying in cash at the post office counter, which remains the preferred way for paying taxes and bills in many countries. The ability to initiate payments in cash provides anonymity, which is sometimes taken advantage of for illicit transfers. The terms 'postal cheque, chèque postal' are therefore largely a misnomer as the payment is effectively a credit transfer. It should be noted that several of these postal banks have today become powerful financial institutions – for instance Die Postbank in Germany and the Post Office Bank in Japan – leveraging the large number of accounts opened by retail customers and small businesses and competing aggressively in those customer segments with commercial banks, by offering a full range of financial services including loans, cards, foreign exchange and even insurance.

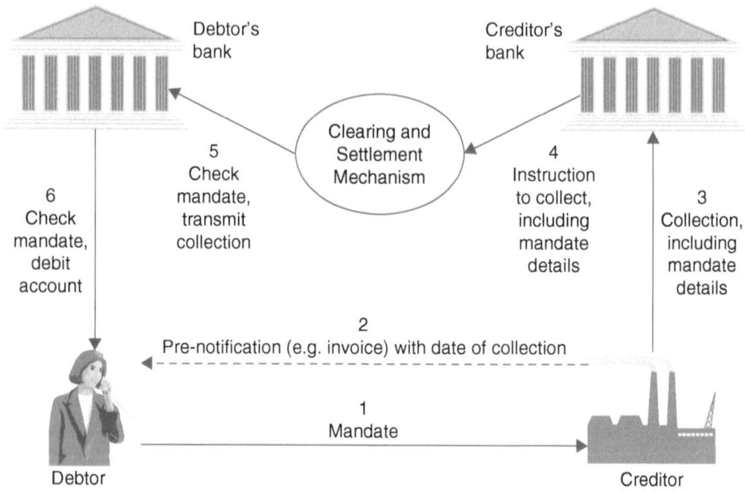

Figure 2.2 Direct debit

5 Direct debits

Direct debits are payments initiated by the creditor through its bank, which collects (draws) the funds from the debtor's account at his/her bank, subject to a legally binding mandate agreed by the debtor (see Figure 2.2). Direct debits generally rely upon a guarantee to the debtor that he will be able to recover the funds collected in case of error or dispute within a specified time limit. The direct debit is a 'pull' payment and can be used for one-off or regularly occurring payments. In certain countries the creditor's bank charges an interchange fee, also known as a Multilateral Interchange Fee (MIF), to the debtor's bank.

Exceptions, also known as the 'Rs', are:

- Rejects prior to interbank settlement for technical reasons such as formatting error, invalid account numbers, absence of mandate or non-compliance with the mandate.
- Refusals initiated by the debtor before settlement, either by challenging an individual invoice or by withdrawing the mandate; if received after settlement, the refusal will trigger a refund.
- Returns initiated post-settlement by the debtor's bank if the collection could not take place on account of insufficient funds, incorrect account number, account closed or death of the debtor.

- Reversals if the Creditor withdraws the collection, requiring a refund if post-settlement.
- Refunds if the debtor requests reimbursement.

The scheme rules will normally define the following times and deadlines:

- The notification period by the creditor to the debtor, normally an invoice or bill stating the date at which the amount due will be collected from his/her account, expressed in calendar days before the due date.
- The latest reception date of the collection by the debtor's bank for a one-off or first of a recurring sequence of payments, expressed in interbank business days before settlement, to allow verification of the mandate and account number.
- The latest reception date for subsequent collections in a sequence of recurring collections, normally shorter than for the first and also expressed in interbank business days before settlement.
- The latest date for settlement of returns, expressed in interbank business days after receipt of the collection by the debtor's bank.
- The deadline for refund requests by the debtor for direct debits covered by a mandate, which can be different if no mandate has been agreed by the debtor (unauthorized collection).
- The latest date for settlement of a refund.

The mandate must be signed (by hand or electronically) by the debtor and a file of mandates is held by the ACH and both banks. It will contain the names, addresses and account identifiers of the debtor and the creditor as well as the payment reference such as a customer reference identifier. Two possible mandate flows exist (see Figure 2.3):

- Creditor mandate flow, whereby the creditor – for instance an energy utility – will obtain the customer's signature on the mandate and send it to the creditor's bank for onward transmission to the ACH and/or the debtor's bank; and
- Debtor mandate flow whereby the debtor will sign the mandate and forward it to his bank for onward transmission to the ACH and/or to the creditor's bank who notifies the creditor.

Direct debits have become the favoured payment instrument for enterprises issuing a large number of invoices/bills, such as financial institutions for mortgage/loan repayments, utilities or telecommunications operators, as it enables them to automatically collect variable

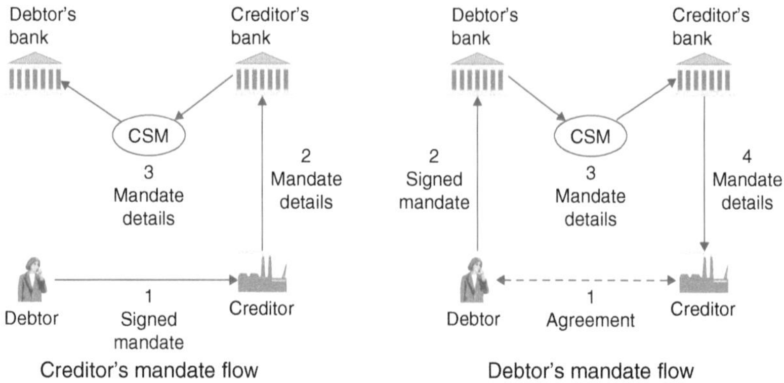

Figure 2.3 Mandate flows

amounts on a predetermined date, thereby optimizing cash flow and treasury management. Most mobile telephone companies nowadays only accept direct debits for subscription customers. Reconciliation is also automatic as the creditor sets the remittance information. Direct debits are gradually replacing standing orders as even 'fixed' amounts, such as insurance premiums, will rise with inflation. Many utilities offer discounts if paying by direct debit to encourage customers to change. Direct debits also reduce time and costs for debtors who, assuming they agree the amount, do not need to initiate a payment by credit transfer or cheque; this also gives them peace of mind that the bill will be paid and that the electricity or telephone will not be cut off if they miss the deadline while travelling.

Costs are low as processing is entirely automated once the mandate has been set up.

6 Cards

Historically, credit cards originated in the US in the 1920s when hotel chains and oil companies began issuing them to customers. The invention of the bank credit card is attributed to John Biggins of the Flatbush National Bank of Brooklyn who invented the 'Charge-It' scheme between the bank's customers and local merchants in 1946.[6]

Cards are operated under schemes whereby banks issuing cards to their customers rely upon the understanding that these cards will be accepted at merchants acquired (or signed-up) by other participating banks.

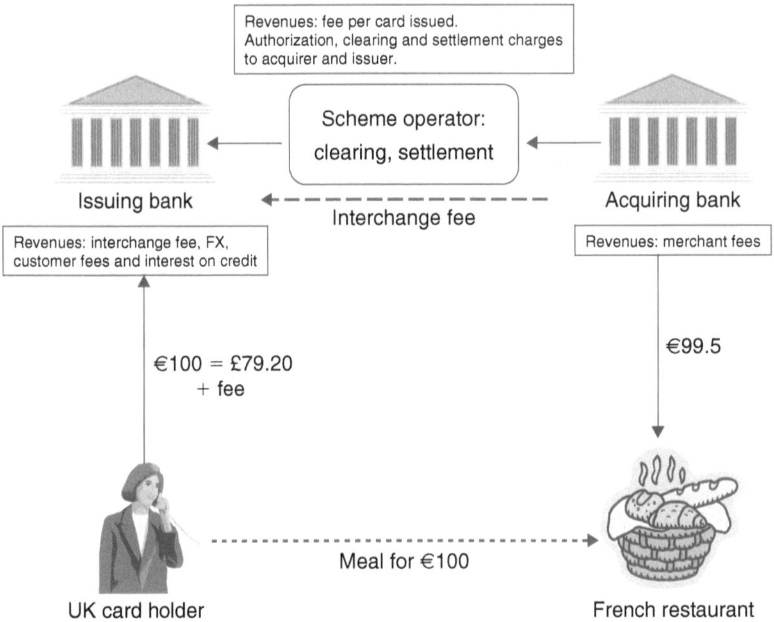

Figure 2.4 Cards

Figure 2.4 illustrates the typical example of a British tourist paying for a meal in France at a restaurant displaying the logos of the cards it accepts (for instance Visa and/or MasterCard). The acquiring bank will credit the restaurant, within an agreed deadline, with the amount of the bill less a merchant fee, in our case 0.5 per cent which he cannot charge to the customer. The acquiring bank will obtain refund through the scheme's clearing and settlement mechanism from the issuing bank, which will debit the cardholder by the full amount of the restaurant bill, converted into his/her currency, plus a commission. An interchange fee is also paid by the acquiring bank to the issuing bank. The scheme owner gains revenues from fees per card issued under its brand and charges for authorizations, clearing and settlement.

The same principles apply when cards are used to withdraw cash at ATMs (automated teller machine, or cash dispenser) operated by a different bank than the issuer.

6.1 Card types

The most commonly used card is the *debit card* which is linked to a bank account, allowing the holder to withdraw cash at ATMs and pay for goods and services at retail outlets, petrol stations, restaurants, etc. The amount of the purchase or withdrawal is debited near-instantly from the holder's account. Some debit cards are only intended for withdrawals at ATMs and therefore called *cash cards*. A *cheque guarantee* feature (see sec. 3 this chapter) is often incorporated with debit cards.

The same applies to *deferred debit cards* except that the amounts are accumulated, up to an agreed ceiling or limit, until the monthly date at which the full amount of the purchases since the last statement is debited from the holder's account through a direct debit. *Credit cards* offer revolving credit facilities whereby the holder, upon receipt of his monthly statement, can choose to settle the full amount or pay only part (subject to a minimum), in which case the issuing institution will charge interest on the outstanding balance. Deferred debit cards are sometimes assimilated to credit cards as the holder benefits from a credit facility for a maximum of one month, but they do not offer true credit that enables the holder to postpone part payment beyond the monthly settlement date, even if willing to pay interest.

Prepaid cards (or *stored-value cards*), either for a fixed amount at purchase and disposable or re-loadable, are an alternative to cash and the stored amount is reduced by each purchase. They are mostly closed systems used for public transport (for example the contactless Octopus in Hong Kong, Oyster in London, Z-pass on US toll roads) and increasingly for mobile telephones. In Hong Kong, the Octopus card has reduced the weight of coins handled daily from 60 tons to 1 ton.

Electronic purses are prepaid cards accepted at a wider range of outlets or even country wide. They have been extremely successful and are commonly used at a national level in Belgium and the Netherlands (Proton and ChipNick respectively) for purchases, public transport, parking meters, etc., but the Moneo card in France has met with only limited success as small retailers refuse to pay the merchant fee which would reduce their slim profit margins.

Corporate purchasing or procurement and Travel and Entertainment (T&E) cards are issued to enterprises to pay for supplies and services, either to the company itself and/or to selected employees for business travel and entertainment.

Affinity cards are linked mainly to charities which collect a fraction percentage of the purchases.

Finally *private cards* are issued mainly by retail chains and petrol companies for use at their stores and outlets, with or without revolving credit facilities.

6.2 Card technologies

Technology has moved forward since, up until the 1970s, the merchant would telephone for authorization for sales above a predetermined floor amount, the cardholder would sign a 3-part paper voucher (one copy for him, one copy for the merchant, one copy for the acquirer), printed by the imprinter with the amount added by hand, which was read optically when sent to the acquirer, giving him/her a very generous float by the time the details appeared on his statement. The identity of the card holder was verified by comparing his signature on the slip with that on the reverse of the card, a weak security had the card been stolen! Card details were subsequently registered on a magnetic strip at the back of the card and swiped through a point-of-sale (POS) terminal which would dial up an on-line authorization centre and, upon acceptance, print the slip for signature. This reduced costs and float while enabling 'on-line authorization to the issuer' to verify the available credit and whether the card had not been lost or stolen, but did not significantly reduce fraud or solve the problem of identity verification.

The next step was the chip card, which originated in France in the early 1970s, where an electronic chip is embedded in the card enabling identity verification by the cardholder entering a secret PIN (personal identification number) on the POS numeric keyboard. With the exception of the US, this chip and PIN technology is being adopted worldwide under the EMV (Europay, MasterCard, Visa) standard and has significantly reduced fraud. In addition to increased security (the chip destructs if tampered with), the programming facilities of the chip enable the card to be used for a multitude of additional functionalities, such as contactless cards which need only be waved close to the POS terminal, loyalty schemes and mobile payments by interfacing with the SIM card of mobile telephone handsets. Prepaid cards and electronic purses could not have been introduced without the chip card which also enables several functions to be combined onto one card, the holder choosing whether each purchase should be charged to his debit card, credit card or electronic purse.

6.3 Card schemes

The card business is dominated by the two International Card Schemes (ICS) or networks, MasterCard and Visa. Visa was originally launched by Bank of America as the BankAmericard in 1956 while MasterCard was established as a competitive alternative in 1966 as the Interbank Card Association (ICA). They initially offered credit cards and subsequently created schemes for debit cards, offering an interoperability framework and cobranding with national debit card schemes such as Carte Bancaire in France or Bancomat in Italy; through these it has become possible for travellers to draw cash from an ATM virtually worldwide.

By September 2006, financial institutions had issued 1.51 billion Visa cards, used for annual purchases and cash withdrawals amounting to $4 trillion.[7] In 2007, MasterCard's customers had issued 916 million cards and purchases on a local currency basis amounted to $2.3 trillion.[8]

Some banks are dual-issuers, issuing cards from both schemes. Several anti-monopoly and anti-collusion lawsuits have been launched against them in the US and in Europe by merchants and the EC, resulting in multi-million dollar fines and leading both schemes to abandon the cooperative bank-owned governance model. MasterCard, headquartered in Purchase (!) NY, floated in 2006 and Visa achieved the richest initial public offering in US history, raising $17.9 billion on 18 March 2008 in the midst of the credit crunch from the sub-prime crisis.[9] Visa Europe remained however independent of the new Visa Inc. and retained its ownership structure by its European member banks. We should remember that the networks, which are in effect processors, are not affected by customer defaults as credit is extended by the issuing banks.

The power of the ICS's brand has become a sensitive issue, but it is clear that a merchant accepts payment from an unknown customer, presenting a card issued by an unknown bank but bearing the MasterCard or Visa logo, solely on the certainty that he will be paid through his acquirer from the same scheme. Some years ago Citibank, arguing that their brand was stronger than Visa's, demanded that the Visa logo be printed on the back of the card; Visa refused and Citibank temporarily stopped issuing Visa cards.

Other noted brands are American Express who operates a successful closed credit card scheme, sometimes in partnership with a local bank or airline, Diners (once owned by Citigroup) and Discover, originally launched by the Dean Witter retail brokerage firm and floated in 2007 following the merger with Morgan Stanley. In April 2008 Discover announced a deal to acquire Diners from Citi. These are mainly targeting high-net worth individuals and the corporate segment. Their fees are higher than MasterCard's and Visa's which explains why fewer merchants accept them.

Japan operates the JCC scheme and China has recently launched the China Union Pay cards: with such a large domestic customer base, they do not feel the need to join the ICS's. European banks created Europay featuring the Eurocard in conjunction with the EC debit card in the 1970s which they sold in 2002 to MasterCard Europe; we will see when talking about SEPA in Chapter 6 (sec. 7.5) how short-sighted the move was.

6.4 Operational and commercial considerations

Card payment processing costs are low and driven by economies of scale. All basic functions (issuer and acquirer processing, queries and investigations, replacement of lost/stolen cards) are generally outsourced to shared service centres – some at national scale – large volume financial institutions or third-party processors; however, the scheme owners retain the clearing and settlement functions.

From the customer's standpoint, cards are cheap and convenient when used as a payment instrument, much less however as a source of credit. They also offer the best reconciliation facilities through statements listing full details of all transactions: date, name of merchant, amount in foreign and home currencies, and lately under regulatory pressure exchange rate and fees. These statements are generally sent by mail but also recently electronically, allowing automated reconciliation through home-finance or corporate accounting packages; for corporate cards, issuers will even sort the payments by cost centre and/or expense type (travel, procurement, etc.).

From the merchant's standpoint, sales volumes rise as consumers are more prone to impulse buying if payment is deferred. The merchant fee paid to the acquirer is effectively an insurance premium that he will be paid, providing it has followed the security and anti-fraud measurers dictated by the scheme. Retailers also benefit from the reduction in cash handling and safekeeping costs. Nevertheless, merchants are in constant dispute and even litigation to reduce the merchant fees.

For banks, cards can be an extremely profitable activity. The word 'can' is used intentionally as profitability depends on services offered and sophisticated customer relationship management (CRM). Profitability is negligible on the basic domestic payment functions for debit cards and deferred debit cards, which explains why there is little competition in countries where those instruments prevail and why customers there rarely carry a card not issued by the bank holding their current account. The high interest charged on revolving credit cards is, on the other hand, an extremely lucrative source of revenue giving rise to fierce competition and aggressive marketing, where issuers seek to differentiate themselves through rewards (principally air miles), the credit limit, the interest rate and interest moratoriums on balance transfers when customers switch. In January 2008 a survey showed that an estimated 2.6 million British consumers (7 per cent of credit card customers) planned to transfer credit card debt run up over the Christmas shopping season to a new card, taking advantage of 0 per cent interest rate introductory offers by no less than 169 cards![10]

As mentioned in Chapter 1 (sec. 2.1), several non-banks have entered this market: retail chains, automobile associations, sports clubs, airlines, etc. Particularly in the US and the UK, individuals will therefore carry several cards and draw on all available credit lines for payments leading to high levels of personal debt, creating a social and economic problem which has raised the concern of central banks.

Issuers endeavour to segment their customers by offering cards with low limits (for youths and students) and 'gold', 'platinum' or 'diamond' cards to the more affluent customers, appealing to status-consciousness and linked to profitable value added services: high credit limits (in some cases unlimited), insurance, concierge services for priority travel, theatre or restaurant bookings, etc. Issuers are also mining the accumulated data on their customers' expenditure preferences and patterns; the first efforts were mainly aimed at fraud reduction, attempting to detect card thefts through unusual behaviour. Major efforts are now devoted to CRM to fine-tune product and service offerings according to perceived individual customer preferences, as well as to detect utilization patterns which, correlated with peer behaviour, might indicate potential delinquency or propensity to switch to another card.

In summary, profitability for the issuer is mainly driven by foreign exchange gains on cross-currency purchases, interest revenues for revolving credit cards and the targeted marketing of value-added services.

7 Payment channels

Payments can be initiated through a variety of channels. Few, except for high value transfer requests by retail customers, originate today from a visit to a branch or a free-format letter. Cheques and credit transfers are still sent by mail, but most banks now encourage customers to initiate domestic and international credit transfers up to a certain amount, set up mandates for direct debits and pay bills for pre-established beneficiaries such as utilities or telecommunication operators through proprietary ATM's, banking kiosks, telephone banking and internet banking.

In addition, the dramatic increase in internet shopping and procurement has demanded the implementation of secure payments over the internet.

We will discuss in Chapter 4 (sec. 4) the security measures that have been introduced to prevent fraud.

8 Statistics and comparative trends

Inertia is a major factor in the choice of payment instrument: habits die hard and any plan to shift customers away from one instrument towards another (for instance move to direct debits, withdrawal of cheques) requires a concerted effort between banks, regulators, industry bodies and consumer associations extending over several years. This inertia is compounded by the fact that cross-subsidization between instruments and customer segments is rife and that pricing is generally not transparent, particularly to retail customers.

8.1 Cash

More than any other instrument cash is profoundly anchored in collective habits and mentalities and profound differences can be observed from country to country. Measured as a percentage of GDP, the value of payments in cash is relatively stable. This explains why new instruments aimed at replacing cash, such as electronic purses, are slow to gain acceptance, even if they offer obvious benefits such as immediate availability of funds combined with reduced handling costs and improved security for retailers who would hold less cash on their premises. Small retailers such as bakers or newsagents are obviously reluctant to pay merchant fees for card transactions of any type: credit, debit, prepaid or purse. Cash payments are more common in Germany than in any other European country; Germans are used to paying large amounts for substantial purchases such as cars in cash, as opposed to cheque or transfer. It was under pressure from Germany that a €500 note was issued, the highest denomination in any currency, while it would have perhaps been more logic to provide a €1 note.

Taking the total value of notes and coin in circulation divided by the population as an indicator, Japanese will hold \$5,541 in contrast to \$2,736 in the US and \$2,700 in the euro-zone. We note the similarity between the US and the EU according to this indicator, while the ratio between cash and GDP shows a slight difference: 6.2 per cent in the US and 7.7 per cent for the euro-zone. At the other extreme the British use relatively little cash (\$1,443 per capita, 3.4 per cent of GDP and 4.5% of M1 money supply), remembering that the cheque was invented by Scottish bankers. Two countries diverge substantially from others, Switzerland and the US. The amount of cash per inhabitant is \$5,007 in Switzerland and 9.4 per cent of GDP. The ratio of cash to M1 money supply is 59 per cent in the US, in contrast to 17.2 per cent in the euro-zone and 21.6 per cent in Japan. This can be explained by the role of the

Table 2.1 Cash statistics 2006

	Cash value per head of population	% of GDP	% of M1 money supply
Japan	5,541	16.6	21.6
UK	1,443	3.4	4.5
US	2,735	6.2	59.0
Euro-zone	2,700	7.7	17.2

Sources: BIS, CPSS, *Statistics on Payment and Settlement Systems in Selected Countries*, March 2008

US dollar and the Swiss franc as refuge currencies. Half of US dollar notes and coin are held by non-residents. Similarly, at the time of the conversion of European currencies to the euro, the Bundesbank discovered that close to half the stock of large denomination Deutschmark notes were held in Eastern Europe. We should also remember that the US dollar has also often been substituted to the local currency (dollarization) by some countries to fight hyperinflation, as was the case in Argentina. Table 2.1 summarizes the above statistics for 2006.

From the above statistics we can also derive the turnover of the total value of payments (M1/GDP) and the velocity of money (or speed of circulation) which is the inverse (GDP/M1). Historically one observes a decrease in velocity: money supply increases faster than GDP over centuries in line with monetarization of the economy. The trend reverses in practically all countries after World War II as more money was deposited at banks and money supply increased slower than GDP.

8.2 Non-cash instruments

The use of non-cash payment instruments is increasing relative to cash in all countries producing reliable statistic, but usage of scriptural instruments varies from country to country. The volume of credit transfers remains relatively stable, direct debits are growing slowly but steadily, but the major trend is the decline of cheques, replaced by cards for face-to-face retail transactions and credit transfers or direct debits as well as cards for remote payments. E-payments are still marginal, except in Singapore where they represent over 84 per cent of the total number of transactions. This is the result of a deliberate policy to create a cashless society. Some statistics include e-payments, but there is not always agreement on what the term includes. Other countries with significant proportions of e-payments include Belgium (4.9 per cent), the Netherlands (3.9) and

Table 2.2 Use of non-cash payment instruments in the EU and selected countries in per cent (2006), excluding e-payments

	Credit transfers	Direct debits	Cards	Cheques
Austria	47.5	35.7	15.2	0.3
Belgium	42.5	11.7	43.0	0.7
Bulgaria	68.2	1.6	30.2	0.0
Cyprus	14.8	15.9	32.3	37.0
Czech Republic (2004)	52.9	34.8	10.9	0.0
Denmark	21.6	14.2	62.6	1.6
Estonia	39.7	7.1	53.1	0.0
Finland	42.5	5.1	52.3	0.0
France	17.5	18.3	37.6	25.6
Germany	42.2	42.8	14.2	0.6
Greece	20.0	11.2	49.0	19.0
Hungary	76.7	9.3	13.8	0.0
Ireland	27.6	18.0	33.8	20.6
Italy	29.6	13.3	34.3	12.6
Japan*	33.1	0.0	62.5	10.7
Latvia	63.7	2.2	34.1	0.0
Lithuania	52.1	3.9	43.0	0.0
Luxemburg	48.3	10.1	38.5	0.3
Malta	17.2	3.1	27.0	52.8
Netherlands	32.7	27.2	36.3	0.0
Poland	71.3	1.1	27.5	0.0
Portugal	10.1	11.3	63.6	15.0
Romania	75.7	10.6	9.5	4.0
Singapore[1]*	1.0	2.5	6.5	4.6
Slovakia	66.8	16.1	17.0	0.0
Slovenia	54.9	12.6	32.2	0.3
Spain	14.5	44.7	35.7	3.5
Sweden	29.2	10.0	60.7	0.0
UK	21.2	19.8	46.6	12.3
US*	6.6	9.2	51.6	32.6

Note: [1] E-payments represent 84%
Sources: ECB, Payment Statistics, November 2007; * BIS, CPSS, *Statistics on Payment and Settlement Systems in Selected Countries*, March 2008

Switzerland (1.7). Table 2.2 shows the distribution of non-cash payments across the various instruments in the EU and selected economies.

We can observe the difference between countries where electronic instruments dominate as opposed to cheque countries such as the US (32.6 per cent), France (25.6), Italy (12.6) and the UK (12.3). Credit transfers are highly used in Germany, Benelux and Nordic countries. They are

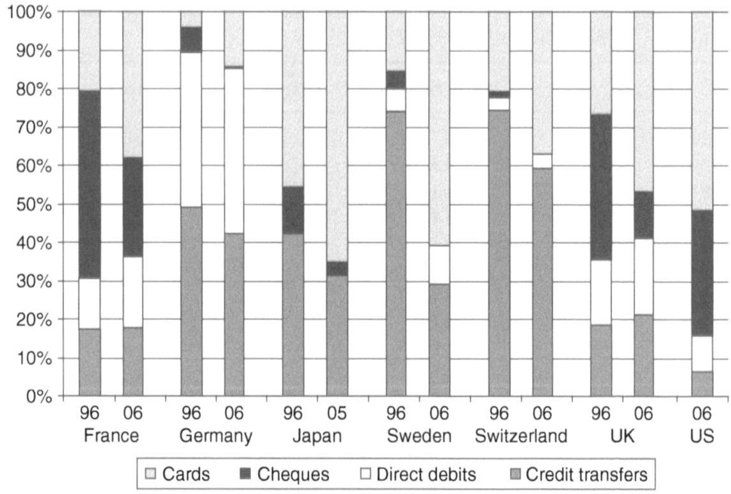

Figure 2.5 Trends in payment instruments in various countries

also heavily used in Eastern Europe, possibly as a heritage of the Soviet economy which imposed cash for individuals and credit transfers for enterprises. If a person in some countries wished to cash a credit transfer, he/she had to go to the issuing branch. Direct debits are a sign of maturity and a logical follow-on from a high usage of credit transfers. We can observe their strong growth in countries having undergone a change in political and economic regime such as Spain (44.7 per cent) and the Czech Republic (34.8 per cent). The majority of Eastern European and Baltic countries wisely chose to leapfrog cheques.

Figure 2.5 shows trends in selected countries over 10 years.

The decline of cheques is immediately visible and some countries have either eliminated them (Sweden, The Netherlands) or reduced their number to insignificance (Belgium, Germany, Japan, Switzerland). Cards show the strongest growth, particularly debit cards as they replace cheques. Sweden and Switzerland show a strong reduction of credit transfers as cards show strongest growth whilst direct debits remain stable.

3
Cross-Currency Payments and SWIFT

We have so far been talking about payments involving one currency, be it US dollars, euro or Japanese yen. International trade and mobile individuals increasingly demand payments to be effected to settle debts in a different currency than that in which the initiator holds his account, for instance a Japanese manufacturer invoicing a US importer in yen. These used to be called 'international payments' or 'cross-border' payments, but since the advent of the euro which is now the legal currency in 15 of the EU countries, it is more correct to distinguish between *cross-currency* payments for our example above and *cross-border payments* when creditor and debtor are located in different countries but the payment is in a common currency – for instance a euro payment between euro accounts in the Netherlands and Spain.

Generally speaking, 'currencies do not travel': the settlement of payments in a given currency takes place at the central bank which issues it. A presence in the country of the currency is therefore required. Credit cards which can be used outside their country of issue are the payment instrument most used by individuals when travelling or ordering goods from abroad (see ch. 2 sec. 6), but credit cards are a relatively new instrument and not suitable for commerce or financial markets. Cheques can be presented abroad, but the beneficiary would have to wait a long time before his account is credited as the cheque has to be *recovered*: physically (before the advent of electronic imaging and transmission) sent back across the oceans to the drawer's bank to verify the signature and availability of funds.

1 Correspondent banking

To satisfy the demand for international payments, banks developed the system of correspondent banking, opening accounts in the local currency

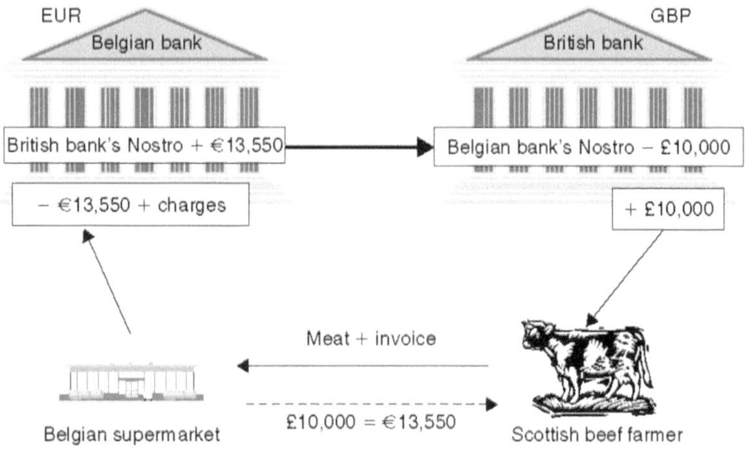

Figure 3.1 Correspondent banking – direct relationship

with each other, called *nostro accounts* (from the Italian 'nostro' meaning 'our').

Figure 3.1 illustrates the case of a Belgian supermarket chain ordering Angus beef from a Scottish cattle farmer, who invoices it for GBP 10,000. The debtor's Belgian bank will convert the £10,000 into euros at the prevailing exchange rate (say €13,550), credit his British correspondent's nostro account in euros and debit the supermarket's account by the same amount plus charges. He will instruct the British bank to credit the farmer's account with GBP 10,000, which the British bank will first debit from the Belgian bank's nostro account.

This case is relatively simple in the sense that the Belgian bank's correspondent, also referred to as its sterling *clearer*, happens to also be the Scottish farmer's bank. This is not always the case as banks normally only entertain correspondent relationships with only two or three correspondents per currency. We can well imagine that the farmer will hold his account with a bank in Edinburgh which will not be the Belgian bank's clearer in the City.

In this case (see Figure 3.2), the Belgian bank will:

- Instruct the Scottish bank to credit the farmer, indicating that *cover* will come from his named sterling correspondent;
- Instruct his correspondent to credit the beneficiary's bank with the £10,000, which will be effected through the UK clearing and settlement system.

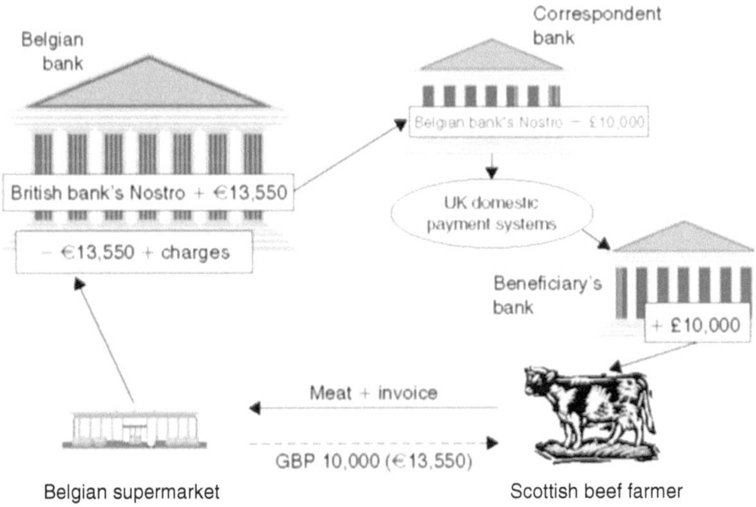

Figure 3.2 Correspondent banking – no direct relationship

An even more complex case arises when the payment must be effected in a third currency other than the debtor's and the creditor's. Like most commodities, oil is traded in US dollars, and Figure 3.3 overleaf illustrates the case of a French chain of petrol stations ordering oil from Saudi Arabia.

Payments in US dollars need to be settled at the Federal Reserve Bank in the US, so the ordering customer's French bank will credit the dollars via its US dollar correspondent, the US domestic clearing system and the Saudi bank's US correspondent. Printed and on-line directories indicate the names of each bank's correspondents or clearers in the major currencies.

As for any account, correspondents issue statements for the nostri accounts they hold. The ordering banks will reconcile these statements to ensure that all payments they instruct have been correctly effected and that no payments have been debited by error. The same applies for all intermediary banks along the chain. If we consider that a major clearer will today transact between 50 and 100,000 international payments daily it is obvious that this reconciliation cannot be effected manually.

These procedures reflect a credit transfer. Direct debits are more difficult to implement cross-border on account of the different legal regimes, schemes and consumer protection rules prevailing in each country. We will see in chapter 6, (sec. 6.2) how cross-border euro direct debits will be available from 2009 within the SEPA framework.

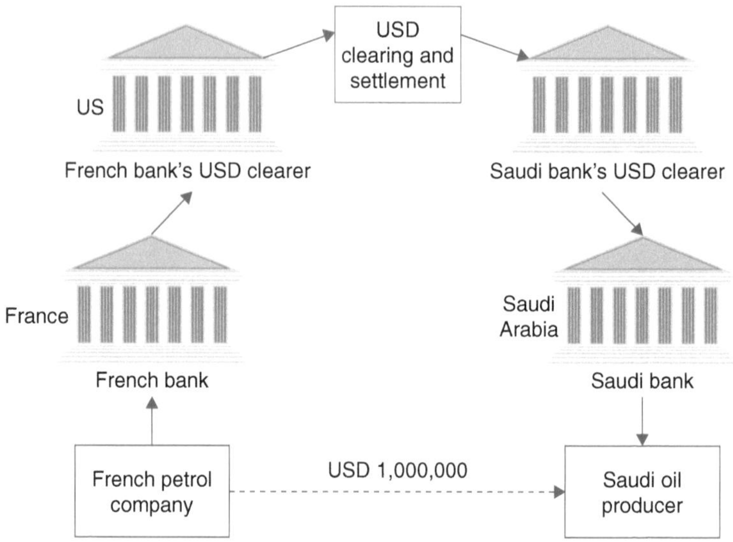

Figure 3.3 Correspondent banks – payments for goods quoted in a third currency, e.g. commodities

2 The SWIFT network

Up until the 1970s, international (as all cross-currency payments then were) payments were transacted between banks by telegram and telex (hence the name *wires* sometimes given in the US to international payments), secured by a system of manually calculated sequential test keys. While standards had been developed by each country for domestic payments, international payments were the last to be automated on account of the differences in language, formulation and practices.

To overcome this problem, Citibank in the early 1970s (then The First National City Bank of New York) started to develop the Marti (Machine Readable Telex Input) system, based on a standardized structure for telex messages to effect payments. Out of fear of a major competitive threat, a group of European banks launched the MSP (Message Switching Project) with the view to develop a standardized automated electronic communication system for international payments. To achieve critical mass, the project was rapidly extended to the major 69 banks across Western Europe and North America (including Citibank which abandoned Marti). The Society for Worldwide Interbank Financial Telecommunication was incorporated as a non-profit bank-owned cooperative in Belgium in 1973 and the SWIFT[1] network cut over to live operation in May 1977, after arduous negotiations with the European postal authorities who then held a monopoly on telecommunications and could foresee the disappearance of a lucrative market.

Although the implementation of a secure international private network was in those days a technical prowess, SWIFT's main achievement lies in the development of internationally accepted standards for financial transactions. Messaging standards were first developed for customer payments, interbank payments and nostro account statements. Standardized bank addresses were also published known as the *BIC codes* (Bank Identifier Code), composed of a unique 4 character bank code, a 2 character country code, a 2 character location code and an optional 3 character branch code: BBBB CC LL (bbb). The SWIFT system would validate conformity with the standards and reject any message submitted with errors, ensuring therefore that the sender need only capture the data once and that messages delivered could be processed automatically by the recipient. With strict guidelines for referencing, this enabled full end-to-end automation of the processes and flows described in the previous section, including automated nostro reconciliation. Messages are encrypted and sophisticated authentication algorithms guarantee origination, integrity and non-repudiation. Subject to compliance with defined operating rules and procedures SWIFT also accepts some liability for the messages it processes. From early on SWIFT offered a range of interfacing terminals and software to the network, originally to provide connectivity to its users confronted with the lack of solutions from the marketplace. The network subsequently expanded geographically to include all major financial centres and, at the end of 2007, connected nearly 8,300 financial institutions in 208 countries.

SWIFT extended in parallel the standardization of messages to cover virtually all financial transactions: payments and cash management, treasury (foreign exchange, money markets) and derivatives, securities and trade (collections and documentary credits). The major breakthrough occurred in 1987 after the banks who owned SWIFT accepted, after protracted hesitations as they feared dilution of their custody business, that securities broker dealers and fund managers could connect to the network to enable the automation of cross-border securities clearing and settlement. In 2006 the SWIFT membership also approved the participation of major corporations to communicate with the bank which sponsored their participation. Figure 3.4 shows the evolution of the distribution of SWIFT traffic between markets from 1996 until the first two months of 2008.

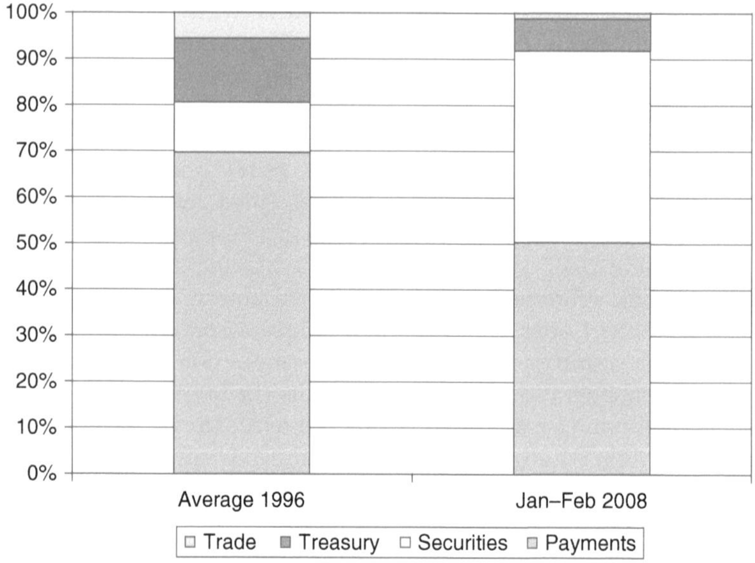

Figure 3.4 Evolution of SWIFT's traffic distribution
Sources: SWIFT 1996 annual report; www.suift.com

We can see how securities messages have grown to almost equal payments in volume and have become the strongest contributor to growth.

In 1986 SWIFT entered value-added services by developing and operating, on an outsourced basis, a netting system for the Ecu (the basket currency precursor to the euro), which subsequently evolved as the EBA's EURO1 netting system (see ch. 6 sec. 5). Several others followed such as an automated matching service for confirmation of foreign exchange trades (ACCORD) and solutions for cash reporting, corporate actions, exceptions and investigations, etc. In addition, SWIFT maintains directories of the BIC codes, correspondents and settlement agents.

SWIFT also now transmits files without format validation; the current SWIFTNet platform is IP-based and messaging standards are gradually migrating towards the XML syntax. SWIFT maintains its leading role in standards development.

SWIFT itself is not a payment system, but serves as transport network for virtually all major payment and securities market infrastructures and is arguably today the leading global provider of financial messaging and processing services. During 2007, SWIFT processed an average daily volume approaching 14 million messages, a five-fold increase from the 2.7 million messages in 1996. Aided by strong volume growth, SWIFT has pursued a systematic policy of tariff reduction to fend off competition from other networking service providers and the internet, while constantly striving towards maximizing operational resilience. Finally, SWIFT organizes the annual SIBOS conference and exhibition, the major venue for debate, networking, self-congratulation and lavish entertainment for the payments and securities processing fraternity.

3 The correspondent banking and clearing business

Correspondent banking and clearing has become increasingly concentrated and competitive since the introduction of the euro, as nostro accounts are no longer required in 15 legacy currencies. The trend to reduce correspondents accelerated and it is rare that banks will maintain relationships with more than two to three clearers per currency. Global banks aggressively market their wide local presence and access to payment systems in several currencies. Nostalgia abounds on 'the good old days of correspondent banking' based on balances, reciprocity (each bank giving the other approximately equal volume of business in their respective currencies), exotic trips and personal relationships cultivated over liquid lunches and days on the golf course. Remuneration is nowadays negotiated around interest on balances, credit lines and above all transaction fees based on STP: the ability for a clearer to receive the payment over SWIFT and process it straight through to final reconciliation without any human intervention. Exceptions and investigations caused by non-compliance with standards or agreed practices are penalized heavily, up to ten times the fee for an STP payment.

4 Remittances

This is the term given to low-value payments transferred mainly by migrant workers to their families back home for amounts ranging between $100 and $500. Volumes and values are difficult to estimate as a large number are effected by 'informal' channels such as *hawala* which are estimated to add around 50 per cent to some 175 million officially recorded remittances which exceeded $232 billion in 2005; countries contributing the largest value are the US and Saudi Arabia.[2] In 20 of the largest recipient countries, these remittances amount for over 10 per cent of GDP.[3]

Cross-currency transfer services from banks, based on the correspondent banking model, are expensive and also assume that payers and beneficiaries, often in remote areas, hold bank accounts which is not always the case.

These services were originally offered by non-banks: Western Union – leveraging their telecommunication infrastructure – and MoneyGram. Funds can be sent and received from accredited service points which accept payment and disburse the funds in cash during longer opening hours than bank branches. Fees are low, but the total cost should be considered including the exchange rate and any fees from the disbursement agent. Substantial revenues are derived from 'emergency' services: transferring money urgently to travelling children stranded penniless following the theft of their wallet on Machu Pichu. Commercial banks have woken up to this opportunity and several now offer low-priced services over 'corridors' between countries taking in large numbers of migrant workers from specific areas for historical or cultural reasons: US to Mexico, France to Africa, Gulf to Middle East and Asia, Spain and Portugal to South America, UK towards India, Pakistan and Africa, etc.

The hawala system is typical of how the informal channels work. A person in the UK wishing to remit funds to Pakistan will approach a 'hawaladar' indicating the amount he wishes the beneficiary to receive in rupees. The hawaladar will calculate the equivalent to be paid in sterling and add a commission. He will then contact a hawaladar close to the beneficiary who will pay him/her. How the hawaladars settle between them is unclear: several intermediaries might be involved and settlement could await an offsetting transfer of funds in the reverse direction, for instance paying for goods imported in the country of the first beneficiary. The system is based on trust and a code of conduct and seldom fails. It is also cash based and therefore offers anonymity.

This raises of course the issue of compliance with Anti Money Laundering (AML) and Counter Terrorist Financing (CTF) legislation, customer identity and transfers to black-listed individuals. The major non banking systems listed above certainly comply with these measures and are licensed. In the UK, HM Revenue and Customs maintains a register of these operators and conducts regular site visits.[4] The BIS published the following principles in 2007 shown in Box 3.1:

Box 3.1 The General Principles and related roles[5]

The General Principles are aimed at the public policy objectives of achieving safe and efficient international remittance services. To this end, the markets for the services should be contestable, transparent, accessible and sound.

Transparency and consumer protection
General Principle 1. The market for remittance services should be transparent and have adequate consumer protection.

Payment system infrastructure
General Principle 2. Improvements to payment system infrastructure that have the potential to increase the efficiency of remittance services should be encouraged.

Legal and regulatory environment
General Principle 3. Remittance services should be supported by a sound, predictable, non-discriminatory and proportionate legal and regulatory framework in relevant jurisdictions.

Market structure and competition
General Principle 4. Competitive market conditions, including appropriate access to domestic payment infrastructures, should be fostered in the remittance industry.

Governance and risk management
General Principle 5. Remittance services should be supported by appropriate governance and risk management practices.
Roles of remittance service providers and public authorities

A. *Role of remittance service providers.* Remittance service providers should participate actively in the implementation of the General Principles.

B. *Role of public authorities.* Public authorities should evaluate what action to take to achieve the public policy objectives through implementation of the General Principles.

Fundamental to success is a distribution network covering remote areas. This is probably the major obstacle facing banks. Even the major global banks generally only maintain branches in major cities. Agreements with local banks operating a large branch network are therefore essential, but few will match the capillarity of the official money transfer systems or even less that of the informal networks.

It should be noted that the demand for remittances also exists domestically in countries where workers in the major cities wish to send money to their unbanked families in less developed rural areas. An innovative system was developed by a Turkish bank based on mobile telephones. After the amount has been debited from the sender's account, the beneficiary will receive an SMS message indicating the amount and a one-off PIN with which the cash can be drawn at any one of the bank's ATMs.

4
Risks in Payment Systems, Oversight and Security

Intermediating and evaluating risk is the essence of banking and the basis for remunerating financial services. The Florentine banker Cosimo de Medici (1389–1464) would instruct his foreign representatives not to lend to princes who never repaid, but to limit themselves to financing reputable and competent merchants, relying upon reputation and the judgement of his staff as no rating agencies were active then.

The second half of 2007 saw the subprime mortgage crisis erupt on the front pages of the financial and popular press as top-10 institutions wrote down billions of dollars worth of debt, forcing them to seek assistance from Gulf and Asian sovereign wealth funds to restore their depleted capital ratios. In spite of the much publicized liquidity shortage, all payment systems had settled normally in the major financial centres up until the date of writing these lines.

On 11 September 2001 the World Trade Centre and the Wall Street financial district in New York were devastated and thousands lost their lives when terrorists flew two planes into the Twin Towers. The cash and securities settlement systems, some of which were located at the foot of the Twin Towers, were rapidly restored for some users from back-up sites. The Federal Reserve, the Bank of England, the European Central Bank and most central banks announced that they would meet all liquidity demands. The ECB injected liquidity the next day through 'quick tenders'. On the thirteenth, the Fed and the ECB published details of a 50 billion dollar swap agreement reached the previous day, to counter the risk of a dollar liquidity shortage. Overnight overdrafts granted by the Fed soared from a daily average of nine million dollars throughout August to four billion on 12 September. Payment systems extended their opening hours. On 12 September the ECB put 69 billion euros on the market and 40 the following day. Half of the swap between the Fed and the ECB was used before refund. The next day everything returned to normal and payment operations were functioning. A banking and stock market crash had been avoided.

On 7 July 2005 terrorists again struck in London, albeit on a smaller scale, but no disruption was reported to the payment systems: the lessons had been learned.

These examples demonstrate both the vulnerability of payment systems to financial and external events, as well as the resilience which has been built up over the years in the light of experience.

1 Analysis of risks in payment systems

The exposure to risk and its management within payment systems are subject to several factors:

The amounts and volumes involved: we have seen how RTGS systems account generally for over 90% of the monetary value, settling in a few days the equivalent of their country's annual GDP, while ACHs are constantly seeking to increase volumes to achieve economies of scale. In other words, the more successful a payment system becomes, the greater the concentration of risk.

Technical and financial innovation: payment and securities clearing and settlement systems must maintain technological leadership to handle increasing volumes and new instruments while reducing execution times and fees as well as complying with demanding risk limitation algorithms. On the other hand, financial institutions are constantly developing more complex products, assisted by (supposedly!) increasingly sophisticated risk models. A key measure is the *value at risk* (VAR), an estimate of the maximum losses a product or portfolio might incur over a given period with a specified confidence level (for example: this asset has a 95% probability of not losing more than 5% of its value over the next 30 days). The subprime crisis mentioned above illustrated painfully how the repackaging and securitization of low quality debt gave birth to instruments which, instead of reducing and/or spreading risk, gave rise to greater financial losses over a longer period of time than were thought possible.

Diversity of expertise and skills: payments stretch across the entire banking organization, functionally and geographically (retail and wholesale banking, securities and FX trading, etc. across all branches and subsidiaries) calling for cooperation between a multitude of disciplines: IT, telecommunications, operations, legal, audit, marketing and finally risk management. Few specialists grasp all issues and their interrelationship, and interfaces between the various systems are particularly sensitive.

Transparency: payment systems must be auditable and individual payments must be traceable end-to-end in case of disputes or investigations. Payment services rely on cooperative systems (for instance ACHs) as well as value-added services, processes and technology through which providers seek to gain competitive advantage. This 'cooperation vs. competition' dichotomy does not always lead to full end-to-end transparency.

Achieving the right balance between costs and security: maximum security and minimum risk are achieved at a cost in terms of investments and operating costs, as well as the opportunity cost of securities immobilized for collateral. Firm criteria are often developed and imposed by central banks and supervisory authorities after an incident as we will see in the following paragraphs.

Effecting payments and managing the related risks are among the core competencies of commercial banks. Central banks, on the other hand, are at the heart of payment systems as final settlement agent, liquidity providers and, ultimately, lenders of last resort. They have therefore naturally assumed responsibility for the oversight of payment systems and cooperate on this topic within the Committee on Payment and Settlement Systems (CPSS) of the BIS.

The CPSS has identified that 'A range of risks can arise in payment systems, taking the following forms in that context:

- *credit risk*: the risk that a party within the system will be unable to fully meet its financial obligations within the system either when due or at any time in the future;
- *liquidity risk*: the risk that a party within the system will have insufficient funds to meet financial obligations within the system as and when expected, although it might be able to do so at some time in the future;
- *legal risk*: the risk that a poor legal framework or legal uncertainties will cause or exacerbate credit or liquidity risks;
- *operational risk*: the risk that operational factors such as technical malfunctions or operational mistakes will cause or exacerbate credit or liquidity risks; and
- *systemic risk*: the risk that the inability of one of the participants to meet its obligations, or a disruption in the system itself, could result

in the inability of other system participants or of financial institutions in other parts of the financial system to meet their obligations as they become due. Such a failure could cause widespread liquidity or credit problems and, as a result, threaten the stability of the system or of financial markets.'[1]

2 Risk management

2.1 Financial risks

Financial risk arises when there is a delay between acceptance of the payment by the system and final settlement. This can be caused by a temporary failure (liquidity risk) or, more seriously, definite inability by a participant to meet its obligations, for instance in case of default, suspension or bankruptcy (credit risk).

These intraday settlement risks are significant in Deferred Net Settlement Systems (DNS) when final settlement occurs at designated times, mostly at the end of the operating day. In addition to the imposition of minimum capital and credit rating requirements as part of the membership criteria, this has led to the introduction of limits on the maximum level of risk that a participant can create. These can be bilateral limits imposed by each participant on the other direct members, an overall multilateral net debit limit imposed by the system (the maximum difference at any point in time between the sum of the values of payments received minus the payments sent by a participant), or a combination of both.

Measures must therefore be taken to ensure that a DNS system can settle daily even in case of default of one or more of its members. The ultimate remedy would be *unwinding*, which implies removing some – up to the point where the defaulting participant's multilateral net debit limit can be met – or all payments entered by the defaulting participant since the last settlement and recalculating the net positions. This is, however, a measure of last resort used extremely rarely as removal of these payments might leave the surviving members with insufficient funds to meet their own obligations. The regulators have therefore imposed that participants bear the responsibility for covering eventual losses; two arrangements prevail, either individually or in combination:

- *Defaulter pays*: the defaulting participant must secure collateral to cover at least the multilateral net debit limit imposed on him;
- *Survivors pay*: a *loss sharing agreement* which stipulates how the surviving participants will share the loss, generally in proportion to the

bilateral limits they have placed on the defaulter, thereby reflecting the risk they were assuming towards it. These commitments will also be secured by collateral.

In RTGS systems credit risk is considered to have been eliminated as final settlement takes place gross for each payment in real-time, particularly if Y-copy routing is adopted (see ch. 1, sec. 3.4) when the receiving bank is only notified after settlement, eliminating the possibility of it crediting the beneficiary's account prematurely. Liquidity risk does however remain, as payments will be queued if insufficient funds are available at the settlement account and ultimately returned if not settled by day end. This risk is however reduced by the provision of intraday liquidity from the money market or collateralized credit lines from the central bank, as well as the implementation of increasingly sophisticated queuing algorithms and liquidity saving features (see ch. 1 sec. 3.3). These modern systems, which combine real-time gross settlement of urgent payments while lower priority payments are deferred awaiting netting or offsetting, are referred to as *hybrid* systems. Early RTGS systems suffered liquidity problems as participants tended to delay entering payments (particularly high value ones), waiting for received payments to supply their liquidity: obviously nothing much happened and the system gridlocked as everybody waited for everybody else! Pricing incentives were introduced, whereby late payments were subject to a much higher tariff, but most RTGS systems now impose minimum percentages of the total daily value that must be entered by specific times throughout the operating day.

All systems rely therefore on a *collateral pool* owned by its members to guarantee obligations and/or credit lines. The assets constituting this pool must be extremely liquid, such as government securities (for instance Gilts, T-bills, and Bons du Trésor), cash or other instruments used by central banks for their open market operations. They can be immobilized or, to reduce opportunity costs, pledged or made available through repurchase agreements (repos) covering the operating day. A *haircut* (generally around 10 per cent) is normally imposed to guard against fluctuations in market value. Direct computer links are also implemented between RTGS payment systems and the securities depositories to ensure rapid availability of the collateral should a participant wish to increase liquidity.

All payment systems must therefore include comprehensive information and control facilities enabling participants, the operator and/or the central bank to monitor balances, limits and collateral valuations in real time and take the necessary action.

2.2 Legal risks

Legal uncertainty can arise out of:

- the contractual agreements between participants, system owner, system operator(s) and eventual subcontractors;
- the legal framework establishing finality of settlement;
- insolvency and bankruptcy legislation; and
- the ability to use collateral posted.

These issues should not be underestimated. In particular for systems operating crossborder, legal fees to ensure enforceability in all relevant jurisdictions have amounted to a substantial proportion of the development investment.

A payment system relies upon a series of contractual agreements:

- The *statutes*, defining the incorporation, shareholding, jurisdiction, objectives, governance and eligibility criteria. Payment systems can be private (normally in majority owned by its participants as shareholders), public (owned by the central bank) or mixed when shareholding includes the central bank.
- *Management and service level agreements* if the operation is subcontracted to one or more service providers. Even if the owner(s) operate the system themselves, subcontractors are always involved for telecommunications, energy and cooling, IT services, maintenance, etc.
- The *operating manual* defining the standards, procedures and processes which must be followed by the operator(s) and the participants, to include performance criteria, security and business continuity.
- The *settlement convention* between the clearing system and the settlement entity, defining in particular the cut-off times and the rules applying to the settlement accounts, credit lines and collateral.
- *Agreements between participants* regarding netting, bilateral credit lines, loss recovery procedures and provision of liquidity, in particular eventual automated lending/borrowing between long and short members to facilitate settlement.

We will see the importance of service level agreements and performance criteria in the section 2.3 covering operational risk.

The legislation surrounding settlement finality must cover payments settled gross and payments which are netted in a DNS system. The implementation of RTGS systems required the abolition of the previously widespread 'zero hour rule' which decreed that in a case of bankruptcy, all transactions by the participant from the start of the day (hour zero) were void, thereby reinstating credit risk after what was considered to be final settlement at the central bank. In addition, legal uncertainty existed in the case of payments accepted by a DNS and netted, which might have to be unwound.

Finally, a reliable legal framework, known as the *laws of secured interests*, must surround collateral to ensure that assets pledged, or subject to a repurchase agreement, can be effectively and rapidly realized in case of bankruptcy.

It should however be stated that sound legal frameworks are now in place for all major currencies, for example the EU Settlement Finality Directive[2] and the Article 4A of the US Uniform Commercial Code.

2.3 Operational risk

Managing operational risk is intimately linked to security and business continuity. Reducing risk in these areas demands the implementation of coordinated and harmonized end-to-end procedures as, to quote the cliché, 'a chain is only as strong as its weakest link'. Security and availability must therefore extend to all components (staff, procedures, IT hardware and software, telecommunications, power and cooling supply, etc.) not only at the central system, but also at subcontractors and each participant: most systems insist on technical and process qualification tests before a participant can operate live. This section will concentrate on operational resilience and business continuity; security will be discussed in section 4 of this chapter.

Design specifications should ensure no 'single point of failure': several institutions discovered, at their cost after a major outage, that the same power grid served main and back-up sites or that telecommunication links, in spite of entering a building at different points, rejoined in the same cable at the end of the street! Service level agreements usually specify execution time under peak volume requirements, as well as response times to information requests such as authorizations for card payments or calls for collateral. Regarding business continuity, criteria include the minimum availability during operating hours (normally over 99.9%), allowable down time for maintenance and system updates, as well as the maximum delay to resume service in case of failure.

The 9/11 terrorist attack highlighted dramatically the need to cope with multiple failures and showed that it was unrealistic to rely upon personnel moving to a back-up operating site following a major regional disaster. It also prompted an industry wide reappraisal of business continuity procedures not only for payments, but taking a holistic view across the entire financial system including exchanges, securities settlement systems and other critical market infrastructures, covering operational issues and provision of liquidity to avert a financial crash. The US regulators (Federal Reserve System, SEC and OCC) and the ECB published stringent new guidelines to guarantee business continuity. Although all critical infrastructures operate primary and secondary sites, both stress the requirement for 'out of region' fully staffed back-up centres for the central system and critical participants (institutions which contribute substantial volumes or value). The ECB guidelines apply to Systemically Important Payment Systems (SIPS) defined as 'A payment system is systemically important if a disruption within that system could trigger or transmit further disruptions amongst participants or systemic disruptions in the financial area more widely.'[3] They recommend 'that SIPS should aim to recover and resume critical functions or services (including critical services outsourced to third-party providers) no later than two hours after the occurrence of a disruption.' Regarding critical participants, the ECB also recommends that operating a secondary site should be part of the requirements to join the system and states: 'At a minimum, relevant participants should be able to close one business day and reopen the following day on the secondary site'.

In addition to staffing issues, the operation of distant sites poses technical problems with respect to data logging and integrity as 'synchronous disk mirroring', to ensure that identical data is available in 'hot standby' mode at both sites, has physical limitations with respect to distance. Secondary sites should also be sized to absorb higher volumes as experience shows that flows exceed the daily average following a serious disruption.

Regulators also demand the implementation of contingency arrangements to ensure that, at a minimum, critical payments (for instance settlement of other payment systems or related to monetary policy) can be handled even in case of catastrophic unavailability of primary and back-up sites: 'The provision of a 'minimum service level of critical functions' could be achieved, for example, through a combination of predetermined business authentication procedures based on manual, paper-based processing, authenticated facsimile messages, or a basic PC-based system using physical media for data transfer.'[4]

Finally, the regulators stress the need to thoroughly document and regularly test and rehearse contingency plans under a variety of scenarios. Industry-wide contingency tests are conducted by the supervisory authorities at random intervals.

2.4 Systemic risk

Systemic risk is the central bankers' terminology for the 'domino effect', the risk that failure of one or more participants to settle might spread to other institutions and degenerate into a major financial crisis. The CPSS therefore published in 2001 the Core Principles for Systemically Important Payments Systems, as defined in the previous paragraph. The core principles are detailed in Box 4.1.

Box 4.1 Core principles for systemically important payment systems[5]

I. The system should have a well-founded legal basis under all relevant jurisdictions.

II. The system's rules and procedures should enable participants to have a clear understanding of the system's impact on each of the financial risks they incur through participation in it.

III. The system should have clearly defined procedures for the management of credit risks and liquidity risks, which specify the responsibilities of the system operator and the participants and which provide appropriate incentives to manage and contain those risks.

IV. The system should provide prompt final settlement on the day of value, preferably during the day and at minimum at the end of the day.*

V. A system in which multilateral netting takes place should, at a minimum, be capable of ensuring the timely completion of daily settlements in the event of an inability to settle by the participant with the largest single settlement obligation.*

VI. Assets used for settlement should preferably be a claim on the central bank; where other assets are used, they should carry little or no credit risk and little or no liquidity risk.

VII. The system should ensure a high degree of security and operational reliability and should have contingency arrangements for timely completion of daily processing.

VIII. The system should provide a means of making payments which is practical for its users and efficient for the economy.

IX. The system should have objective and publicly disclosed criteria for participation, which permit fair and open access.

X. The system's governance arrangements should be effective, accountable and transparent.

* Systems should seek to exceed the minima in these two core principles.

The key issues for Principles I – VII have been discussed in the previous section. The asterisk* for Principles IV and V, indicating that 'Systems should seek to exceed the minima in these two core principles', refer to the recommendations of the CPSS that countries should at least implement an RTGS system for high-value payments and that multilateral netting payment systems should be able to withstand the inability to settle by more than one participant.

Principle VIII, which might initially appear as 'motherhood and apple pie', is a reminder that cost efficiency should include all costs: fees, liquidity, joining investment and operating costs. Operators should also consider that institutions of different size might wish, or be compelled, to join and that economic interfacing solutions must be made available to low-volume participants.

Principle IX clarifies that access criteria must be transparent and objective, for instance minimum capital requirements or market share.

The definition of 'systemically important' might appear subjective; the ECB[6] considers that all RTGS systems, high value systems and retail payment systems for which there is no national alternative, for instance ACHs handling credit transfers and direct debits irrespective of the value, must be defined as SIPS.

2.5 Settlement risk in financial markets

All trading operations include two steps: the actual trading when the price is struck, and the settlement which consists of delivering the currencies or securities brought or sold. It is important that this takes place simultaneously to avoid a *settlement fail*, for instance the cash for securities being paid but the securities not being delivered. All securities are today dematerialized: shares are no longer physically printed and handed over, but ownership exists as accounting records in a Centralized Securities Depository (CSD) which are modified when the trade is settled. To eliminate settlement risk, regulators have mandated the implementation of Delivery versus Payment (DVP). This is normally achieved by interlinking the CSD with the relevant RTGS system which sends confirmation that the payment has been irrevocably settled following which the change of ownership will be registered. This concept will be further enlarged in Chapter 11, while Chapter 10 will look at the elimination of settlement risk in foreign exchange trading.

3 Regulatory oversight

Until the 1990s, central banks were solely responsible for supervising commercial banks, while separate bodies, such as the SEC in the US, supervised securities trading. The emergence of global and universal banks combining retail, commercial and particularly investment banking and securities services prompted the devolution of supervision to independent bodies such as the Financial Services Authority (FSA) in the UK, the Bundesaufsichtsamt für Finanziellen Instituten (BaFin) in Germany. Arguing that they issue money which is the fundamental means of exchange, that it is essential to maintain stability of the financial system and that safe and efficient systems are vital for the implementation of monetary policy, the central banks maintained oversight of the payment and settlement systems: 'Oversight of payment systems is a public policy activity focused on the efficiency and safety of systems, as opposed to the efficiency and safety of individual participants in such systems... In many countries, the central bank's oversight role is considered an integral element of its function in ensuring financial stability',[7] clearly separating oversight over the payment system from supervision of its participants.

Oversight is defined as: 'Oversight of payment and settlement systems is a central bank function whereby the objectives of safety and efficiency are promoted by monitoring existing and planned systems, assessing them against these objectives and, where necessary, inducing change'.[8] As mentioned previously, central banks cooperate on these issues and define guidelines within the CPSS at the BIS which are defined in Box 4.2.

Principle E is of particular importance as payment and securities systems increasingly offer their services internationally and the above publication further specifies that 'there should be a presumption that the central bank where the system is located will have this primary responsibility'. Under this principle, oversight of SWIFT for example rests with the National Bank of Belgium where SWIFT is headquartered.

Banks also cooperate in national bodies to define payment services and monitor performance of the various systems, such as APCA (Australian Payments and Clearing Association) in Australia and APACS (Association for Payment and Clearing Services) in the UK. We will see in Chapter 6

Box 4.2 General Oversight Principles[9]

A. Transparency: Central banks should set out publicly their oversight policies, including the policy requirements or standards for systems and the criteria for determining which systems these apply to.
B. International standards: Central banks should adopt, where relevant, internationally recognized standards for payment and settlement systems.
C. Effective powers and capacity: Central banks should have the powers and capacity to carry out their oversight responsibilities effectively.
D. Consistency: Oversight standards should be applied consistently to comparable payment and settlement systems, including systems operated by the central bank.
E. Cooperation with other authorities: Central banks, in promoting the safety and efficiency of payment and settlement systems, should cooperate with other relevant central banks and authorities.

(sec. 1) how banks also established the European Payments Council (EPC) to address the Single Euro Payments Area (SEPA). These organizations are often blamed for preserving the interests of the banks and ignoring the demands from their customers. A novel approach was taken in the UK in 2007 through the creation of the Payments Council, whose Board includes external directors, alongside the Bank of England as an observer (see ch. 6 sec. 8).

4 Fraud prevention, security and anti money laundering

As payment services develop, security measures must take account of the wider range of payment means and channels that emerge, bringing with them new opportunities but also introducing new risks.

A comprehensive study of the security procedures and technology across all instruments and channels, starting with measures to prevent counterfeiting of banknotes, would be beyond the scope of this book. We will attempt however to provide an overview of the principal risks and fraud prevention measures surrounding electronic payments and cards.

Security and fraud prevention centre principally around four issues:

- *Authentication*: is the originator of the payment or the payment instruction the account owner or a person authorized to effect payments from that account, credit card or payment instrument? Is the beneficiary or receiver of the payment or information the intended recipient? At both ends of the communication link we need assurance that the 'real' and 'asserted' identities are correct.
- *Confidentiality*: has any outside third party gained unauthorized access to the payment information, or to any data which would allow it to subsequently fraudulently access the account or modify any instruction?
- *Integrity*: has any unauthoriszed third party fraudulently changed any of the information: amount, beneficiary, account holding bank, account number(s), etc.?
- *Non-repudiation*: could the originator, or any authorized party, deny having taken any action he/she has actually undertaken?

Major concerns lie with identity theft, or phishing, whereby fraudsters attempt to acquire passwords, usernames, dates of birth, PINs, etc. by posing as a trustworthy counterparty. Methods range from the sophisticated, whereby criminals insert a dummy banking or on-line retailer website to capture payment information, to simplistic requests, by e-mail or SMS, purporting to come from trusted entities such as banks or government agencies requesting details such as passwords or PINs. Other scams have been based on capturing card details and PINs by installing fraudulent readers and/or cameras at ATMs. Most of us will have received e-mails from Nigerians suffering from a terminal illness requesting our account details to transfer their wealth to someone they can trust to use it for the greater benefit of mankind! These simplistic scams, including miraculous lottery wins, often deliberately target vulnerable segments of the population such as the elderly. Most banks state on their websites, or in the opening messages from call centres, that they will never ask for information such as card PINs.

In the retail space growing volumes and the proliferation of new internet payment methods linked to e-mail or pre-payment schemes, some of which shift the security issues away from the financial institutions to new players, can alter the underlying security for the user.

Although banks enhance their security continuously, organized crime is constantly adapting and developing new ways to collect and use identity information, bank account and credit card details. This can include collusion with staff within the financial institution or it's customers, hacking of databases, recuperating confidential information from waste bins or stealing data in transit e.g. CD-ROMs, tape back ups and laptops. Banks and merchants need to constantly review their technical and organizational security procedures to maintain and enhance the level of security they achieve.

In the business to business space, payments are becoming more and more embedded in the exchange of data that encompasses the complete trade chain; this has brought new routes through which payments are initiated and therefore the need to create trust schemes that can handle these.

In addition to these security and fraud prevention issues, an increasing regulatory burden is imposed on payment service providers in terms of customer identity verification or Know your Customer (KYC), Anti Money Laundering (AML) and Counter Terrorism Finance (CTF). These issues are overarching, irrespective of the payment instrument and/or channel used.

4.1 Internet banking

The implementation of internet banking websites requires varying levels of security depending on the value of the information and transactions that can be undertaken. Many different methods of authentication are available in the marketplace now, for example:

- username and password;
- partial PINs and passwords;
- one-time passwords based on using a 'grid' or 'matrix' of stored values on a plastic card;
- one-time passwords generated by a time synchronized device (such as 'key fob' type devices;
- one-time passwords generated from a pseudo-random sequence (including EMV-CAP cards and readers);
- a manual (disconnected) device in conjunction with an on-line challenge/response protocol;
- an automatic device (for instance connected via a USB port) with a similar challenge/response protocol; and
- a device which is capable of storing keys and performing asymmetric cryptography, such as a smart-card or USB token, and which therefore can be used as client in a Public Key Infrastructure (PKI: see next section).

4.2 Wholesale banking and trust schemes

Frequently, higher levels of security and fraud prevention measures are implemented on account of the values and volumes transacted, particularly for direct computer-to-computer links. The objective is to combine authentication (at both ends), confidentiality, integrity and non-repudiation. Much of this is achieved through *Public Key Cryptography* which is based on the use of a private key and a public key that are inextricably linked. The private key can be used to sign a message and the public key, available to all counterparties, can then be used to check the signature. The mathematics ensure that the private key cannot be used check the signature, or the public key to create the signature. These keys can also be used to encrypt data using either the private or public key that can only be decrypted using the public or private key respectively. Through the use of various protocols this technology also provides non-repudiation. The Internet Banking Application itself should also ensure that the user with the correct level of authority is initiating the transaction and, where appropriate, enforce dual and multiple signatures.

Throughout the development of payment services, individual payment messages and files of payments initiated by the bank customer have always been sent to the Bank itself or the Automated Clearing House (ACH) directly. In trading terms this has meant that the payment message has been created, signed and sent to the Financial Institution by the buyer/payer. Except in limited EDI message types, the payment has often been divorced from the underlying information or trade cycle which requires extensive communication between the trading enterprises.

As discussed previously, banks are seeking to develop services which enhance their position in the trade cycle and compensate for loss of revenues on the commoditized basic payment services. These required the development of a new trust model to allow messages and eventually payments initiated by one bank's customers to be checked and trusted by another bank and its customers. This has been achieved by linking the development of individual Public Key Infrastructures (PKI) at banks across the world to a single Trust scheme such as IdenTrust. IdenTrust has developed a legal framework alongside a set of policies, procedures and technical standards for authentication and to issue trusted identities worldwide. Reverting to the classical four-corner model a customer who has been issued a Digital Certificate, confirming that their public key has been issued to it by a third party whom all the recipients can trust such as an IdenTrust member bank, can conduct trusted business with a trusted customer of another IdenTrust member bank. Schemes such as IdenTrust provide a global framework for the provision of certificate authority services, enabling financial institutions to extend their full range of services onto the internet and become trusted third parties for e-commerce transactions. Through this they can develop new lines of business as the internet becomes a preferred transaction medium and their customers will have the ability to leverage a single bilateral relationship with a financial institution for all e-commerce dealings. At the same time this offers businesses and financial institutions a way to add value by proactively managing the risk associated with e-commerce.

4.3 Cards

With the exception of the US, chip card technology combined with a PIN under the EMV (Europay, MasterCard, Visa) scheme is gaining worldwide acceptance and fraud is significantly reduced in comparison with signature and magnetic stripe. In any case, signature or PIN verification can only take place when the card holder is physically present in the retail outlet at the moment of purchase.

The expansion of telephone ordering and internet shopping has also required the development of security measures to enable Card Not Present (CNP) transactions. The most common is the CVV2 (Card Verification Value 2) code, generally referred to as the 'security code', which is a three or four digit number most often placed on the reverse of the card. It does not however offer protection should the card be stolen. Visa and MasterCard have therefore developed additional security procedures such as Verified-by-Visa and SecureCode for MasterCard to be used on the internet.

In addition to ensuring the authenticity of the card holder, card providers have sophisticated transaction monitoring systems that ensure they detect unusual activity or behaviour patterns on an account and can take the appropriate actions to stop fraud as early as possible.

The Payments Card Industry Standards Council, regrouping the major brands (Amex, Discover, JCB International, MasterCard, Visa), have also developed comprehensive requirements for a Data Security Standard (PCI DSS) covering security management, procedures, policies, network architecture, software design and backed by comprehensive self-assessment questionnaires. All issuers, merchants and acquirers have to prove they abide by these rules and undergo specific assessments to prove it.

4.4 Anti money laundering (AML) and counter-terrorism finance (CTF)

Since 9/11, legislation and regulation to counter AML and CTF have multiplied and placed an increasing burden on the banks.

The Financial Action Task Force on Money Laundering (FATF) was established by the G-7 Summit as early as 1989 and, up until the time of publication, was endorsed by 34 countries and had published 40 Recommendations against money laundering supplemented by nine Special Recommendations against terrorism finance. The principal focus is on Customer Due Diligence (CDD): not maintaining anonymous accounts; verification of identity of retail customers; and business purpose and identity of beneficial owners of corporate and correspondent banking relationships. Accurate and meaningful originator information must be included on all funds transfers and preserved throughout the entire payment chain. Records must be maintained for at least five years. Financial institutions should report any suspicious activity, customer or financial institution.

The USA Patriot Act (Uniting and Strengthening America by Providing Appropriate Tools Required to Intercept and Obstruct Terrorism) of 2001, among other provisions, strengthens most of the FATF recommendations by incorporating them into law.

Ordering customers and beneficiaries must be checked against stop lists of embargoed persons, entities or countries; each country maintains its own, the most commonly used being issued by the US Office of Foreign Asset Control (OFAC). These measures have forced many banks to invest in substantial developments to ensure compliance, adequate audit trails and investigation tools.

5
The Role of Payment Systems in the Economy

Except under a barter economy, an exchange of money is necessary to settle any purchase of goods or services, whether in fiduciary (cash) or in scriptural money. In the latter case, the bank can choose to settle via a payment system or directly with the creditor's bank. This practice, where banks held correspondent accounts with each other, has largely disappeared for domestic payments within the same currency, but was widespread until technology enabled the introduction of electronic payment systems during the second half of the twentieth century. The correspondent account system would have in any case become unmanageable because of the necessity to reconcile all the accounts and the opportunity cost of maintaining idle balances scattered around the banking system. Payment systems have enabled banks to centralize the settlement of liabilities and reduced demands on liquidity and processing costs through economies of scale and the networking effect.

1 The economic role of payment systems

The role of payment systems is to ensure the convertibility of liabilities on commercial banks, otherwise known as commercial bank money, embodied by the balances (or credit lines) customers hold on their bank accounts. The commercial bank assumes a claim acceptable over the market on behalf of its client, followed by the central bank which substitutes it for a claim in central bank money acceptable by all banks. This role was, until the second half of the twentieth century, assumed in London by the Accepting Houses which, subject to a fee, rendered 'acceptable' by guaranteeing it a bill of exchange between two customers drawn on a foreign bank. In a modern payment system, the commercial banks use their settlement account with the central bank to guarantee finality. The payment system substitutes all interbank settlements by one settlement in central bank money.

We noted in Chapter 1 (sec. 2.5) that an efficient money market is indispensable to the smooth functioning of payment systems, as it enables banks to fund their end-of-day settlement positions in DNS systems and to access intraday liquidity in RTGS systems. The centralization of settlement and clearing operations contributes to the pricing of money on the domestic market (interest rate) and of currencies on the international markets (exchange rate). Even in a DNS system the bank's treasurer will follow the position throughout the day and, if required, start funding an anticipated short position early on to avoid higher interest rates at closure if the market dries up or the spread between the lending and borrowing rates has widened.

The main impact of a payment system is to unify the market. This was observed at the launch of the euro and the TARGET high-value RTGS system. Within a few months interest rates converged across the eurozone, except for minor differences due to country credit ratings. The ECB was able to implement its monetary policy effectively through an efficient payment system.

Much was written during the subprime crisis about the 'interdependencies' of risk between institutions and instruments across geographies. The central banks responded by coordinated interventions which they were able to implement, and measure the impact, through the relevant payment systems and securities markets whose settlement systems interconnect. Will the major high-value payment settlement systems interconnect in the same way as we progress towards harmonization of standards and procedures? Would that provide a more effective tool for central bankers coordinating their interventions to avoid systemic risk, or would the risk of single point of failure arise?

2 Payment systems and money velocity

Money velocity can be influenced by the performance of payment systems in terms of execution speed, cost and security. Money supply is equal to the value of payments multiplied by money velocity. For a given value of transactions, a highly efficient payment system will reduce the speed of execution and increase the turnover of money supply. Conversely, for a given value of transactions, the demand for liquidity will diminish as money velocity increases, payment systems become more efficient and execution time reduces. Theoretically, money supply should diminish for a given velocity, but increased demand from a growing number of transactions is more than compensating the effect of a higher velocity from technological advance: the growth of money supply is slower than the growth of the GDP.

Central banks will use the information provided by payment systems to determine their monetary objectives and to measure the delay in reaction to their interventions. As settlement institutions, they have visibility on all operations, not only payments but also government debt. The monetary channel measures the diffusion of interest rates on the markets by arbitraging between the different maturities on the yield curve or between different financial instruments. The balance sheet channel reflects the impact of monetary policy on the value of the collateral and consequently collateralized credit lines. The payment systems are therefore one of the channels through with central banks transmit monetary policy and can measure the impact of their interventions. As banks require liquidity during the final phases of the settlement cycle, the availability of central bank money is critical. They rely on the central bank for day-to-day supervision of the markets and as lender of last resort.

In theory, money velocity depends short term on interest rates and long term on economic growth as the number and the value of transactions increase. Historically, money velocity slowed until the 1950s and accelerated thereafter. This deceleration can be explained by the monetarization of the economy. That phase ended after World War II and was followed by economic growth and the widespread adoption of bank accounts: money velocity accelerated to stabilize since the turn of this century.

Looking at Fisher's equation $MV = PT$ (Money supply $\times$ Velocity $=$ Price $\times$ number of Transactions), an increase in performance of payment systems, given a constant money supply, should reduce the number of payments (or limit their growth) required to effect the transactions. The leverage of monetary policy should be reinforced by shrinkage of the money supply or its lower growth than GDP. As velocity increases, the number of transactions diminishes. At the extreme hypothetical case, an infinite velocity (nil execution time) would result in a number of transactions declining to zero: we would revert to a barter economy with networks of supercomputers swapping goods and services in real time; money would have been substituted by the payment system and the central banks would have lost control of the money supply!

3 Network economics

As with all networks, payment systems will benefit from economies of scale and value-added services which increase its attractiveness and profitability. Under a regime of perfect competition, prices will converge towards the marginal cost. As the profitability of the core generic payment service will diminish with competition, competitive differentiation will be dictated by segmented value services through which the service providers will attempt to increase their profits. Ultimately, the core payment service becomes a public utility while value-added services are market-driven.

Networks are driven by economies of scale; costs are largely fixed so additional transactions reduce the unit processing cost. The value of a network depends therefore on the development investments, the services offered and the volume of transactions processed. It is also linked to the square of the number of participants according to Metcalfe's Law. These factors can however exercise a negative influence, for instance when a network reaches saturation, obsolescence or even becomes a de facto monopoly leading to complacency and reluctance to invest in new developments.

We have seen in Chapter 1 (sec. 2.2) how payment system owners can vary the various pricing components (joining fee, annual charge, transaction fee) according to their objectives at each phase in the life-cycle of the system. Once a network has reached critical mass, the *feedback effect* kicks in: unit costs diminish with growing volumes; new adherents seek to join; and investments can be devoted to the development of new products and services. Telecommunication operators for instance decided to invest in mobile telephony in the full knowledge that it would cannibalize their revenues from fixed lines calls and sought alternative revenues from mobile and other services such as broadband and value-added telecommunication services. Similarly, SWIFT launched its file transfer services knowing that the revenues from the individual message charge would suffer.

Some systems, such as SWIFT, become immune to new entrants competing on their core transmission services owing to the sheer numbers of participants and geographical coverage: the barriers to entry are too high. Volume in payment systems is however highly concentrated among a small number of large institutions: in the UK for example, the five largest participants represented 80 per cent of the number of payments over the CHAPS RTGS, 76 per cent of cheque clearing and 76 per cent of the BACS ACH volumes in 2006[1]. With the exception of RTGS systems, payment networks are therefore constantly under the threat of a couple of large users deciding to exchange payments bilaterally, settle the net amount over the relevant RTGS and retain participation to transact with the rump of small volume users or remote geographical locations. Each bank merger generates more 'on us' payments which are removed from payment systems. Payment systems and networks are therefore constantly seeking to develop value-added services to lock-in customers.

The trading and settlement of European securities is currently dominated by three systems, interconnected to other major financial markets. New entrants are likely to concentrate on niche markets and trading platforms have emerged, such as Turquoise. In spite of the backing of major participants, few survive and most eventually retreat to specialized instruments, often after the incumbents have reduced fees. Mission accomplished some will say, raising the question of whether they were mainly launched as a scarecrow. Another example is the ill-fated attempt by Eurex, the derivatives exchange, owned jointly by Deutsche Börse and the Swiss Exchange, to set up a trading and settlement platform in Chicago which closed after two years. One consequence was the merger between the two local incumbents: the CBOT and the CME.

By their very nature networks become a monopoly used by an oligopoly of participants. Rising volumes, declining unit costs, product and technological innovation contribute to this concentration. The barriers to entry to compete on the core service becoming too high, new entrants are constantly seeking value-added services attacking the Achilles heel of the incumbent to establish new networks. They will establish a temporary monopoly before being in turn challenged by a new entrant. Ultimately, as the window of competitive advantage created by new services shortens, the networks regroup and consolidate as we will see in the subsequent chapters.

Part II
Overview of Current Payment Systems

6
European Payments and SEPA

Harmonization of payment practices across the euro zone is seen as the next logical step in a progressive historical sequence: Common Market, Single Market, Monetary Union and the introduction of euro notes and coins. Payments in Europe have undergone a profound transformation since the late-1990s, when all systems and back-office applications had to be converted as countries joined the euro single currency, starting with the first 12 in 1999. It wasn't until 2008 that the seismic change from a business viewpoint occurred with the advent of the Single Euro Payment Area (SEPA). SEPA should clearly be understood as a political move initiated by the European Commission (EC) and the European central Bank (ECB), within the vision of the Lisbon Agenda, to systematically strengthen the Single Market and the euro as a currency.

1 SEPA

The fragmentation of the European payments landscape, where each country maintains its own national payment schemes, standards, practices, infrastructures and legislation, was considered an obstacle on the road to the Single Market. 'SEPA will be the area where citizens, companies and other economic actors will be able to make and receive payments in euro, within Europe (currently defined as consisting of the 25 EU member states plus Iceland, Norway, Liechtenstein and Switzerland), whether between or within national boundaries under the same basic conditions, rights and obligations, regardless of their location.'[1] SEPA is viewed as the next logical step after the introduction of the euro notes and coins and all euro payments within the EU become domestic within the concept of the European Single Market.

Practically speaking, SEPA will enable for instance:

- A Dutch citizen who owns a holiday apartment in Spain to transfer funds to his builder and set up direct debits for the local electricity and telephone companies from his bank in the Netherlands, without opening a bank account in Spain, as well as use his/her Dutch debit card at all Spanish POS terminals.
- A multinational French insurance company to pay all salaries and settle all invoices for its subsidiaries and affiliates in the EU, as well as collect insurance premiums from all its EU customers via direct debits, through one bank as opposed to maintaining banking relationships in each country in which it operates.

It is worth remembering that the attention of the European authorities was first drawn to payment systems by much less lofty ideals. As early as the 1990s employees of the European institutions in Brussels and Luxemburg were shocked by the high fees charged by the banks when they transferred part of their salaries back to their home countries to meet their remaining commitments, such as allowances for children left studying at local universities. Surveys were conducted showing lengthy and unreliable execution times, as well as high charges levied by the sending and receiving banks, resulting in the beneficiary most often not receiving the full amount originally transferred. The banks, unwisely, did not deign to react which led the European Parliament in 2001 to enact Regulation 2560/2001 which, in essence, imposed maximum execution times, forbade banks from charging more for cross-border payments in euro than for domestic ones – including electronic transfers up to €12,500 rising to €50,000 and cash withdrawals at ATMs – and dictated that the full amount had to be remitted to the beneficiary unless specifically agreed.

From then on the EC had the bit between their teeth and, supported by the ECB, relentlessly pushed towards harmonization and standardization. The banks reacted appropriately this time by creating the EPC: 'The European Payments Council (EPC) is the decision making body of the European banking industry in relation to payments whose declared purpose is to support and promote the creation of the SEPA'.[2] In a rare show of unity, the EPC regroups the commercial, savings and cooperative banks, operating through a lean but highly effective secretariat that drives expert working groups whose recommendations are ultimately approved by the EPC Plenary. It duly delivered schemes for SEPA credit transfers (SCT) and direct debits (SDD), as well as a framework for cards (SCF). These will apply to all payments in euro within the EU, and all payment service providers adhering to the SEPA schemes must be reachable by each other. Subsequently, the EPC created a Scheme Management Committee to approve admissions and resolve eventual disputes.

It rapidly became apparent that legal harmonization was required in order to implement standardized schemes. After protracted discussions between the EC, the EPC and the national communities and many revisions, the European Parliament adopted the Payment Services Directive (PSD) in 2007; it must be transposed into national legislation by November 2009 at the latest and will apply to all payments within the EU, including non-euro currencies such as UK sterling or the Swedish kroner.

SEPA was officially launched on 28 January 2008 with the SCT and the SCF. We will explain in the following paragraphs why the implementation of the SDD had to be delayed until November 2009 pending transposition of the PSD. Existing national schemes cannot however be switched off overnight. They will operate in parallel with the SEPA schemes until these reach a 'critical mass', at which point the national schemes will be discontinued. We will see in section 7 of this chapter the implications of this coexistence period and the uncertainty surrounding its duration.

2 The Payment Services Directive (PSD)

The Payment Services Directive 2007/64/EC[3] aims to harmonize legislation surrounding the provision of payments services within the EU, increase competition, as well as reinforce consumer protection through transparency of information and charges and by defining the rights and obligations of the payment service providers and their users. All entities offering payment services are referred to under the generic term of Payment Service Provider (PSP) and their customers are designated as a Payment Service User (PSU).

The PSD opens the door for non-banks to provide payment services, either as a sole activity or alongside their core business, such as mobile telephone operators: these PSPs, designated as Payment Institutions (PI), will be subject to much lighter capital requirements and regulatory supervision than credit institutions which, as could be expected, met with much resistance from the banking sector. The supervision of these PIs is left to the discretion of each Member State and they can offer their services throughout the EU if authorized by one Member State (EU passporting principle).

In terms of scope, the PSD covers all payments, domestic and cross-border when both sending and receiving PSPs operate within the EU, in all EU currencies including cross-currency payments such as between sterling and Danish kroner accounts. Cheques are however excluded.

Payments must be executed on the business day following the day and point in time of receipt of the payment order by the PSP, known as D+1. Parties may however agree on D+3 until 2012. These are maximum times and existing shorter execution cycles at national level remain valid so as not to introduce service degradation. Value dating is not allowed, prohibiting backdating of debits and enabling the beneficiary to use the funds and receive interest immediately after being credited.

The Directive requires PSPs to communicate to the customer the terms under which his/her instruction is accepted, the execution time and a breakdown of the charges, including, where applicable, exchange rates and commissions. The full amount must be received by the beneficiary, unless agreed between the PSP and the beneficiary in which case charges must be itemized separately. Variations prevail depending on the amount, between one-off transactions as opposed to payments under framework contracts and whether the PSU is a consumer, a micro-business or a business.

Customers have up to 8 weeks to claim refunds if an authorized payment was executed incorrectly or, in the case of direct debits, the amount debited exceeded the amount that the payer would have expected to pay. The deadline for lodging claims is extended to 13 months for unauthorized debits, for instance in the absence of a mandate. The PSP must accept or dispute the claim within 10 business days of receipt. Exemptions and opt-outs are allowed for business users. These clauses explain why implementation of the SDD was delayed pending transposition of the PSD into national legislation as different customer protection and guarantees prevail today in each country. Nevertheless, the PSD embodies a marked shift of responsibility and burden of proof towards the PSPs.

PSD transposition into national legislation must be completed by November 2009, allowing Member States limited discretion during implementation. It is anticipated that the EEA countries will also introduce legislation in line with the PSD. A detailed legal review of the PSD and the various exemptions, including the areas of uncertainty at the time of printing and the interaction with related national and EC legislation is beyond the scope of this book. Readers should therefore seek legal advice on compliance with the PSD.

3 The TARGET2 RTGS system

In the run-up to monetary union and the introduction of the euro in January 1999, it rapidly became apparent that a pan-eurozone RTGS system was required for the execution of the Eurosystem's (the ECB and the national EU central banks) monetary policy and to settle high-value payments. Time did not allow for the development of a new supranational system, so the ESCB implemented TARGET (Trans-European Automated Real-time Gross settlement Express Transfer) by *interlinking* the participating national RTGS systems. The system worked well but suffered from variations in service levels, operational requirements and pricing, as the service and user interface ultimately depended on the national RTGS system to which each bank connected. The Eurosystem therefore launched TARGET2 in November 2007 based on a Single Shared Platform (SSP), providing a harmonized service level at a uniform price, over a standard interface with access via the SWIFT network (Y-copy) using SWIFT messages. In retrospect, TARGET2 can be seen as the first tangible step towards SEPA. One of the principal challenges of this concentration was the connection of over 50 Ancillary Systems which settle through TARGET: ACHs, national and international securities settlement systems, CLS (see ch. 10 sec. 3), etc. The development and operation was entrusted to the Banca d'Italia, the Banque de France and the Deutsche Bundesbank (the 3CBs).

Banks can access TARGET2 as direct or indirect participants. It should be noted that although the system is operated by the 3CB on behalf of the Eurosystem, banks maintain the 'business relationship' with their respective central bank for participation, liquidity and collateral management, billing and oversight. TARGET2 therefore offers an optional Home Accounting Module for central banks which would like to continue to offer some basic payment services without having to maintain local home accounts which could be expensive to manage.

The system processes credit transfers and direct debits. Three levels of priority are available:

- Highly Urgent (HU) reserved for payments between central banks and between central banks and commercial banks for the implementation of monetary policy, as well as 'systemic' payments for settlement of ancillary systems, which are settled gross in first-in-first-out (FIFO) sequence.
- Urgent (U) payments which are also settled gross and FIFO.

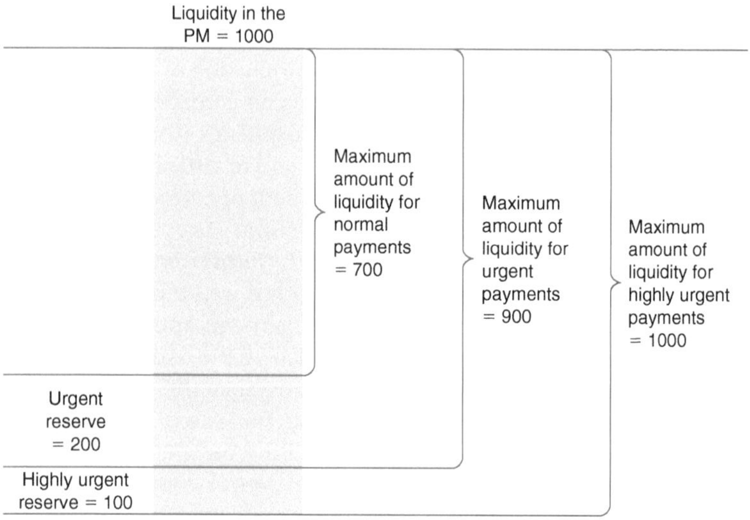

Figure 6.1 TARGET2 liquidity reservations
Source: ECB: TARGET2 UDFS Book 1 – Version 2.3.

- Normal (N) payments which are settled subject to liquidity saving procedures, bypassing FIFO.

Effectively, TARGET2 is a hybrid payment system incorporating state-of-the art liquidity optimization facilities:

- Participants can specify earliest and latest debit times: this is especially useful when payments are subject to a time constraint, for instance to settle CLS short positions;
- Liquidity reservations can be set for HU and U payments, as well as for settlement of ancillary systems (see Figure 6.1);
- Each participant can set a bilateral limit towards an individual bank (see Figure 6.2) and/or a multilateral limit against a group of banks; and
- Offsetting of Normal payments, whereby the FIFO sequence might be breached if the simultaneous settlement of a payment to be sent and a payment to be received is possible, or will result in an increase in liquidity, subject to time and limit constraints.

Figure 6.3 illustrates the sequence of settlement checks:

'1. The system checks whether there are already operations of an equal or higher priority level in the queue (exception: if the submitted

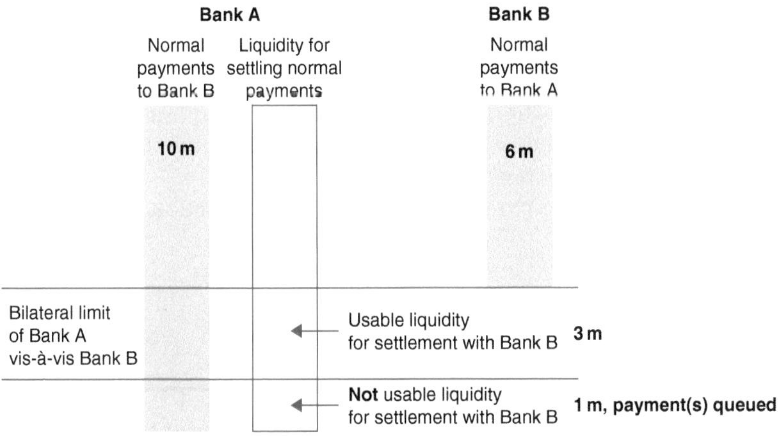

Figure 6.2 TARGET2 bilateral limits
Source: ECB: TARGET2 UDFS Book 1 – Version 2.3

transaction is a normal one, it is not checked whether the "normal" queue is empty, because the FIFO-principle can be breached for normal payments).

2. If the highly urgent and urgent queue is not empty, a bilateral algorithm named "offsetting check with liquidity increase" takes place.

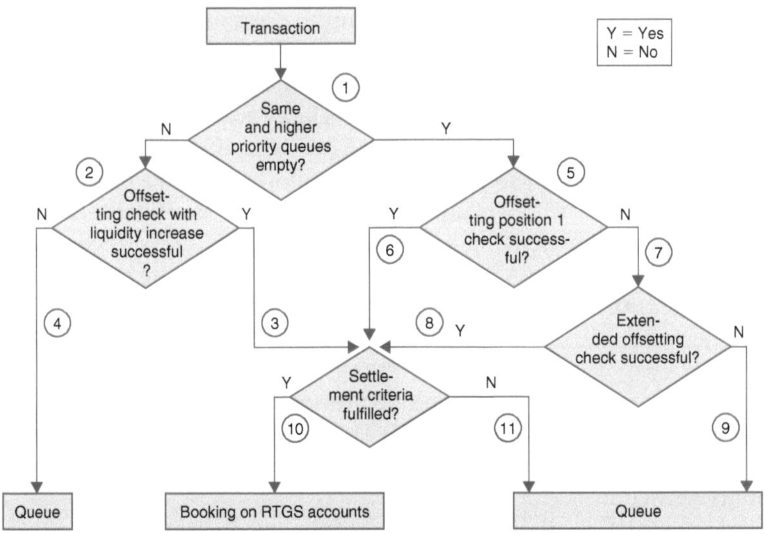

Figure 6.3 TARGET2 payment settlement steps
Source: ECB: TARGET2 UDFS Book 1 – Version 2.3

This algorithm is only successful if offsetting payments from the receiver are available and the sender will afterwards have an increased liquidity position.

3. If offsetting transactions exist, it is checked if the submitted transaction fulfils the other settlement criteria (i.e. bilateral or multilateral limit and liquidity reservations not breached).
4. If no such offsetting transactions exist, the transaction is put in the queue.
5. If the highly urgent and the urgent queue is empty, a bilateral algorithm, the "offsetting position 1 check" takes place. This algorithm is only successful if offsetting payments on top of the receiver's queue are available.
6. If the offsetting check is successful, it is checked if the submitted transaction fulfils the other settlement criteria (i.e. bilateral or multilateral limit and liquidity reservations not breached).
7. If the offsetting check is not successful, a bilateral algorithm named "extended offsetting check" takes place. This algorithm is only successful if offsetting payments from the receiver (not only on top of the queue) are available and the receiver will afterwards have an increased liquidity position.
8. If the extended offsetting check is successful, it is checked if the submitted transaction fulfils the other settlement criteria (i.e. bilateral or multilateral limit and liquidity reservations not breached).
9. If the extended offsetting check is not successful, the transaction is put in the queue.
10. If the other settlement criteria (i.e. bilateral or multilateral limit and liquidity reservations not breached) are fulfilled, then the operation(s), is (are) settled on the RTGS accounts.
11. If the other settlement criteria are not fulfilled, then the operation(s) is (are) put in the queue until sufficient liquidity is available and the other settlement criteria are fulfilled. If there is not sufficient liquidity available and/or the other settlement criteria are not fulfilled till the time of covering is reached, the payments not settled will be rejected.'[4]

Sophisticated queue resolution algorithms are applied to minimize delaying payments while taking into account the priorities assigned, the settlement requirements of ancillary systems as well as any timing and limits restrictions.

Prior to settlement and as long as payments are not included in a queue resolution algorithm, participants can change priorities between

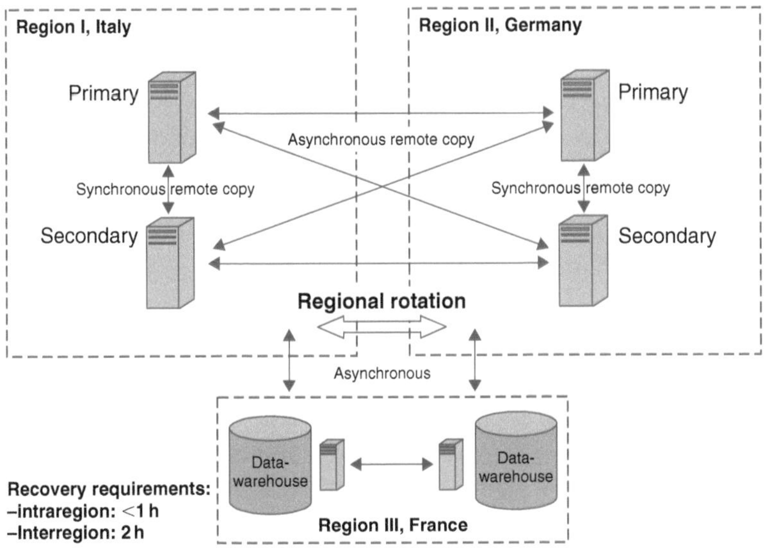

Figure 6.4 TARGET2 architecture

Urgent and Normal, reorder payments within a priority, change timing parameters and even cancel the payment.

Direct participants can transfer liquidity from their Home Account to their Settlement Account at the start of each day, which they can replenish or withdraw during the day as the settlement balance fluctuates. Banks from the same group can pool liquidity cross-border.

Participants and central banks have access to the system through an Information and Control Module (ICM) for statements, reports, liquidity management, enquiries, entering and changing timing and limit parameters, track-and-trace, etc.

In line with best practice for SIPS, TARGET2 operates out of two active regions, Germany and Italy, with data warehousing located in France (see Figure 6.4). The role of primary and secondary regions alternates at regular intervals to ensure that technical staff remains at even levels of competence. A Contingency Module will run in the region not active if an incident occurs. The use of the Contingency Module is only envisaged for the processing of very critical payments in case of catastrophic unavailability of one region, and before the second region is up and running.

TARGET2 settled daily on average over 366,000 payments for a value exceeding €2.4 trillion during 2007.[5]

4 Clearing and settlement mechanisms (CSMs)

The multitude of ACHs in the EU is seen as a major source of inefficiency and the EC and the ECB are driving towards open competition and consolidation, following the separation of schemes and infrastructures mandated by the authorities: the scheme owners define the standards and rules allowing infrastructures to compete.

The EPC defines two levels of compliance for clearing and settlement mechanisms (CSMs):

- Level 1: SEPA scheme compliant
- Level 2: PE-ACH compliant ACH: 'A PE-ACH compliant ACH is a business platform which will include the provision of the clearing and settlement of SEPA Scheme payments with full reachability throughout SEPA and made up of governance and operational rules, the necessary technical platform(s) and related services'.[6]

The reachability can also be provided by interlinking SEPA scheme compliant ACHs or CSMs, the European Automated Clearing Houses Association (EACHA) has defined an Interoperability Framework to achieve this. Recognizing that some PSPs will wish to clear by bilateral file exchange with some counterparties and not through an ACH (as in Germany at national level), the SEPA schemes refer generically to 'Clearing and Settlement Mechanisms' (CSM). PSPs are free to choose any CSM irrespective of its country of location and we will see in section 7.5 of this chapter how this competitive environment is changing the landscape.

5 The EBA payment systems

The Euro Banking Association (EBA) started life in 1985 as the Association Bancaire pour l'Ecu (ABE), a private banking association established in Paris with the objective of developing a settlement system for the Ecu, the precursor of the euro. The Ecu was a basket of EU currencies and, as such, did not therefore have a 'national' settlement system, or an obvious settlement agent. The system was launched in 1986 with 18 banks and settlement taking place at the BIS. Development and operation were subcontracted to SWIFT. As the euro single currency was introduced in 1999 the Ecu netting system became the EURO1 netting system and the ABE changed its name to EBA-ABE (Euro Banking Association – Association Bancaire pour l'Euro). The EBA is a 'discussion forum for payments practitioners ... The initiation and development of cost-effective and efficient euro clearing systems are core activities of the association and have led to the creation of Europe's leading private large-value clearing system EURO1, the low-value payment system STEP1 and the first PE-ACH (pan-European automated clearing house) STEP2.'[7] These are owned and operated by the EBA Clearing Company whose shareholders are the clearing banks.

5.1 The EURO1 system

EURO1 is a same-day deferred net settlement (DNS) system processing single payments. The operation is subcontracted to SWIFT. Messages are transmitted over SWIFT using the Y-copy feature. Multilateral net balances are updated after each payment, but EURO1 does not operate as a central counterparty. Instead, a Single Obligation legal structure, validated in all EU countries, ensures that 'each participant has a single obligation (in the case of a negative amount) or a single claim (in the case of a positive balance) towards all other participants. The single obligation is valid and enforceable at each and any time throughout the day'.[8] This implies that each payment is irrevocable and final upon being processed and unwinding is therefore not possible. The system processes credit transfers and direct debits.

Cut-off time is 16.00 CET to allow for settlement, through the national central banks (NCBs) and the ECB, to complete prior to TARGET's closing time at 18.00 CET. Balances are sent out and each short participant (with a debit position) instructs his NCB to debit his account in favour of EURO1's settlement account at the ECB. When all payments from short participants are received the ECB, upon instruction from EBA Clearing, instructs the relevant NCBs to credit the long participants (with a credit position). Each participant grants a limit to the others (subject to a mandatory minimum of €5 million and a maximum of €25 million) and is allocated a debit cap (the sum of the limits received from all other participants) and a credit cap (the sum of the limits he has granted). Debit and credit caps are subject to a maximum of €1 billion and a collateral pool of €1 billion has been established at the ECB in case one or more short participants fail to meet their obligations.[9] Payments which would breach the credit and/or debit caps are queued.

During 2007, EURO1 processed a daily average of over 211,000 payments for a value of €228 billion from 70 participants.[10]

5.2 The STEP1 system

The STEP1 system was launched in 2000 to enable banks which did not meet the EURO1 capital and credit rating admission criteria to effect payments following the implementation of regulation 2560/2001. STEP1 participants connect directly to the EURO1 system, but settlement is effected through a EURO1 participant of their choice which provides liquidity and settles on their behalf (indirect participation with direct connectivity). The system is restricted to payments which would not present systemic risk: credit caps are limited to €25 million and payments which would result in a negative position are queued (zero debit cap). The cut-off time is 14.30 CET to allow STEP1 participants to fund their balances with their settlement bank which will settle via EURO1.

At the end of 2007, STEP1 processed daily an average of 24,000 payments for a value exceeding €800 million.[11]

5.3 The STEP2 system

STEP2 was launched as a euro bulk payment ACH in 2003 under the CREDEURO scheme (up to €50,000) in preparation for SEPA. Development and operation is subcontracted to SIA SSB, the Italian infrastructure operator. An SCT service was duly launched in January 2008 and an SDD solution is under development. With over 3,000 direct and indirect participants, as well as interoperability agreements with 15 infrastructures in 12 countries,[12] STEP2 is considered to be the first PE-ACH.

At the end of 2007, STEP2 was processing over 360,000 transactions per day.[13]

6 The SEPA schemes and frameworks

6.1 The SEPA Credit Transfer (SCT) and SEPA Direct Debit (SDD) schemes

The SCT and SDD will replace the existing fragmented national schemes. They are defined in Rulebooks laying out the rules, standards, practices, rights and obligations between participants in the scheme and Data Models specifying the data requirements at the business, process and physical layers. The schemes have adopted the UNIFI (ISO20022) XML standard, the BIC (see ch. 3 sec. 2) to identify the banks and the International Bank Account Number (IBAN) made up from a country code and a check digit, followed by the national bank account number including any sorting or routing code.

The EPC schemes[14] define the rules and data models between banks, PSPs and CSMs, allowing the PSPs to manage the communication and relationship with their customers in a competitive environment. The EPC recommends however the adoption of the UNIFI (ISO20022)

XML standards for customer communication to facilitate end-to-end interoperability.

The SEPA schemes could obviously not incorporate all the features and data of the existing national ones. They allow therefore individual or 'communities' of participants, at the national level for instance, to offer Additional Optional Services (AOS) as long as they do not jeopardize interoperability of the participants.

For the SCT, the scheme specifies a maximum execution time of D+3, D being the date of acceptance. This will need to be reduced to D+1 from 2012 to comply with the PSD and service providers can naturally agree to a shorter time in the meantime.

The SDD will introduce more significant differences with the majority of national direct debit schemes, as changes extend beyond standards to deadlines, message and mandate flows. Referring to the concepts introduced in Chapter 2 (sec. 5) the following times and deadlines will apply:

- As the practice of value dating is no longer legal under the PSD:

  D = due date = debit (or collection) date = settlement date

  assuming that the banks and CSM are operating on that day.
- The notification date of the collection must be at least 14 calendar days before the collection date.
- The debtor's bank must receive the collection from the creditor's bank 5 interbank days (D–5) before the due date in case of a one-off or first-time debit, reducing to 2 interbank days (D–2) for subsequent recurring collections, but not earlier than 14 calendar days.
- Settlement of returns must occur within 5 interbank days following the due date.
- Refund requests must be introduced 8 weeks following due date for authorized debits, for instance if a consumer challenges the amount charged by a utility, and 13 months in case of unauthorized debits.

The SDD scheme operates under a Creditor Mandate Flow and the EPC is pursuing the development of electronic mandates.

The SDD is strongly consumer oriented. At the request of the corporate sector, the EPC plans to implement a business-to-business (B2B) direct debit scheme along the following lines:

- no right of refund from bank, disputes to be solved between businesses without involvement of the service providers;

- the mandate must be sent to the Debtor Bank in advance of the first collection for verification and stored by it on account of the potentially large amounts involved;
- shorter time cycle, D+1; and
- optional bank participation and no reachability requirement, so creditor and debtor's banks must agree bilaterally to use the scheme.

6.2 The SEPA Card Framework (SCF)

The SCF is principally aimed at enabling the use of debit cards at merchant POS terminals across the SEPA area, as the International Card Schemes already provide near-worldwide acceptance of credit cards at merchants and debit cards at ATMs. Unlike the SCT and SDD schemes which aim at replacing existing national schemes, the SCF is an adaptation framework enabling existing card schemes and operators to achieve interoperability across the four domains:

- cardholder to terminal interface;
- card to terminal (EMV);
- terminal to acquirer interface (protocols or minimum requirements); and
- acquirer to issuer interface, including network protocols (authorization and clearing).

The principle of separation between schemes and infrastructures is maintained, allowing merchants to select acquirers outside their national borders on a competitive basis and POS terminals to be standardized through a common interface, enabling use of all debit cards at all merchants across the eurozone. The EPC is developing standards in the four domains.

6.3 Other instruments and channels

In conjunction with the Eurosystem, the ECP has developed the Single Euro Cash Area Framework (SECA), defining common processes and service levels for cash (notes and coins) functions at wholesale level, as well as investigating ways to encourage consumers and merchants to migrate to more efficient payment instruments, in particular cards.

The EPC is also developing frameworks and schemes for E-payments (payment initiation at on-line merchants) and payments via mobile phones (M-payments) based on the core schemes.

7 Business and operational impact of SEPA

SEPA marks the beginning of the end of what we called 'the established order' for payments in Chapter 1, as several paradigms will be overthrown and competition will increase at all levels.

Firstly, corporate and retail customers will no longer need to hold accounts with a bank in the country in which they need to effect payments: the pan-euro standardization introduced by the SEPA schemes and frameworks will enable them to send and receive euro payments, whether domestic or cross-border, from any payment service provider in the EU using the same schemes, therefore offering opportunities to concentrate relationships and processing while negotiating the most advantageous conditions.

More significantly, the banks' monopoly on payments will be broken when the Payment Services Directive (PSD), which will allow non-bank payment institutions to enter the market, is transposed into national legislation by November 2009.

Banks will also no longer be compelled to use in-country clearing and settlement mechanisms as the standardization and reachability requirements allow ACHs to offer clearing services outside their country of operation. Consolidation in this area has already started.

7.1 Banks

Banks derive significant revenues from payment services which are expected to reduce as a result of pan-European competition. Fee and profitability models vary today from country to country and even from bank to bank within country, depending on instrument and customer mix (corporate vs. retail), execution times, value-dating practices and interest rates. There is however no doubt that revenues will diminish as a result of the abolition of value dating, shorter execution times and cross-border competition: 'Payments volumes in the eurozone will rise between 2003 and 2010, but SEPA's impact could reduce banks' direct payments revenue by between €13 and €29 billion (30%–60%) below expected 2010 levels'.[15] As the profitability of basic payment services will diminish to practically zero, banks will need to develop value-added services around payments to recover revenues.

Substantial investments are required to implement the ISO20022 XML standards and achieve compliance with the SEPA schemes and frameworks, as well as the PSD. Mainly as the result of SEPA, the top 75 European banks are expected to invest between $6 and $9 billion until 2010, or $80 to $120 million each in their payments business.[16] It is anticipated therefore that several banks which lack critical mass or merely offer payments as an indispensable by-product of deposit-taking or credit services will, while continuing to offer payments services under their own brand, outsource the processing of payment operations to larger institutions or specialized service providers. Several large banks are offering to 'white-label' their payment services.

The benefits of SEPA are undeniable and will be developed further by customer segment and payment instrument. These will not however materialize as long as banks and customers have to support the SEPA schemes alongside the prevailing national ones. It is therefore essential to rapidly achieve a critical mass of SEPA payments to keep the coexistence, or transition, period as short as possible. At the time of publishing, few National SEPA Plans had committed to a deadline and some banks were calling for an EC regulation imposing an end date for the transition period. The EC is also driving the widespread adoption of e-invoicing as a value-added service to justify and accelerate the adoption of the SEPA schemes (see ch. 12 sec. 2).

Banks were slow to react, the majority adopting a cautious minimum compliance attitude before the launch of the SCT in January 2008. A few however saw SEPA as a major strategic opportunity to expand their geographical coverage and gain market share by developing value added services, one being conversion from the old to the new schemes and standards. The implementation of the SDD in November 2009 will however force most banks to reach some crucial decisions and launch projects to implement them. The authors recognize however that it will probably be too late for most by the time this book is published.

7.2 Corporate customers

Most major corporations have centralized their European treasury and cash management operations since the introduction of the euro and SEPA will enable them to concentrate their payment processing and debt collection activities into shared service centres and achieve economies of scale as single files of domestic and cross-border payments can be sent and received on a single platform. Prior to SEPA several major corporations had outsourced payment processing, debt collection and reconciliation of payables and receivables and this trend is likely to accelerate.

The ability to effect and receive payments cross-border from one service provider will lead most corporations to restructure their bank accounts and concentrate all payment activities with one or two service providers, not necessarily the financial institutions with which they maintain credit relationships. This will put most accounts held for foreign subsidiaries at risk. Some accounts might still be maintained for cash and cheque transactions, but their importance will diminish particularly if corporations take proactive steps to eliminate cheques in favour of more efficient instruments. In addition to the elimination of value-dating, this concentration will facilitate balance and liquidity optimization to manage working capital more efficiently.

All invoices will need to indicate the IBAN and BIC of the account to which payment should be made. Corporations will also have to modify their applications to comply with the formats and XML standards mandated by the SEPA schemes. Users of major ERP systems such as Oracle or SAP should not experience too much pain as these vendors will introduce the necessary upgrades. Banks offering corporate internet portals for small businesses will no doubt also effect the required modifications. Medium-sized corporations are probably most at risk as their financial software vendors might lack the knowledge or resources to introduce the changes. Several banks are offering format conversion services as a competitive value-added service.

The PSD states that some of the provisions relating to transparency of conditions and the information requirements on charges, execution time and refunds can be waived or modified by mutual agreement for corporate clients. Member states can, however, choose to offer micro-enterprises (defined as businesses with less than 10 employees and an annual turnover of less than €2 million) the same protection as consumers. As the national legislation resulting from the transposition of the PSD emerges, corporations might need to renegotiate contractual arrangements with their payment service provider.

7.3 Government agencies

The public sector accounts for 47% of the EU's GDP and some 20% of the volume of payments. The adoption of the SEPA schemes by government agencies is therefore essential to achieve the critical mass required before existing national schemes can be abandoned. At the time of publication, high-level commitments had been made but without many signs of concrete initiatives.

7.4 Consumers

Consumers will benefit most from SEPA with the minimum investment. Banks will adapt the internet banking portals so that they can effect retail and cross-border payments from one account and new debit cards accepted across the SEPA area will be issued to them. Owners of second homes will be able to close their foreign bank accounts and effect all payments through their home bank.

7.5 Cards

Merchants will be able to accept debit cards from all SEPA area holders and negotiate the most competitive terms and conditions with acquirers within and outside their home country. Transaction and handling costs will reduce as they will no longer be forced to accept cash or credit cards (which incur a higher merchant fee) from foreign customers and common redress and exception procedures will apply. Large merchants, particularly those with outlets in several countries and offering shopping on-line, will benefit most.

Issuing is likely to be little affected beyond reissuing SCF compliant and branded cards, but acquiring will become increasingly competitive with pan-EU acquirers emerging and the ability to acquire without necessarily issuing.

Finally, all parties will benefit from the standardization of protocols, standards and interfaces enabling the development and certification costs of POS equipment and software applications to be spread over a much wider market.

At the time of publication the ECB was exerting strong pressure for the launch of a European debit card brand. European banks are now left to regret their decision to sell the Europay brand and schemes to MasterCard in 2002.

7.6 Clearing and settlement mechanisms and card processors

The provision of clearing services, which used to be a national quasi-monopoly, is now open to competition from clearing houses outside national borders. This has already led to reductions in clearing fees and ACHs and card processors to offer value-added services to compensate for the revenue shortfalls in their core business. Such services can include direct debit mandate handling, back-office payment and card processing for banks, PSPs and corporations, electronic invoicing and billing, electronic commerce, reconciliations, claims handling, customer support, card manufacturing, mobile payments, etc. The distinction is emerging between 'thin' ACHs concentrating on core payment clearing – therefore avoiding competition with their members – and 'thick' ACHs developing valued-added services.

As mentioned in previous paragraphs, the use of an ACH for credit transfer and direct debit clearing is not compulsory and several major banks (for instance Deutsche Bank, Deutsche Postbank and ING)[17] have announced their decision to exchange bilateral files with principal counterparties, settle through TARGET2 and/or the EBA EURO1 and use the EBA STEP2 for clearing with remaining banks. Large volumes of interbank clearing are likely therefore to move away from traditional clearing houses and we should not forget that each bank merger results in payments between the banks concerned to become 'on us' and withdraw from external clearing.

Clearing and card processing are principally a fixed costs business demanding large volumes to keep costs low. In 2006 the CEO of Interpay, the Dutch ACH and card processor, stated that 1 billion transactions per annum – approximately 40 million per day – were required to achieve sustainable efficiency. The majority of national ACHs do not process such a critical mass and are likely to disappear once the national schemes are discontinued. As early as 2007 Belgium announced that it would not migrate its national clearing to the SEPA schemes and the banks in Luxembourg transferred their domestic clearing to the EBA STEP2, alongside six major Italian banks. In 2006 the Italian, German and Dutch credit card processors announced their merger. In 2007 Interpay merged with TAI, a major German payments processor, to form Equens which subsequently announced a joint venture with Seceti in Italy. In early 2008, BGC, the Swedish ACH, outsourced the clearing of euro payments to VocaLink in the UK. Global card processors have initiated aggressive acquisition campaigns. This consolidation is expected to continue and, at the time of printing, it was anticipated that no more than six or seven clearing houses and processors would survive at the end of the transition period.

7.7 Impact and opportunities for banks outside the EU

Non EU-banks which have subsidiaries and/or branches offering payment services within the EU will have to comply with the PSD for all payments and the SEPA schemes for payments in euro. Those who have so far refrained from offering payment services in the EU, because they might not have a critical mass of customers or business volume (for instance from expatriates and/or subsidiaries of their local corporate customers) within any one country, may wish to reconsider their strategy as they would be able to leverage investments and operating costs across the entire eurozone.

When effecting transfers into the EU, banks are recommended to use the IBAN to facilitate straight through processing and payments staff are advised to familiarize themselves with the PSD and the SEPA schemes.

Countries which are considering implementing new schemes or revising their current ones are strongly recommended to adopt the EPC schemes (with the appropriate currency code) to benefit from the available solutions for ACH and bank back-office applications, reducing fragmentation and costs.

8 The UK payment systems

The UK payment systems present a contrast between one of the most efficient high-value RTGS systems (CHAPS), as befits the world's leading financial centre, opposed to a heavy reliance on cheques and an archaic three day clearing house cycle. Under regulatory pressure to improve execution times for retail payments, the banking industry launched the Faster Payments Service in May 2008. As the UK has not adopted the euro, a sterling RTGS system must be maintained and service providers are not compelled to adopt the SEPA schemes, although compliance with the PSD will be required.

8.1 CHAPS

The CHAPS system was launched in 1984 as a decentralized system (direct member banks and the Bank of England each operated their own platform and exchanged payments with each other) with end-of-day multilateral settlement through accounts at the Bank of England. It now operates as a centralized RTGS system with access via the SWIFTNet system over Y-copy. It is operated by the Bank of England on behalf of the CHAPS Clearing Company Ltd, owned by its direct members and the Bank of England. Other financial institutions can use CHAPS through agency agreements with direct members and bank customers can route urgent payments via CHAPS, for instance solicitors for property purchases. CHAPS also operated an RTGS euro settlement system, CHAPS euro, which attracted significant volumes and value but ceased operation with the advent of TARGET2.

Intraday liquidity is provided either through non-interest bearing Cash Ratio Deposits held by members at the Bank of England, or repurchase agreements (repos) of eligible assets. These must be reinstated at the end of the day and a penalty is applied on overnight overdrafts at the settlement account. For TARGET2, UK banks will use facilities at other European central banks because of restrictions applied to intraday credits in euros granted by the Bank of England as a non-euro area central bank.

8.2 Direct credits and debits

Direct credits, as credit transfers are called in the UK, and direct debits are cleared by VocaLink, born from the merger of the former BACS with Link, the ATM interchange network. Corporate bank customers, known as users, can submit payments directly to VocaLink via high-speed links or internet if sponsored by their account-holding bank, which are processed subject to credit limits. The sponsoring banks are invoiced for the payments submitted by their users and then charge their customers subject to negotiation.

As mentioned earlier, the schemes operate on a three day cycle, with settlement on Day 3 through CHAPS, which will need to be shortened to comply with the PSD. Direct debits operate on the creditor mandate cycle. VocaLink also operates a credit transfer scheme for domestic euro payments. Under pressure to improve account portability, a system is available whereby all standing orders and direct debit mandates are automatically transferred when customers switch accounts. VocaLink is developing a full range of value-added services and, following an aggressive marketing campaign to overcome its 'not in the eurozone' perceived handicap, is gaining customers for its SEPA compliant services.

8.3 Cheque and credit clearing

The UK operates a paper credit scheme, similar to credit transfers, but where payment must be effected by cheque if sent to the creditor or cheque or cash at a bank or Post Office. The credit clearing form cannot be used to debit the debtor's account and effectively serves as standardized support for transmission of remittance information. These paper credits and cheques are cleared by the Cheque and Credit Clearing Company under rules for each scheme.

Cheques received by the collecting banks are magnetically encoded and/or digitally imaged and sorted by paying bank to whom the data is transmitted over the IBDE network (Interbank Data Exchange) operated by VocaLink. The funds can then be applied to the beneficiary's account. The physical cheques are bundled and sent to the Clearing Exchange Centres where they are handed over to the paying bank. The Cheque and Credit Clearing Company calculates the net amounts which are settled via CHAPS. Paying banks implement their own procedures for signature verification and fraud detection.

The dates at which funds were posted to accounts, started earning interest and were available for withdrawal varied from bank to bank. Under mounting customer and regulatory pressure, maximum timescales were established in November 2007 according to the 2–4–6 scheme:

- Day 0: cheque presented.
- Day 2: creditor starts earning interest and debtor ceases to earn interest.
- Day 4: creditor can withdraw money against the amount of the cheque.
- Day 6: funds belong irrevocably to the creditor even if the cheque 'bounces' (approximately 0.5% of cheques presented),[18] unless he/she has been accomplice to a fraud.

Day 4 is moved to day 6 in case funds are credited to a savings account, the cycle being known as 2-6-6. The Cheque and Credit Clearing Company also clears cheques in euros drawn on UK banks.

A Cheque Guarantee Card scheme operates with different levels of guarantee, visible on a hologram on the reverse of the debit card.

8.4 Faster payments

The Faster Payments service was launched in May 2008 under pressure from the Office of Fair Trading as consumers had no alternative between a 3–4 day execution time for direct credits and the substantial fees for CHAPS payments. The banking industry responded with an advanced scheme providing a maximum 2 hour clearing for internet and telephone payments while allowing members to compete on access channels, fees and value-added services. The core platform is operated by VocaLink.

Payments can be effected between accounts enabled for Faster Payments. The debtor instructs his/her bank to transfer the funds via telephone banking, internet or, if provided by his bank, mobile telephone. After verification, the sending bank submits the payment to the core platform which debits its account and forwards the instruction to the receiving bank who accepts the payment after verification that it is for a valid account, at which time its account is credited and the sending bank notified that the payment has been accepted. The receiving bank credits the beneficiary and can choose how to notify and make the funds available to him/her, as the sending bank can choose to advise his customer that the transaction is complete.

The service is initially limited to payments up to £10,000 and standing orders up to £100,000. These ceilings are expected to rise and members can set lower limits. Future developments include the possibility to initiate the payment from a branch, access to service providers as agencies

Table 6.1 UK clearing statistics

	Average daily volume (000's)	%	Average daily value (£mns)	%	Average value per item (£)
CHAPS sterling	141	0.5	274,120	93.4	1,948,767
Direct credits and standing orders	10,200	37.8	11,100	3.8	1,088
Direct debits	11,713	43.6	3,492	1.2	298
Cheques and credit clearing	4,829	18.0	4,812	1.6	996

settling through a direct member and the ability for corporate customers to connect if sponsored by a member or agency.

8.5 Cards

Two debit card schemes operate in the UK, Switch and Visa debit. The UK credit card market is one of the most competitive and interest on outstanding balances on revolving credit cards is a major source of income for UK banks. A few banks issue both MasterCard and Visa credit cards and several non-financial entities also offer credit cards: supermarket and retail chains, soccer clubs, automobile associations, etc. Competition centres around interest rates, air miles, loyalty points and consumers are constantly tempted by offers of free balance transfers with moratoriums on interest charges. This results in very high levels of consumer indebtedness with the resulting economic and social implications.

Nearly all ATMs are connected to the LINK network allowing customers of participating institutions to draw cash from their accounts at participating banks from any member's ATM.

8.6 Volumes and trends

Clearing statistics for automated payments in 2007 are summarized in Table 6.1.[19]

The very high share of the total value of payments effected over CHAPS, in contrast to the very small proportion of the number of payments, is due to the settlement of high trading volumes in the City.

Overall payment trends are represented in Figure 6.5.

We see that cash remains king in spite of its declining use, representing 63% of the total number of payments effected during 2006 and anticipated to still account for 43% of all payments in 2016.[20]

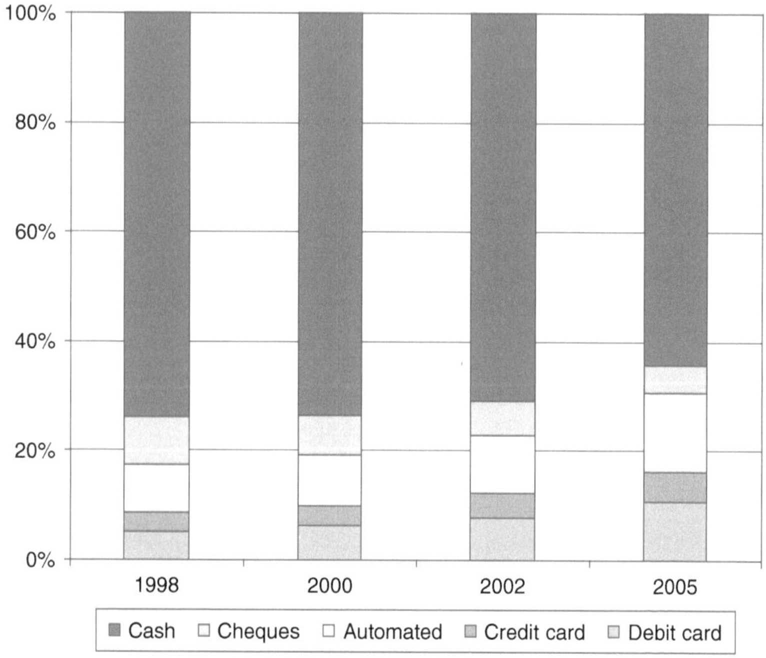

Figure 6.5 UK payment trends 1998 – 2005 including cash
Automated includes: direct credits, standing orders, direct debits and CHAPS
Source: APACS, *Payment Trends 1998–2005: Facts and Figures*, www.apacs.org.uk

Cheque volumes are also declining steadily, from 64% of the number of non-cash payments at their peak in 1990 to 13% in 2006.[21] The decline is accelerating with the year 2007 showing the sharpest fall (9.1%) in interbank cheque clearings.[22] Several retail and petrol chains no longer accept cheques. Non-cash payment usage trends are shown in Figure 6.6.

The debit card is the most popular and fastest growing non-cash instrument, accounting for one in three of non-cash payments in 2006 and its usage is expected to double by 2016.[23] Close to 2.7 billion cash withdrawals were effected from 58,000 ATMs in 2005.[24]

8.7 Governance

The Bank of England is responsible for oversight of UK payment systems. In 1985 the Association of Payment Clearing Services (APACS) was created as the private sector body for payment services. In 2004, the Office of Fair Trading set up a Task Force to investigate payment services in

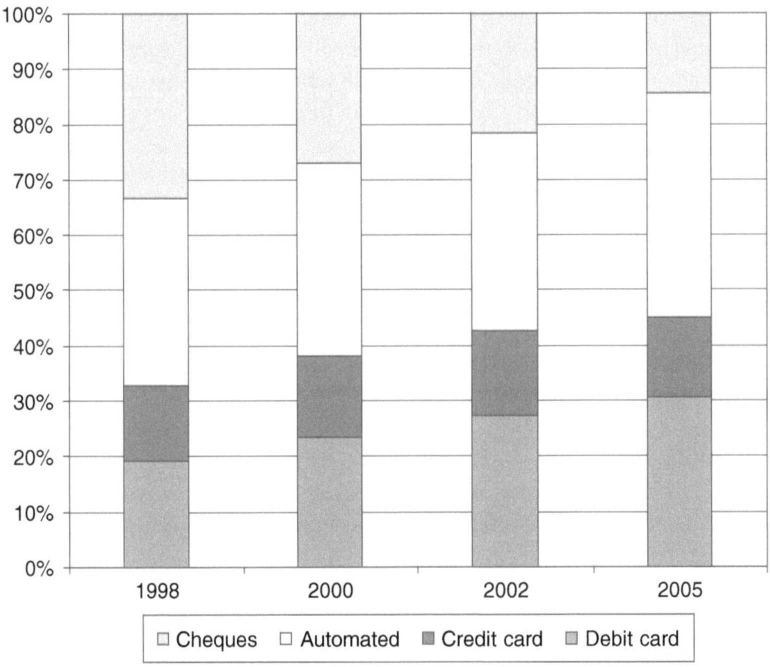

Figure 6.6 Trends in non-cash payments 1998–2006
Automated includes: direct credits, standing orders, direct debits and CHAPS
Source: APACS, *Payment Trends 1998–2005: Facts and Figures*, www.apacs.org.uk

the UK. Out of its work came a proposal from the industry to create a new body, the Payments Council. The Board of the Payments Council includes external directors alongside the Bank of England which acts as an observer and is chaired by a non-voting independent chairman. 'The Payments Council is the organisation which sets strategy for UK payments. It was created in March 2007 to lead the future development of co-operative payment services in the UK in order to ensure:

- Payment systems and services meet the needs of users, payment service providers and the wider economy;
- The operational efficiency, effectiveness and integrity of payment systems in the UK; and
- Payment systems are open, accountable and transparent.'[25]

Following extensive industry and user consultation, the Payments Council published in May 2008 the 'National Payments Plan – Setting the strategic vision for UK payments'. It charts the direction for payment services over a decade, focusing on efficiency, innovation, integrity and the need to ensure that the needs of all users, including the disadvantaged, are considered. Covering all schemes and instruments, the National Payments Plan highlighted the following priority areas:

- Proactively managing the decline in cheque volumes; while stopping short of setting a deadline for closure of cheque services, the plan sets a comprehensive programme to determine one focusing on understanding all users' requirements, ensuring the availability of alternatives, planning and education.
- Developing a mobile payment service between bank accounts.
- Defining a roadmap for the alignment of domestic message standards with the SEPA schemes.

This initiative will hopefully be followed by other countries as it enables all stakeholders, including service providers and technology vendors, to plan and manage investments and resources within the same strategic vision and timeframe.

7
The US Payment Systems

The US payments systems are the largest and most varied in the world: highest volumes, largest number of participants (over 17,000 commercial banks, savings institutions and credit unions in 2007) and a variety of instruments and settlement mechanisms. We should remember that the US had no central bank until the early twentieth century when the Federal Reserve was created. A central bank had been created with a 20 year mandate after independence in 1796. Its mandate as Second State Bank was renewed for a further 20 years but a second renewal, although approved by Congress, was vetoed in 1836 by President Andrew Jackson. The debate raged between the supporters of central banking and free banking, as part of the wider argument between federalism and anti-federalism, the Hamilton/Jefferson conflict and the populist contempt of banks. Monetary policy was devolved to the state Reserve Banks, leading to differences in policies and interest rates and opening opportunities for arbitrage. The cheque clearing houses operated with one of the participants acting as a settlement institution, moving funds between accounts held with it by the other banks. One of the reasons behind the Federal Reserve Act by Congress, which created the Federal Reserve System on 23 December 1913 as a 'Christmas gift to the nation', was disruptions in payments as many banks and local clearing houses refused to accept cheques drawn on certain institutions following The Bankers' Panic in 1907. The Federal Reserve System, including the 12 regional Federal Reserve Banks which issue the dollar notes, was given authority by Congress to create a nationwide cheque clearing system. In addition to the distribution of notes and coin minted by the US Treasury, the Federal Reserve has responsibility for monetary policy, the provision of payment services and the regulation and supervision of banks. It is interesting to note how the word 'bank' has been avoided; the Fed waited until 1935 to be

Table 7.1 Clearing systems for high value and retail payments by sector

	Public: Federal Reserve Financial Services	**Private: The Clearing House Payments Company LLC**
High value	Fedwire	CHIPS
ACH	FedACH	EPN
Cheques	Reserve Banks	SVPCO

given responsibility by the Roosevelt administration for monetary policy by fixing the commercial banks' reserve requirements, hence the name Federal Reserve. See also Box 7.1 at end of this chapter.

Legal harmonization across State legislation is provided by model statutes of the Uniform Commercial Code covering banking activities.

While in most advanced economies the central banks will leave the clearing of low-value payments to the private sector, a unique feature of the US payment systems is the duplication of competing clearing systems for high value and retail payments offered by the public and private sectors as shown in Table 7.1.

To ensure fair competition, the Federal Reserve is required by the Monetary Control Act of 1980 to set fees for payment services on a full cost recovery basis and to include a Private Sector Adjustment Factor to reflect the taxes and cost of capital it would incur were it a private sector corporation.

In terms of terminology, readers are no doubt aware that cheques are spelled *checks* in the US and that high-value payments over Fedwire and CHIPS are often referred to as *wires*. Not all financial institutions are direct participants in these systems, the smaller ones often using domestic *correspondent* and clearing services offered by *money centre banks*.

1 Fedwire

The Fedwire Funds Service operated by the Federal Reserve is an RTGS system, offering therefore immediate settlement finality, accessible to any bank holding an account within the Federal Reserve system. Access is on-line via direct link, IP, or for smaller institutions off-line via the telephone. Opening hours have been extended and now span 21.5 hours to ensure overlap with Asian and European systems, as well as the CLS schedule (see ch. 10 sec. 3).

As liquidity to facilitate settlement, the Fed grants eligible participant banks daylight-overdraft credit on their settlement account. The Fed monitors each account balance at the end of every minute. Even though a maximum limit, or net debit cap, had been imposed on each institution since 1985, average peak daylight overdrafts reached close to $140 billion in 1993. To reduce this risk, the Fed charges interest at 36 basis points since 1994 on the average of the negative balances throughout the day, with no credits for positive balances but minus a deductible based on eligible capital and an assessment. The peak daylight overdrafts fell to $60 billion following the introduction of this measure. In February 2008 the Fed issued a proposal for consultation to allow 'healthy depository' institutions to secure intraday overdrafts with collateral, subject to an increased fee on uncollateralized daylight overdrafts.

At the end of 2007, some 6,800 Fedwire participants exchanged daily an average of 534,000 payments for a settlement value of $2.8 trillion. The average value per transfer was $5.2 million.[1]

2 The Federal Reserve national settlement system

To reduce settlement risk and provide settlement finality to private-sector clearing systems such as cheque clearing houses, ACHs or card processors, the Federal Reserve operates the National Settlement Service which allows multilateral net settlement between the accounts held by participating banks at the Federal Reserve. The clearing system transmits a settlement file containing the list of the participants and the amount to be debited or credited to each. Settlement is effected subject to the same rules as for Fedwire on an all-or nothing basis: credits are posted once all debits have been successfully applied; settlement is then final and irrevocable and the clearing system is notified accordingly.

3 CHIPS

The New York Clearing House (NYCH) started operation of the Clearing House Interbank Payments System (CHIPS) in 1970 as an electronic replacement for a high-value paper clearing service. It was originally a multilateral end-of-day net settlement system to which sophisticated risk management procedures were gradually added: bilateral credit limits; net debit caps; and a loss sharing agreement. Since 2001, CHIPS operates as a real-time final settlement system providing final settlement for released payments, and is now operated by The Clearing House Payments Company LLC, as the NYCH is now named. CHIPS is principally used for large corporate payments and to cover international payments in US dollars when the beneficiary's account is not held by the ordering bank's correspondent.

CHIPS opens at 9.00 pm ET (Eastern Time) on the previous day and by 9.00 am each participant must pre-fund, over Fedwire, their CHIPS' account at the Federal Reserve Bank of New York. The amount for this opening position is determined by CHIPS and revised weekly, based on the previous six weeks' activity. Additional funding transfers can be made throughout the day. A reservation facility is available for priority payments. Banks transfer payments individually or in batches, which the CHIPS algorithm attempts to net on a bilateral or multilateral basis subject to each bank maintaining a positive balance (no daylight overdraft) and a credit limit set at twice the pre-funded balance. Released payments are final and unresolved payments can be deleted by the sending bank at any time.

At 5.00 pm the credit limits are removed and CHIPS attempts to settle all remaining payments, but still subject to the positive balance rule. If payments remain unresolved, CHIPS calculates a multilateral net balance for all participants which will be combined with the position on its account to create its *closing position*. If negative, the participant may transfer this *closing position requirement* over Fedwire within 30 minutes. If the closing position requirement is met, payments are then released and positive closing positions are returned to the participants, so all CHIPS accounts are reset to zero at the end of the day. Unresolved payments expire at end-of-day.

The number of CHIPS participants has decreased dramatically over the years, from a peak of 142 in 1984 to 45 in 2007. This reduction can certainly be attributed partly to the wave of mergers and acquisitions since the restriction on interstate banking was lifted, leading to the disappearance of some famous names – Irving Trust, Manufacturers Hanover, Chemical Bank, First National Bank of Chicago, Security Pacific, Bankers Trust – to name but a few. A retired senior American banker remarked whimsically that 'not one of the banks I have worked for exists today, my pensions are paid by institutions I have never worked for!'. It is clear however that, with the exception of the global and first league institutions driving payments as a profit centre, many banks shy at the liquidity and risk implications, IT investments and operational discipline demanded by a system such as CHIPS and prefer to use the services of a correspondent participant.

During 2007, CHIPS processed daily on average close to 348,000 payments for a value just over $1.9 trillion. It is extremely efficient in terms

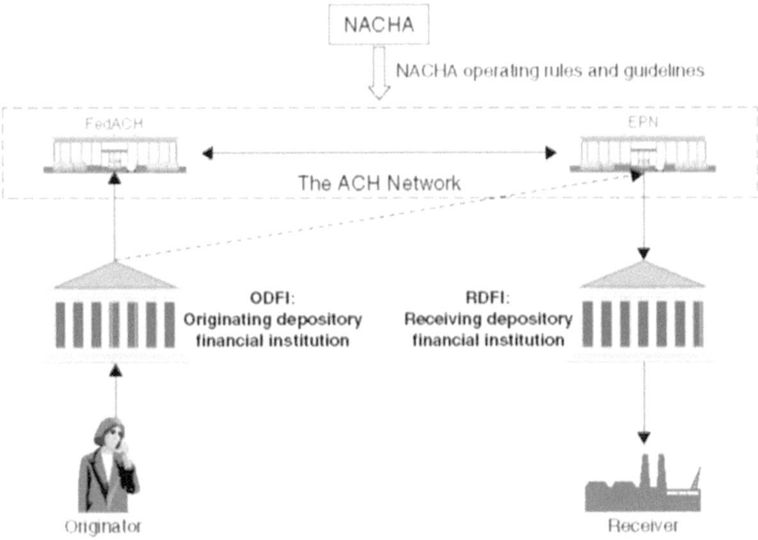

Figure 7.1 The ACH Network

of liquidity, requiring around $3 billion pre-funding to settle $2 trillion.[2] The average value per transfer was $5.6 million.

Between them, Fedwire and CHIPS settle daily approximately 35 per cent of the annual GDP of the US; these high-value systems turn over the entire country's annual GDP in less than three days.

4 The ACH Network

The ACH Network today processes credit transfers, direct debits and electronified cheques (see following section). It operates under rules and business practices established by NACHA, a not-for-profit organization representing some 11,000 financial institutions. NACHA is in effect the scheme manager, driving standardization, education and marketing efforts, and the infrastructure is operated by the FedACH in competition with EPN, a service of the Payments Company LLC which also operates CHIPS. Banks can choose to work with one or both and each operator will transfer payments to the other, subject to negotiated access fees, to provide a unified nation-wide ACH payment system (see Figure 7.1).

On FedACH, banks deliver payment files to the Federal Reserve Banks which are processed by a centralized application. Payments can be submitted for next day or +2 days, the cut-off for next day being 2.15 am ET.

Settlement is final when the amounts are posted to the banks' accounts; normally at 8.30 am ET for credit transfers and 11.00 am ET for debit items. Payments processed over EPN follow the same rules and are settled net over the National Settlement Service.

EPN and FedACH had about equal market share in 2007. Both operators offer a variety of connectivity options and prices have converged, so competition centres on value-added services: fraud detection, centralized OFAC screening, limits, etc. EPN offers the Universal Payment Identification Code (UPIC) published by corporations to preserve the confidentiality of bank account identification and facilitate account transportability.

FedACH also offers international services to Canada, Mexico and selected European countries relying on a network of local Receiving Gateway Operators; execution time varies per country but settlement to the receiving bank occurs within 2 days.[3]

In 2007, the ACH Network processed a daily average of close to 56 million items for a value touching $115 billion, debits representing 65 per cent of the volume on account of the large number of electronified cheques.[4]

5 Cheques

Although their usage is declining, over 33 billion cheques were written in the US in 2006 for an average value of $1,280, of which 0.5 per cent were returned unpaid.[5] Some 20 per cent[6] are presented at the same bank on which they are drawn ('on-us'), still leaving substantial volumes to be cleared. This can take place by exchanging them bilaterally with the drawer's bank, through a local clearing house, using the clearing services offered by the Federal Reserve or SVPCO, or outsourcing to a correspondent.

The Federal Reserve Banks operate cheque processing centres and publish availability schedules indicating when the amount will be credited to the collecting institution, depending on the time to receive settlement from the bank upon which the cheque is drawn. Credit to the institution is normally given same day or next business day and availability of funds to customers is regulated by the Expedited Funds Availability Act. The Federal Reserve runs a highly efficient courier and air transportation logistics operation between participating banks and its cheque processing centres. Bilateral clearings are normally settled via Fedwire or CHIPS, while independent clearing houses settle via the National Settlement Service.

Major efforts have been deployed to reduce paper volumes. NACHA offers corporations the possibility to convert cheques to ACH debits or Accounts Receivable Cheque Conversion items (ARC), which represented 19 per cent of the ACH Network volume in 2007.[7] Large retailers have adopted Point of Purchase (POP) conversion for consumer cheques, whereby MICR readers at check-out capture the cheque details, validate them from the payer's bank (directly or through a processor) and process the debit as an ACH transaction after voiding the cheque and returning it to the customer.

The major breakthrough occurred in October 2004 when the Check Clearing for the twenty-first Century Act took effect, known as Check 21. Subject to specific technical standards, it gives an Image Replacement Document (IRD) the same status as the original paper cheque, enabling banks and processors to handle cheque images more quickly, efficiently and confidently. Cheques collected by merchants or corporations can now be either converted to ACH items or processed as images. An initiative was launched in 2008 allowing users to pay in cheques via pictures taken with the cameras on their mobile phones. Regrettably, not all banks can yet receive cheque images (41 per cent of all US institutions in March 2007),[8] in which case the clearing system or processor will print a legally acceptable substitute.

The Clearing House Payments Company LLC operates the SVPCO Image Payments Network, based on a peer-to-peer architecture allowing banks, the Reserve Banks and processors to exchange cheque image files directly between each other. Integrated settlement is automated through the Federal Reserve Bank.[9] Several other specialized services have arisen, such as the cheque image storage and retrieval utility Viewpoint operated by IBM on behalf of a consortium of major banks.

In 2007, it was estimated that 40 per cent of all interbank cheques involved the replacement of the original paper by electronic information.[10] In view of the reduction in volumes of paper cheques, the Federal Reserve has consolidated the number of its cheque processing centres from 45 in 2003 to 22 in 2007, with the published objective to reach four by 2011.[11]

6 Cards

The US market for revolving credit cards is the most competitive in the world and we are all familiar with the thick card wallets carried by American friends. Debit cards are also widespread, with authorization

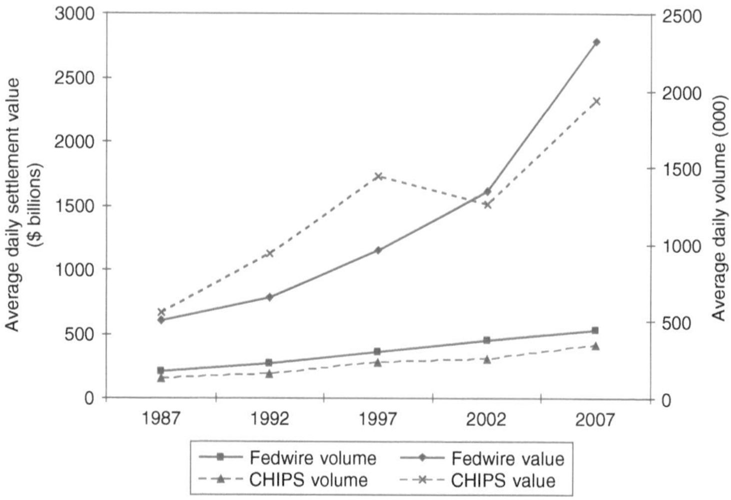

Figure 7.2 Trends in US high-value systems 1987–2007
Sources: www.chips.org; www.federalreserve.gov

by signature or PIN. The credit cards and signature-based debit cards are normally processed through the MasterCard or Visa networks, while the PIN authorizations are processed via the ATM networks, which explains the large difference in merchant fees for debit cards. Most banks outsource processing, whether for issuing and/or acquiring, to large scale processors and operators. Surprisingly, the US had not, at the time of publishing, moved to adopt chip cards, relying on the magnetic stripe technology in spite of rising fraud.

7 Trends

Figure 7.2 shows the comparative evolution in average daily volumes and settlement values between the two high-value systems Fedwire and CHIPS.

The volume progression is unremarkable, but the graph shows that CHIPS originally settled higher values. Fedwire overtook CHIPS in 1999 and has retained its lead since. Increasing regulatory pressures over settlement risk were forcing the settlement payments for foreign exchange and securities systems towards RTGS systems. CHIPS only moved to real-time finality in 2001, after which the advent of CLS shifted the

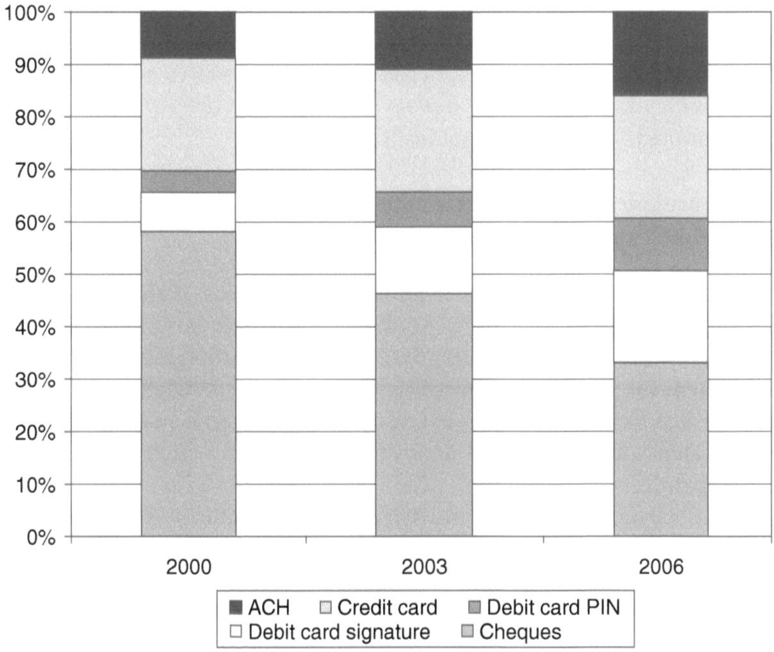

Figure 7.3 Trends in US non-cash payments 2000–2006
Sources: Federal Reserve System, *The 2007 Federal Reserve Payments Study; The 2004 Federal Reserve Payments Study*

foreign-exchange settlement payments, which accounted for a significant proportion of CHIPS payments, to Fedwire albeit, as we will see in Chapter 10 (sec. 5), with much smaller volumes.

For retail payments, cash remains king and the number of cash payments hovers constantly at around 50 billion annually and is expected to remain at that level,[12] while volumes of other instruments are growing, inexorably eroding its market share. Figure 7.3 shows the evolution of non-cash payments between 2000 and 2006.

The usage of cheques is declining steadily. The tipping point occurred in 2003 when the number of electronic payments first overtook the number of cheques.[13] The share of credit card payments remains virtually unchanged, but debit cards exhibit strongest growth, aided by rewards programmes and overtaking credit cards in 2006,[14] with PIN authorization expected to dominate.

Clearing and settlement unit costs stood at 1 cent for ACH items and 6.3 cents for cheques in 2006, expecting to evolve towards 0.7 and 8.8 respectively by 2010.[15] All parties are obviously keen to accelerate the electronification of cheques, but no stated plan to drive them out had been mooted at the time of publication.

8 Overview of the securities clearing and settlement systems

Fedwire operates the Fedwire Securities Service which is the depository for all government securities. Book-entry transfers are effected gross with DVP through Fedwire, providing real-time simultaneous irrevocable settlement for the cash and securities legs. Access is restricted to depository institutions and certain government agencies, so non-bank brokers and dealers must settle via a depository institution which is a Fedwire participant.

DTCC (Depositary Trust and Clearing Corporation) is the world's largest securities depository offering safekeeping, clearing and settlement for equities, corporate and municipal bonds, government and mortgage-backed securities, money market instruments and over-the-counter derivatives. It operates through specialized subsidiaries: the National Securities Clearing Corporation (NSCC), the Depositary Trust Company (DTC) and the Fixed Income Clearing Corporation (FICC).

The Government Securities Division of the FICC offers trade comparison, netting and settlement for the Government securities marketplace. After matching, it acts as a central counterparty and issues a net position statement for each issue. Each net position is replaced by a settlement obligation for the scheduled settlement date which the participants settle over Fedwire ensuring DVP.

Trades in equities are first matched by the NSCC who act as a central counterparty if successful. Net positions for each security are issued to the brokers who instruct their settlement banks to pay or receive funds over Fedwire; DTC transfers the securities upon receipt of funds. Settlement is T+3.

'DTCC's depository provides custody and asset servicing for 2.8 million securities issues from the United States and 107 other countries and territories, valued at $36 trillion. In 2006, DTCC settled more than $1.5 quadrillion in securities transactions'.[16]

Fedwire is currently developing a new platform to: provide corporate actions services; multi-currency processing; incorporate ISIN 15022 standards; and reduce settlement to T+1.

Box 7.1 A country and a currency without a central bank: the US before 1913

The US did not have a central bank until 1913: issuing notes and coins was separated from clearing interbank liabilities. The famous 'greenbacks' created by Lincoln to finance the Civil War in 1862 were issued by the Treasury. Monetary policy was managed by the Treasury who would fund the States and local banks during liquidity shortage, for instance between harvesting and selling the crops. Interbank liabilities were cleared by the New York Clearing House (NYCHA) which was created in 1853 after a banking crisis. Clearing banks would deposit funds at the NYCHA to guarantee their liabilities against clearing house certificates. These NYCHA certificates were very much sought after and circulated alongside the greenbacks as they carried a high return (6 per cent) and were jointly guaranteed by the most important banks. The banks could also use them alongside Treasury bills as minimum reserve capital against assets: they were compelled to stop lending if their capital dropped below 25 per cent. Of the $9.8 million of notes issued by the Clearing Houses, only $180,000 was lost in Philadelphia in 1890, less than 1.8 per cent. Only one failure was recorded at the NYCHA in 1893, mainly owing to one bank refusing to lend to another to eliminate a competitor. The Federal Reserve, whose name does not include the word 'bank' on purpose, was partly created in 1913 as a Reserve to guarantee finality of settlements.

8
Major Asian Payment Systems

Eastern and South Eastern Asia include some the world's most dynamic economies, but the area remains fragmented from every viewpoint: politically, as parliamentary democracies cohabit with totalitarian and communist regimes; and economically, as advanced economies such as Japan, South Korea and Singapore coexist with emerging economies such as China and India. The same applies to the financial services industry with several centres vying for leadership: Tokyo, Hong Kong, Singapore and more recently Shanghai. Betting was split between Singapore and Hong Kong, the latter after having been overtaken, paradoxically regaining the lead after the handover to China which uses it as a springboard. Several Chinese enterprises chose to list on the Hong Kong exchange which boasts some of the most sophisticated infrastructures and access to investors worldwide. Geographically Hong Kong and Singapore suffer from limitations which might prevent them from gaining a sustainable leadership. The main rivalry today lies between Tokyo and Shanghai, but as both suffer from inherent weaknesses it is difficult to predict the outcome. Tokyo is certainly more advanced in terms of technology and financial maturity. It has launched a programme to upgrade its platforms to bring them on par with the other leading financial centres. Other barriers such as language and a certain isolationist tradition sometimes prevent Japan from leveraging its leadership in many areas. Shanghai, on the other hand, was at the time of publication lagging in terms of infrastructure in spite of spectacular progression. The repatriation on the Shanghai exchange of Chinese companies previously listed in New York or Hong Kong, as well as the privatization of large public companies such as the banks, propelled Shanghai in 2007 to the top of the ranking of exchanges by listings. The race is on and betting is open.

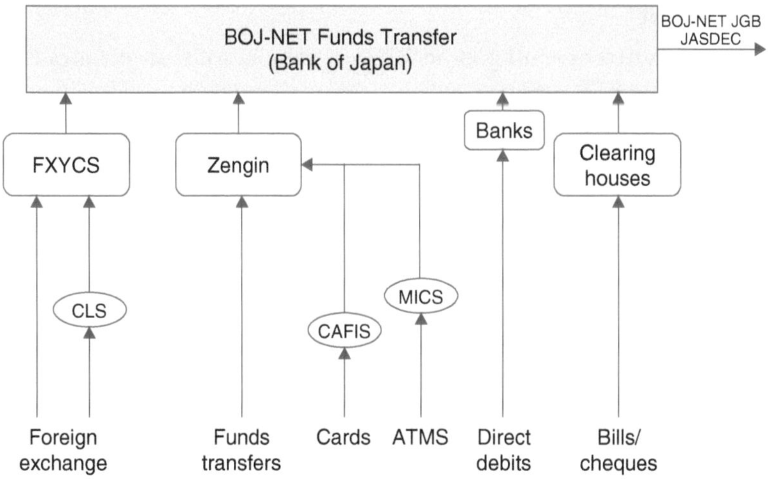

Figure 8.1 Japanese payment systems

1 Payment and securities clearing and settlement systems in Japan

The overall architecture of payments systems in Japan will undergo a radical transformation between 2008 and 2011. The following main clearing and settlement systems operated in Japan:

- The BOJ-NET Funds Transfer system, owned and operated by the Bank of Japan.
- The Foreign Exchange Yen Clearing System (FXYCS) managed by the Tokyo Bankers Association, but the system is operated by the Bank of Japan.
- The Zengin system for low-value payments, also managed by the Tokyo Bankers Association.
- Bill and Cheque Clearing Systems (BCCS).

Figure 8.1 summarizes the overall architecture of Japan's payment and settlement systems.

All systems are sized to handle large peak volumes as, in line with Japanese trading practices pre-scheduled payments such as salaries and commercial payments are executed between the 25th and the end of the month. Japan is also the country where mobile payments are most widely used, as we will see in Chapter 9.

1.1 BOJ-NET

BOJ-NET started operating as an RTGS system in 2001; it includes the BOJ-NET Funds Transfer system for payments and BOJ-NET JGB services for the settlement of Japanese government bonds. 'Simultaneous processing', whereby payments to and from the Bank of Japan are netted out bilaterally and settled simultaneously, takes place at set times throughout the day. The Bank of Japan offers intraday overdrafts, free if repaid at the end of the day, which must be fully collateralized by eligible assets pledged to it; collateral and haircuts are reviewed weekly.

In 2007, BOJ-NET Funds Transfer processed a daily average of 23,300 payments for a settlement value just exceeding Yen 100 trillion, each payment averaging Yen 4.3 billion. During that year, the daily peak of intraday overdrafts at the settlement accounts with Bank of Japan, measured every ten minutes, was Yen 22.2 trillion.[1]

1.2 The foreign exchange yen clearing system (FXYCS)

FXYCS was established by the Tokyo Bankers Association (TBA) to clear the Yen leg of FX trades and cover payments for international transfers when the beneficiary's bank is different from the ordering bank's correspondent. It was originally a paper clearing system but automated operation was entrusted to the Bank of Japan in 1989 and integrated with BOJ-NET.

Until October 2008, FXYCS operated in both an RTGS mode with continuous settlement and a Deferred Net Settlement (DNS) mode. For DNS-mode payments, the TBA acted as a central counterparty (CCP), the obligation between the sending and receiving banks being replaced by two obligations: one between the sending bank and the TBA, the other between the TBA and the receiving bank. Settlement of DNS mode payments took place over BOJ-NET at 14.30 local time. Risk mitigation measures included Net Credit Limits established bilaterally between banks and an overall Sender Net Debit Cap for each participant. A loss-sharing rule guarded against failure of a participant to settle, the amount to be contributed by each survivor being calculated pro-rata to the Net Credit Limits it had granted to the defaulting institution. Major banks acted as Liquidity Providers in case a survivor could not meet its loss-sharing obligation.

In 2007, FXYCS processed a daily average of just under 31,650 payments for a settlement value of Yen 23 trillion, each payment averaging Yen 730 million.[2]

1.3 Zengin

Zengin, the Japanese domestic ACH in operation since 1973, is owned and operated by the Tokyo Bankers Association. Participants are however located throughout the country, although smaller institutions such as agricultural and credit cooperatives operate their own regional clearings which link in to Zengin.

Payments can be submitted individually or in batches. Zengin is a DNS system and, as for FXYCS, the TBA operates as a CCP and the obligation between the banks are substituted by obligations towards and from the TBA. Each participant is allocated a Sender Net Debit Cap which must be fully secured through collateral and/or guarantees. Subject to this limit, Zengin credits the beneficiary bank immediately, which in turn will grant his customers immediate access to the funds thanks to the large collateral posted and guarantees. Net positions are calculated at 15.30 and settlement takes place at 16.15 over BOJ-NET, funds being first debited from the accounts of all the short participants before being credited to the long ones. Should the two participants with the largest obligations default, designated Liquidity Providers will assist with settlement and be subsequently repaid by the TBA through realization of the collateral posted by the defaulting institution.

In 2007, Zengin processed a daily average of just under 5.5 million payments for a settlement value close to Yen 11 trillion, each payment averaging Yen 1.9 million.[3] The collateral pool stood at Yen 11.5 trillion[4] in the first half of 2007.

Interestingly, Zengin does not process direct debits. Mandates are registered with the banks which process direct debits bilaterally.

1.4 The next-generation RTGS-XG system

As volumes and values grew, it became apparent that BOJ-NET required more efficient liquidity management and enhanced settlement risk management. In addition, the spate of mergers between major institutions led to increasing concentration, with the top three participants accounting for 45 per cent of the value settled over Zengin and 60 per cent over FXYCS in 2006.[5] Participants in Zengin could often not clear payments as they were hitting their sender net debit caps and raising them would entail increasing collateral.

Following consultation with the industry, the Bank of Japan therefore launched the RTGS-XG (next generation) project. From October 2008, new Liquidity Saving Features (LSF) will be introduced and all FXYCS payments will be incorporated into RTGS-XG, discontinuing the DNS mode. From 2011, a limit will be set on the value of individual payments submitted to Zengin (currently anticipated at Yen 100 million), above which they will be routed to and processed by RTGS-XG.

From October 2008, transactions with Bank of Japan and the government, settlement payments for DNS systems and the payment leg of securities transactions will continue to be processed in pure RTGS mode. At the bank's request, other payments can be settled through a 'new account' (funded from the standard account) using the new liquidity savings features:

- the system will first attempt to offset the payment bilaterally, subject to both participants having sufficient funds in their respective new accounts for the net amount; this attempt will be repeated at frequent intervals taking into account any change in the liquidity positions; and
- if settlement cannot take place, the payment will be queued for multilateral offsetting, which will run four times per day at predetermined times.[6]

BOJ-NET will effectively become a hybrid system, enabling participants to manage liquidity more effectively and reduce the collateral required for an efficient settlement.

1.5 Bill and cheque clearing

Cheques are fortunately not used by retail customers in Japan, but Japanese corporations issue cheques and bills (promissory notes). These are presented and cleared at a multitude of local privately operated clearing houses. The first was created in Osaka in 1879; from over 540, their number has dropped steadily with volumes and stood at 146 in mid-2007,[7] the largest being the Tokyo Clearing House. Settlement takes place at 12.30 over BOJ-NET, following the same procedure as for Zengin, the payee gaining access to funds from 11.00 the next day in case the cheque is returned. No limits are placed on the value of the items submitted by each participant and unwinding takes place should a bank fail to meet its settlement obligation, recalculating the net positions after excluding items submitted by it.

In May 2007, bill and cheque clearing systems processed a daily average of 577,100 items for a settlement value just above Yen 2 trillion, each item averaging Yen 3.6 million. Volumes have declined since 1979 at an annual rate of 8–9 per cent.[8]

1.6 Cards

Credit and debit cards are heavily used in Japan, consumers being encouraged to reduce cash payments. International credit cards are issued under MasterCard, Visa or the national JCB scheme. Payments are processed by the Credit and Finance Information System (CAFIS) and settlement takes place over Zengin.

A vast network of ATMs exists offering a wide variety of banking services, with a large proportion installed in convenience stores offering easier access during longer hours. These convenience stores also collect local taxes and payments for utility bills. The ATM networks are linked via the Multi Integrated Cash Service (MICS) network, offering access to accounts from ATMs installed by a different institution, with settlement also taking place through Zengin.

In addition, most urban transport and railway companies offer prepaid and stored value cards, mainly contactless or linked to mobile telephone services, to reduce cash handling.

1.7 Future evolution

In December 2007, the Financial Services Agency of Japan published 'The Plan for Strengthening the Competitiveness of Japan's Financial and Capital Markets'. It emphasizes the need to further improve the security, efficiency and ease of use by benefiting from advances in technology and international experiences, focusing on the following areas:

- Minimizing risk and improving efficiency through the introduction of RTGS-XG and the changes to FXYCS and Zengin described above.
- Standardization: Japanese payment systems have evolved until now taking into account the Japanese language and domestic requirements at the expense of interoperability with international standards, which jeopardizes STP. The next generation of the Zengin system, planned to be introduced around 2011, should actively consider adopting ISO 200022 XML and the latest EDI standards to allow more remittance information to be transmitted.
- For retail payments, examine the introduction of payment service provider licenses, as in the European PSD, to increase consumer protection when using prepaid cards, e-money, and points services (loyalty schemes).

1.8 Securities clearing and settlement systems

Several systems effect the clearing and settlement of securities in Japan, mainly owned by the private sector and managed by the Japanese Bankers Association or its members (see Figure 8.2).

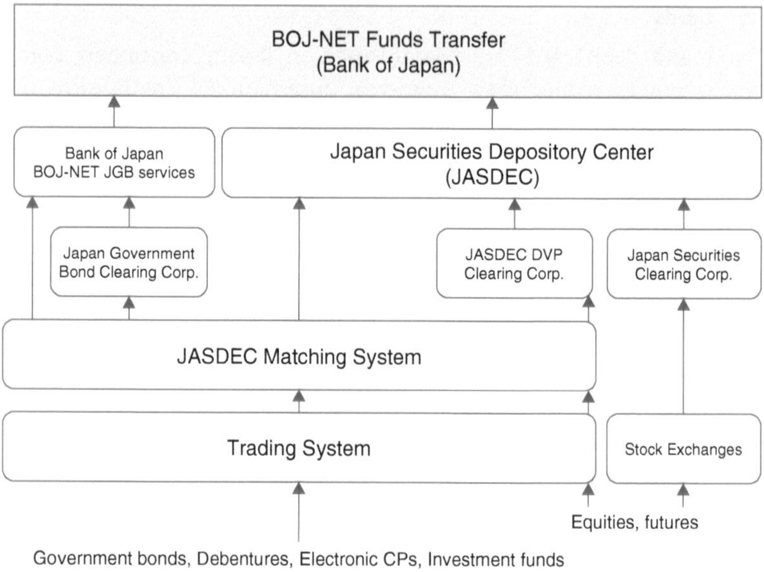

Figure 8.2 Japanese securities settlement systems

The Bank of Japan assumes responsibility for clearing and settling Japanese Government bonds (JGB) over the BOJ-NET JGB Service which operates in DVP mode with the cash leg settled over BOJ-NET Funds Transfer. This system is also used for repos to collateralize overdrafts should participants wish to increase liquidity on BOJ-NET Funds Transfer. Transactions can be settled directly or after clearing through the Japanese Government Bond Clearing Corporation (GBCC). In 2006 BOJ-NET JGB settled a daily average of 15,000 transactions for a value of Yen 75 trillion, of which 31 per cent were cleared through JGBCC.[9]

The Japan Securities Depositary Center (JASDEC), alongside the JASDEC DVP Clearing Corporation (JDCC) and the Japan Securities Clearing Corporation (JSCC), settles all trades on the six Japanese Exchanges (of which Tokyo represents 85 per cent of the volume) by book entry for corporate and other bonds, equities, dematerialized Commercial Paper (CPs) and investment trusts.

Japanese financial authorities are fully conscious of the need to constantly improve the clearing and settlement procedures to retain Tokyo's leading position as a financial centre. They are promoting increased efficiency among participants to improve STP and reduce fails by mandating them to review their processes, IT systems and improve transaction flows. In the same way as for payment systems, they are also striving towards the adoption of international standards to improve interoperability with other financial centres. Although DVP has been implemented, there are still inherent risks due to the current T+3 settlement cycle which they are driving to reduce to T+1 in line with international best practice. This is particularly critical for operations on JGBs which are used in repo operations for liquidity management.

Finally, there is general recognition that Japanese custodians must improve their services and that access by foreign investors to the Japanese markets must be developed in line with other markets.

2 Payment and securities settlement systems in China and Hong Kong SAR

The Chinese economy ranks today as the second in the world after the US and the second exporting country behind Germany. If its growth is sustained, it will take the lead within a few years and China already holds the largest foreign reserves in the world. However until recently, the Chinese payment systems were among the least advanced for reasons not purely economic. China has a long tradition of decentralized economy, owing not only to its size but to the uneven distribution of population, industrial resources and wealth. Historians have long stigmatized the 'celestial bureaucracy' as overbearing, conservative and corrupt. At the end of the nineteenth century however, the number of civil servants per capita was well below comparative figures in Western states which have, since the sixteenth century, developed powerful civil services.

Chinese payment systems are therefore primarily local and national systems are often a federation of regional systems. We should also not confuse the move to a market economy and the privatizations with devolution of power and responsibility. The local officials revealed themselves as extremely conservative, clinging to their authority which was increased by distance from the central authority. At the end of the nineteenth century, innovation and progress was mainly stimulated by provincial governors and capitalist mandarins attempting to emulate progress in the West, in spite of the opposition to change from the Imperial Court petrified in millenary traditions. It took therefore time at the end of the twentieth century to grasp that a liberalization of the economy must entail a recentralization of power and that reform had to be driven top-down.

In spite of its dramatic progress, China remains fundamentally an agricultural country, farmers represent close to 800 million out of total population of 1.3 billion and agriculture accounts for close to 30 per cent of GDP. In spite of numerous 'land reforms', Chinese farmers do not own their land. Agricultural plots are distributed by the village heads, according to the requirements of each family but exclusively to family heads, meaning men. Hence the importance of having a male heir and the high number of abortions. Tensions between cities and the countryside, workers and farmers, inland and seashore have existed throughout the history of China. The communist revolution was led by farmers under a proletarian ideology. Today's economic reforms are led by the seashore city-dwellers from the coast, seeking a more 'harmonious' society in the words of President Hu Jintao, echoing Confucian tradition. These new political orientations are aimed at achieving an improved social equilibrium and redress the dramatic economic imbalance between the richest and poorest provinces.

Readers will appreciate that the economic development of China must be seen in the context of the historical and social background sketched above. This also applies to payment systems and other infrastructures such as telecommunications and data processing. Efficient systems require large quantities of data which are often classified as confidential in a controlled economy.

The 'one country, two systems' philosophy has applied since the return of Hong-Kong and Macao to China. We will therefore examine the systems in mainland China and Hong Kong, which has maintained its role as an advanced financial centre with a large number of foreign institutions and requisite infrastructures.

2.1 Mainland China

The official name of the currency is Renminbi, the 'people's money' (from the characters *ren*: man, *min*: people and *bi*: money), but is popularly known as the Yuan. The choice of payment instruments is strongly influenced by recent history, individuals using primarily cash and businesses credit transfers.

Chinese are traditionally attached to cash, which is understandable considering their history of civil wars, regime changes, property confiscation and bank failures. In spite of record savings rates, $2 trillion or more than 30 per cent of GDP, Chinese are reluctant to deposit their holdings at banks. Most elderly people prefer to hoard their savings under the mattress to pay for a decent funeral to secure a happy reincarnation. New instruments have difficulty in gaining acceptance in the face of those used by the centralized administration. Growth figures might be impressive, but the growth started from a very low base and the market share remains marginal.

The People's Bank of China (PBOC) is a relatively young institution. Under the last years of the Empire, issuing notes and coins was entrusted to the Bank of China (a commercial bank specializing in foreign exchange) and the Imperial Bank of China. The first real central bank was created during the Republic in 1927, following the reunification by Chang Kai Shek of the country divided between the warlords. However, monetary policy was only entrusted to it in 1935. After the victory of the Communists in 1949, banking functions were concentrated into the PBOC, which cumulated the roles of central bank and sole commercial bank, holding the accounts of central and local government agencies, offices and enterprises. During the Great Leap Forward and the Cultural Revolution money was considered a barbaric relic to be disposed of. Local banks served as mere branches of the PBOC, collecting funds from local collectivities and distributing 'credits' according to the centrally issued plan. Payments, as such, were reduced to a strict minimum. Workers and farmers were provided for by their employers or agricultural communities. Any surplus was 'collected' in bank accounts, the only authorized savings instrument. Interest and exchange rates were fixed arbitrarily by the central authorities without any regard to supply and demand as no financial market existed. Monetary policy was limited to adjusting the interest rate to encourage people to withdraw their savings from the payment circuits, thereby neutralizing purchasing power. Payments between enterprises were effected 'on us' between accounts at the PBOC.

The banking sector is currently at the same time highly concentrated and very fragmented. The four large state-controlled banks (Industrial and Commercial Bank of China, Bank of China, China Construction Bank and Agricultural Bank of China) account for two thirds of deposits and credits. Alongside them operate joint stock commercial banks (but still under state control in spite of their name), a few privately owned banks (such as Minsheng Bank), 'policy banks' which have taken over the non-commercial subsidized credits originally granted by the big four, rural credit cooperatives, and the City credit banks controlled by local collectivities whose activities are limited to one city. Some of the latter have been brought by foreign banks as a starting base while awaiting a national licence. Since 2007 in accordance with the World Trade Organization's (WTO) requirements, a small number of foreign banks were allowed to open branches in nine designated cities, albeit under very heavy capitalization requirements. The PBOC nominates the clearing banks and intervenes throughout the entire payment clearing and settlement process. Banks are supervized by the China Banking Regulatory Commission (CBRC).

As explained above, cheques and credit transfers remain the most popular payment instruments. Other instruments are gaining ground, but within a very limited segment of the population. Out of a total population of 1,300 million, only approximately 100 million from the new middle classes are expected to request a credit card, nevertheless a sizeable market! At the other extreme of the social scale, the poorest farmers and the 'mingong', migrant populations seeking work in the cities without the 'hukou' (residence permit) number close to 200 million.

Enterprises are keen users of cheques. The PBOC estimated that 1.8 billion cheques for a total value of Yuan 350 trillion were processed in 2005.[10] A National Cheque Image Exchange System was launched in 2007 with cheques truncated at the bank of deposit and images transmitted to the drawers' bank. Availability of funds varies between one and three days. The maximum amount per cheque was Yuan 500,000 in 2007.

As explained above, credit transfers continue to be favoured by enterprises for historical reasons. Direct debits, still in their infancy, are being heavily promoted by utilities and insurance companies.

Chinese banks have invested heavily in cards with assistance from the international schemes and foreign banks. In 2002 the PBOC and the Big Four state banks launched China Union Pay (CUP) to interlink the various regional card networks and create a national card clearing and settlement system. Around 1.1 billion debit cards were in use in 2006 as opposed to 50 million credit cards, with purchases amounting to Yuan 1.89 trillion,[11] a fraction of the value handled by cheques. The lack of credit history is one of the factors explaining the relatively slow growth of credit cards. The US processor TSYS has taken a significant stake in CUP which is seeking to avoid joining the international card schemes and instead striking agreements with acquirers in specific countries.

The CNAPS (Chinese National Advanced Payment System) was launched in 2002 by the PBOC which also operates it. It has two components:

- a High Value Payment system (HVPS) which operates on an RTGS basis; and
- an ACH, the Bulk Entry Payment System (BEPS).

Institutions join as direct or indirect participants, including some non-banking entities such as central and local government agencies, the

Treasury and the Central Government Bonds Depositary and Clearing Corporation (CDC). Interestingly, in spite of its width stretching over 5,000 km, China operates with one time-zone, which at least facilitates the fixing of cut-off and settlement times.

The PBOC grants HVPS direct participants intraday facilities through free repos or collateralized intraday overdrafts. The minimum amount for a payment through HVPS payment in 2007 was Yuan 500,000. The system started operating in Beijing and Wuhan. The choice of Wuhan is symbolic: an inland city on the Yangtze river in the centre of China, from where the 1911 revolution started which led to the overthrow of the Imperial regime after 2,000 years. It was also the site of the start of the Taiping revolt in the middle of the nineteenth century which spread along the Yangtze up to Nankin, the ancient Ming capital.

BEPS shares the telecommunications infrastructure with HVPS and operates as an ACH processing credit transfers, recurring and one-off direct debits. Payments between banks in the same city are processed in regional City Clearing Processing Centres (CCPCs). Interbank payments between CCPCs take place over the BEPS. Net amounts are calculated at 17.00 local time (remembering that China maintains the same time zone across the width of the country), settlement takes place overnight through HVPS so beneficiary banks are credited next day. A maximum amount of Yuan 20,000 was enforced in 2007.

As in most countries, government bonds are the most liquid instrument used to raise funds for the Treasury and by the PBOC to intervene through open market interventions. They are also used by banks and even enterprises (a heritage from the communist period) to manage their treasury. Settlement is effected end-of-day by the CDC over HVPS and the SD&C (China Securities Depository and Clearing Corporation Ltd) which is also the depositary for shares. There is also an interbank market in bonds, separate from the market open to enterprises and brokers, operated by the PBOC which offers repos and spot trades.

The interbank bond market operates continuously, so there is no clearing. The trades on the Shenzen and Shanghai market are settled over the local branches of SD&C. Clearing and settlement take place in real-time. DVP was not available at the time of publication, so settlement takes place under the PAD (Payment after Delivery) or DAP (Delivery after Payment) principles using a book entry system with internal audit and control systems.

After an initial 'let a thousand exchanges bloom' phase, the government intervened to consolidate them around two in Shanghai and

Shenzen, which trade shares in Chinese corporations. Two types exist: 'A' which are shares in Yuan held by Chinese nationals and 'B' shares which are denominated in Yuan but paid for in US dollars and held by non-residents. The two exchanges are supervised and managed by the China Securities Regulatory Commission (CSRC) who operate the trading and clearing platforms. Settlement and delivery is effected by the SD&C which also handles government bonds. Settlement is effected T+1 for A shares and T+3 for B shares. The SD&C manages a guarantee fund available in case of default of a participant. Members must deposit the guarantees in designated banks and the SD&C is not allowed to lend securities to members of the exchange.

2.2 Hong Kong SAR

The Hong Kong payments landscape presents some interesting particularities. Notes are issued by three commercial banks: HSBC, Standard Chartered Bank and Bank of China. It features a triple-currency large-value settlement system in Hong Kong dollars, US dollars and euro. Finally, the Hong Kong cheque clearing system has concluded reciprocal agreements with the clearing houses in Shenzen and Guangzhou which guarantee acceptance of cheques issued in Hong Kong in mainland China and vice versa: a narrow bridge allowing convertibility between the two currencies.

The Hong Kong Monetary Authority (HKMA) is the central bank of the Hong Kong SAR and is therefore responsible for monetary policy. It also supervises the banks and has oversight responsibilities over payment and settlement systems. It does not however issue notes – this is subcontracted to the three commercial banks mentioned earlier.

The Chinese authorities have gone to great efforts to maintain Hong Kong's position among the world's financial markets since the handover in 1997 under the 'one country, two systems' principle, encouraging the development of new services. More than ever Hong Kong is used as a controlled gateway between mainland China's economy and the outside world as it moves towards a market economy. After the repatriation of Chinese companies listed in Hong Kong to Shenzen and Shanghai, reciprocity agreements have been signed between the three exchanges. Several companies choose to list simultaneously in Shanghai and Hong Kong. This raises convertibility and arbitrage issues between the A shares traded in Shanghai in a closed market environment and the H shares traded in Hong Kong at a distinctly lower price under free market principles. A unification of the markets would immediately raise the problem of compensating millions of Chinese holders of overvalued A shares who would see their value drop.

Payment clearing and settlement which was historically carried out by the Hong Kong and Shanghai Banking Corporation (HSBC) is now carried out by a private company, the Hong Kong Interbank Clearing Limited (HKICL), owned by the HKMA and the Hong Kong Association of Banks (HKAB). HKICL operates the RTGS systems for the three currencies: CHATS HKD, CHATS USD and CHATS Euro as well as the Central Money Market Unit (CMU), which is the CSD and settlement system for government securities (Exchange Fund Bills and Notes, EFBN). It is linked in real-time to CHATS to manage liquidity and facilitate immediate investment of surplus funds.

Cash is widely used in Hong Kong and the cash to GDP ratio is among the highest in the world, comparable to Japan or Switzerland. The Chinese are very attached to cash and a large proportion of high denomination Hong Kong notes circulate in mainland China as refuge currency. The HKD is linked to the RMB by a flexible peg enabling some arbitraging. The RMB not being convertible, foreigners use the HKD to hedge their RMB operations, bearing in mind that the RMB was appreciating slowly but surely against the USD at the time of publication, awaiting full convertibility of the RMB in line with the agreements reached with the WTO.

In spite of the rapid growth of electronic instruments, cheques remain the most popular instrument for retail and corporate payments. The cheque clearing is operated by HKICL for settlement through CHATS with value next day. Bilateral links have been established for clearing HKD and USD cheques between Hong Kong, Guangzhou and Shenzen.

Credit transfers and direct debits are also used. Debit and credit cards are issued under the international schemes. We should also note that Hong Kong introduced the first contactless card scheme for public transport, Octopus.

The CHATS (Clearing House Automated Transfer System) RTGS system is accessed via the SWIFT network through Y-copy which removes all customer data and transmits only the information strictly necessary for settlement (see Figure 8.3).

Payments are settled immediately providing the settlement account with HKMA is funded. Banks can access the CMU for repo operations in EFBNs to replenish liquidity; the payment will be queued if EFBNs cannot provide sufficient liquidity as no overdrafts are allowed on the settlement accounts. This facility is automatically activated to avoid delaying payments and excess EFBNs are returned to the CMU when

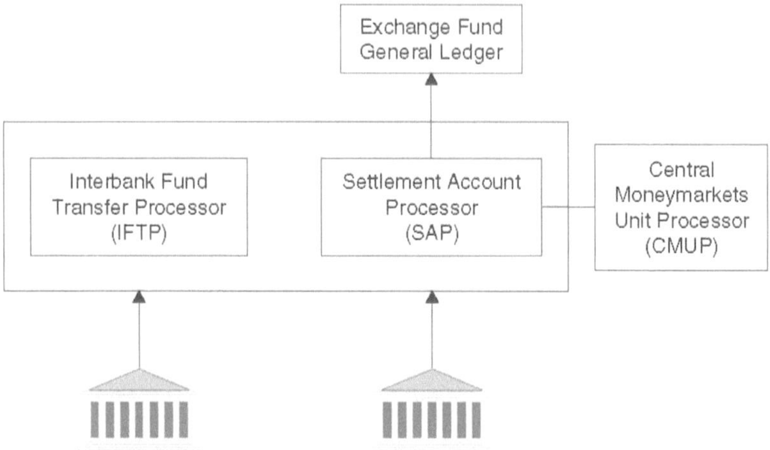

Figure 8.3 The Hong Kong CHATS RTGS system

no longer required. Repos are free if returned the same day, but can be extended overnight by a loan from HKMA through the Discount Window. Participants have full visibility over their queues, including incoming payments. Participants can also obtain liquidity through intraday repos of securities other than EFBNs held with the CMU; these Liquidity Adjustment Window (LAW) operations are however intended as exceptional.

CHATS USD settles through HSBC and CHATS Euro through Standard Chartered (Hong Kong) Bank. They operate on similar principles to CHATS HKD except that intraday credit facilities are available in USD through repos and overdrafts; these are free if the borrowers refund HSBC through their New York clearer before CHIPS closes the following day (which theoretically implies a settlement risk). The cohabitation of the three systems also allows FX trades to be settled on a Pay versus Pay (PVP) basis. The HKD/USD settlement facility was the first PVP system in existence and also facilitates liquidity management as funds are immediately available for re-use.

As introduced above, the CMU is the CSD for government debt instruments and also offers some custody services. It has signed reciprocal agreements with Clearstream and Euroclear, as well as the CSDs in Australia, New Zealand and South Korea. This provides direct access by foreign investors to the Hong Kong markets. It offers two settlement modes: Delivery versus Payment (DVP) and Free of Payment (FOP).

The CMU does not act as a central counterparty and does not extend credit, therefore not guaranteeing settlement. Participants are exposed to replacement risk. The cash leg is settled via CHATS through the link between them. Intraday repo facilities are available through the HKMA for HKD and HSBC for USD.

The Hong Kong Securities Clearing Corporation (HKSCC), a private company, controls the Central Clearing and Settlement System acting as CSD for non-government debt and equities; it is operated by the Hong Kong Exchange and Clearing Ltd (HKEx). It is linked to CHATS to provide DVP. Trades are settled T+2 and those for which payment has not been received are set aside. HKSCC acts as central counterparty and is therefore exposed to replacement risk on trades not settled. All trades are therefore market-to-market daily and HKSCC can initiate margin calls as well as call for collateral from a broker if it considers that its exposure poses excessive risk. Brokers contribute to a guarantee fund to cover any defaults; their contribution is based on their average position during the previous month.

In conclusion, the 'one country, two systems' regime has allowed Hong Kong to strengthen its payment and securities settlement systems in order to maintain its position as major financial centre and act as gateway for the mainland's economy. The Chinese systems were not on par with Hong Kong's at the time of publication, nor compatible with China's position as economic powerhouse. The sophisticated Hong Kong systems set an example China can follow. The establishment of bridges between the payment systems in Hong Kong and the mainland are typical of the pragmatic and gradual approach adopted by the government.

9
New Entrants

As mentioned in Chapter 1 (sec. 2.1), several non-financial institutions are offering payment services, breaking in to the cosy monopoly the banks enjoyed up until the end of the last century. Each one can present the following threats:

- Brand disintermediation: will the new entrant substitute itself in the mind of the customer to his/her bank as first choice when thinking of effecting a payment or initiating the transaction? Who defines the customer experience?
- Loss of revenue, be it fees, float or interest on revolving credit, etc.
- By-pass: does the non-banking service provider use conventional payment systems and providers, adding value at the periphery, or does it create a totally new scheme?
- Risk: does the scheme operated by non financial institutions present risk to its customers or create systemic risk?

This chapter attempts to describe the most aggressive new entrants and examine the potential threat under the above criteria.

1 Remittances service providers

These organizations offer low cost services to migrant workers wishing to send funds to relatives in their country of origin, who often do not hold bank accounts. They also offer emergency funds transfers to, for instance, travellers who would not hold accounts in the countries through which they are travelling. As mentioned in Chapter 3 (sec. 4), the main providers are Western Union, MoneyGram and Travelex. Funds can be sent and received from accredited service points displaying their logo, generally retail outlets at convenient locations with long opening hours. They by-pass the conventional schemes and represent a total loss of revenues to the banks, as well as brand disintermediation. The amounts transferred would not represent systemic risk and the customers benefit from redress procedures and guarantees.

Chapter 3 also mentioned the parallel systems such as Hawala. They present the same competitive threats as the organizations identified earlier, but without the contractual guarantees to customers, although they do rely on a strict 'code of honour'. They are however open to suspicion of money laundering and identity verification.

2 Non-bank issued credit cards

Many retail chains have been issuing store cards with a revolving credit facility for use at their own outlets since the middle of the twentieth century. They were originally intended as a plastic identification, using the standard dimensions, for accounts that stores have offered their regular customers for centuries. As many chains originally refused to accept any other credit or debit card, these store cards represented a loss of revenues for the banks in terms of merchant fees, interchange fees and interest on revolving credit. Even the amounts spent at Harrods in London would not pose any systemic risk and the store assumes the risk that their customers could default, generally insuring against any losses.

The threat increased however when many retail chains, such as Marks & Spencer and amazon.co.uk, started offering general credit cards in conjunction with MasterCard or Visa and linked to loyalty schemes. The loss of revenues to the banks then spread to any purchase the holder might charge to his/her card at any accepting merchant worldwide, coupled with total brand disintermediation and the loss of opportunities created by analysis of the customer's spending habits. Retailers analyse their customers' purchases to bombard them with targeted mailings focusing on items they are likely to be of interest. It should be noted however that the processing of these store cards is generally assumed by a bank or a card processor, but the lost income by far outstrips these outsourcing revenues.

3 Transport cards

Most cities operate prepaid stored-value contactless card schemes for public transport, Hong Kong having led the way with Octopus. Readers will be familiar with the ones operated by cities in which they live: MetroCard in New York, Oyster in London, Navigo in Paris, Suico in Tokyo. These were originally closed systems, some extending to other related transport networks such as suburban railways. Their acceptance is now often extended to some other local retail outlets such as convenience stores or newsagents which also offer reloading services, as well as fast-food restaurants and vending machines. Although the prepaid issuer benefits from the float, losses to the banking industry are not really significant as the amounts involved are low, thus removing any concern about risk. Brand disintermediation is not really an issue as it is an area where banks have a minimal presence. The owner however runs the risk of losing the remaining stored value in case of loss or theft. An interesting alliance was announced in the UK between Oyster and Barclaycard Visa whereby the Oyster functionality is imbedded with the card.

4 Mobile phones and mobile payments

The statistics are overwhelming: over 2.75 billion mobile phone handsets worldwide in 2007, as many as debit/credit cards, twice the number of internet users, 80 per cent of the European population,[1] or one for every two adults worldwide. In several countries such as India and China, mobile telephony is leapfrogging land line provision.

The technology is proven. Near Field Communication (NFC) provides contactless connectivity and the purse or credit/debit card details can be imbedded in the SIM card in the GSM world, in the NFC chip in the CDMA world and even in a separate SD card used today to store gp or mp3 files. All stakeholders use GlobalPlatform standards for services management in SIM cards and the 'rich' NFC chip.

The key issues surrounding mobile banking services and payments revolve around security and . . . the sharing of revenues between the bank and the mobile phone operator.

Security solutions are improving: SMS messages can be encrypted; the PIN for financial services can be used in addition to the code used to open the mobile phone. Opportunities for biometrics exist with voice recognition, face recognition with the camera included in most handsets and fingerprinting which will be available shortly, remembering that consumers change handsets on average every 2 years.

Several banks are today offering SMS services for alerts, balance enquiries, confirmations, and some limited bill-payment services as the savings compared to the cost of calls from support staff are substantial.

Mobile payments are seen as the Holy Grail to strive for. Throughout this book, we define mobile payments as the initiation and or confirmation of a payment transaction from a wireless device such as a mobile phone, PDA or similar. Mobile payments originated in Japan with services pioneered by NTT DoCoMo. The scheme started as a stored value purse scheme, giving DoCoMo the benefit of the float, with some purchases carried over to the mobile telephone bill. Mobile payments can even offer the anonymity of cash through the use of prepaid cards.

This brings us to the heart of the problem. Banks' skills lie in handling a relatively small number of payments per consumer for amounts normally exceeding $20, but most importantly in credit assessment. Mobile operators, on the other hand, have the technology to itemize a very high number of calls costing very little. They do not however have the banks' experience in credit assessment for allocating spending limits should they wish to allow purchases such as clothes, household appliances, travel and entertainment to be added to their monthly invoice, in other words manage credit risk beyond the average $150 on a mobile phone consumer bill. A solution could lie in a cooperation between mobile operators and banks, whereby small amounts such as urban transport, parking fees, cinema tickets, etc. are charged to the mobile bill while purchases above an agreed floor amount would be charged to the debit or credit card issued by the bank.

This would involve installing a credit/debit card applet allowing the customer to decide. Banks would share space on the SIM card with the operator, but an issue arises: who is the landlord and who is the tenant? The SIM card belongs to the operator and the bank is therefore at his mercy and could be expelled! The banks should remain masters of the space they rent, accessed through their branded security feature. In Korea, the SIM card is issued by the bank to the customer who chooses his mobile operator. Both parties should cooperate to provide value-added services such as SMS confirmations of payments over the internet or when using card at ATM abroad to counter skimming.

Mobile payments are spreading in emerging economies with a largely unbanked population and poor infrastructure. Vodafone launched M-PESA in Kenya through its subsidiary Safaricom in 2007, in cooperation with a commercial bank and a microfinance institution. Transactions include Person-to-Person, Person-to-Business and loan repayments. Payments can be initiated from a bank account or by depositing cash with an agent. The recipient can either receive the funds on his bank account or in cash from an agent by showing the amount and a code received by SMS. Full statements and audit trails are available for all stakeholders.

The major threat is the mobile operators acquiring Payment Institution's licence, as allowed under the PSD in Europe, and issuing cards.

They will rapidly gain the skills to assess credit risk, or find an insurance scheme to cover them. Brand disintermediation and revenue losses to the banking industry would be total. Systemic risk is negligible and credit risk could be limited if they imposed low limits which would be acceptable to their target customer segments: technology-savvy youths and Generation Y.

5 Paypal

Paypal originated in 1998 from the need to effect person-to-person payments when individuals purchased objects from unknown counterparties through internet auction sites such as eBay. The problem was twofold: most of the individuals selling objects such as old books or used appliances were not registered as merchants to receive credit/debit card payments, while buyers were reluctant to send cheques or post their account details or credit card numbers to an unknown counterparty or on the internet. PayPal acts as an intermediary whereby individuals register their account indentifiers or credit/debit card number with PayPal when opening an account, but which remain known to PayPal only. When PayPal customers wish to send a payment they indicate the e-mail address of the beneficiary and the amount. The system is viral as an account is automatically opened for the beneficiary based on his e-mail address if no PayPal account is associated with it. The amount will be, at the sender's choice, debited from his/her PayPal account subject to funds, his bank account or charged to his credit/debit card. The funds will be deposited in the beneficiary's PayPal account who can leave them there, or transfer them to his/her regular bank account. A mobile payment initiation service was launched in 2007.

Businesses have the choice between two types of merchant accounts which enable them to place a PayPal button on their website which buyers can click to initiate the payment. Should the merchant not have a PayPal account but indicates that MasterCard and/or PayPal are accepted buyers can use a 'PayPal Debit Bar' facility which creates a one-time virtual MasterCard number to complete the purchase. PayPal payments can also be initiated via mobile phones.

PayPal was acquired by eBay in 2002. At the end of 2007 it held 141 million accounts worldwide, of which 57 million (40 per cent) were active, and processed 2 million transactions daily for a value totalling $17 billion during the last quarter;[2] annualized revenues ran at $2.3 billion.[3] This makes it the largest account-holding institution in the world ... Its revenues derive from the balances left in PayPal accounts upon which it pays no interest, but itself placing the funds in interest-bearing bank accounts. PayPal charges merchants a fee plus a monthly account maintenance charge.

PayPal is an interesting example of brand disintermediation and revenue loss (principally float and deposit base), with partial bypass as the purchase uses classical payment channels (ACH, credit/debit cards) unless the funds are transferred from a PayPal account. PayPal is not an FDIC-insured bank, but claims to hold funds in regulated and insured banks. The safety of customer funds in PayPal accounts in case of failure of PayPal is unclear.

6 Earthport

Earthport positions itself as 'The International Bank-2-Bank Payments Service'.[4] It transfers funds between customer accounts held with high-street banks over its proprietary Universal Payments Network (UPN) and aims 'to become the independent utility of choice for payment and collection of funds for national and global money movements'.[5]

Earthport maintains Segregated Accounts for each client with banks, in line with FSA regulations, and a Virtual Account within the UPN mapping onto the Segregated Account. It holds banking relationships with 35 banks enabling it at the beginning of 2008 to effect payments in 190 countries. Earthport is connected to SWIFT as a corporate enabling it to extend its reach to countries beyond its UPN's coverage. The UPN uses a least cost routing algorithm enabling Earthport to offer lower fees than banks. Payments can also be initiated using cards.

As customers initiate payments and view positions and statements through the Earthport website, it strikes with brand disintermediation and at the banks' and SWIFT's revenues from international payments. Customer funds are held in the Segregated Accounts with commercial banks and Earthport insures against error and fraud.

The authors recognize that the above selection may be obsolete by the time this book is read, but have attempted to present a representative sample at the time of publication. Generally speaking, these new entrants have displayed more innovation than banks which have most often been reduced to playing catch-up or enter into alliances from a position of weakness. We will see in the final chapter how they will affect the future of the payments industry.

Part III
The Settlement of Trading Activities

10
The Settlement of Foreign Exchange Trades and CLS

As outlined in Chapter 4 (sec. 2.5) all trading operations include two steps: the actual trading over the telephone, or more commonly today computer screens, and the settlement which consists of delivering the currencies and/or securities traded and ensuring that ownership has effectively and irrevocably passed from seller to buyer on both legs. The general public is mostly aware of the trading operations through TV interviews of financial 'experts' captured in trading rooms, or films such as 'Wall Street'. Much less glamorous and exciting, but nevertheless demanding exacting care to avoid fails, are the back office operations necessary to settle the trades struck by the 'masters of the financial universe'.

1 The settlement of foreign exchange trades and settlement risk

Figure 10.1 illustrates the processes after a foreign exchange (FX) trade has been struck. Trades can be agreed for various settlement dates: 'spot' or forward: seven days, thirty days, etc, spot being the shortest and settling two working days after the trade has been struck, or T+2. It is technically possible to trade same day by adding the interest over two days.

Details of the trade are recorded on a *ticket*, the name of the sheet of paper having survived although trades are mostly nowadays recorded electronically. The positions and limits are immediately updated to reflect the latest risk status by trader, currency, country and trading counterparty. Trading details include the counterparty, the amount traded, the exchange rate agreed and the settlement deadline (spot by default). If necessary, the nostro correspondent or clearing banks which the counterparties will use are added, remembering from Chapter 3 that if a foreign currency is involved, settlement will have to take place in the

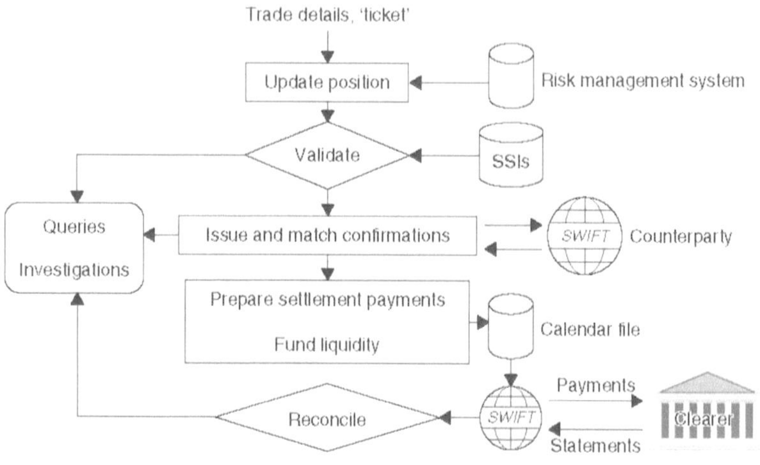

Figure 10.1 After the trader has put the phone down ...

country of the currency. These are generally known beforehand and drawn from Standard Settlement Instruction (SSI) files. After validation, counterparties exchange confirmations of the trade details, each normally being the mirror image of the other, which are matched. Confirmations are mostly transmitted over SWIFT which also offers a confirmation matching service ACCORD reporting exceptions to reduce back-office overheads. Assuming no discrepancy, payments are set up and funding is secured for the settlement date when payment is effected. The trading entities then await the statements from their respective clearers for final reconciliation.

Figure 10.2 shows the classical settlement chain taking the example of a British and a French bank striking a US dollar/Japanese yen trade, both having to resort to their Japanese and US clearers as neither are trading their home currencies.

A *fail* occurs if one leg of the trade does not settle, in our case the yen are delivered but not the dollars. Our example shows the most extreme case of *settlement risk*, linked to the asynchronous settlement of the two legs.

Due to the time-zone differences between Tokyo, Europe and New York (see Figure 10.3), the French bank would have probably instructed its Japanese clearer the day before settlement day to ensure settlement when the Japanese payment systems opened at 9.00 am Tokyo time, when the amount is irrevocably transferred between the two Japanese clearers. The dollars would expect to be settled at the latest when CHIPS closed at 4.00 pm in New York, some 20 hours later! Had the British

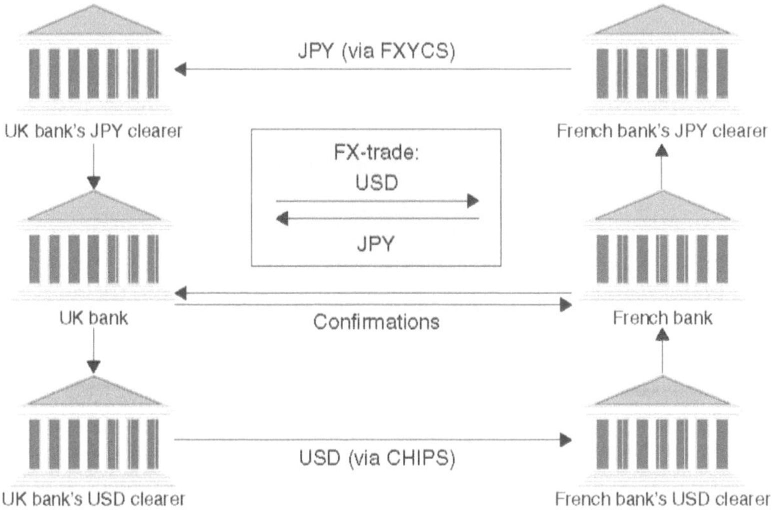

Figure 10.2 Traditional FX settlement

Figure 10.3 Settlement (or Herstatt) risk

bank failed at around 2.00 pm London time or been unable to meet its obligations, the French bank would no longer have been able to cancel its payment instruction as the Japanese systems would have long closed and it will have paid out the yen without any chance of receiving the dollars. Settlement risk is therefore the combination of the principal risk (the amount traded) over a period of time, taking into account the time to receive and reconcile the nostro statements.

This is not a hypothetical case. On 26 June 1974 the Bundesbank withdrew Bankhaus Herstatt's banking licence. Herstatt, a small German family private bank aggressively active on the foreign exchange market, had sold dollars for Deutschmarks to meet its settlement obligations in Germany. Its counterparties duly delivered the marks via their German clearers but Herstatt, following suspension by the Bundesbank in the middle of the business day, had not paid the dollars, leaving several institutions with a loss. This ensured that Herstatt entered banking history as the term *Herstatt risk* has since become synonymous with FX settlement risk. The events were repeated in subsequent years following the failures of Drexel Burnham Lambert in New York and BCCI in London.

Trading volumes were peaking at around 1.7 trillion dollars in the 1990s, so FX settlement risk raised serious concerns with the regulators and major market players. 'You [the banks] put this risk into the market, you take it out!' thundered Lawrence Sweet of the Federal Reserve Bank of New York at the 1996 SIBOS conference. Settlement systems in the major currencies extended their opening hours, but achieving only minimum overlap windows. Various multilateral netting systems sprung up (notably ECHO) which failed to fully meet the concerns of the central banks as some 30–50 per cent of settlement risk subsisted. The BIS published a landmark report in 1996 'Settlement Risk in Foreign Exchange Transactions', known as the *Allsopp Report* after Peter Allsopp from the Bank of England who headed its publication. It concluded that the simultaneous and interdependent settlement of both legs was the only way to minimize settlement risk, which gave birth to CLS under the leadership of the 20 major FX trading institutions worldwide.

2 CLS

CLS, which stands for 'Continuous Linked Settlement', acts in effect as a trusted third party or escrow holder. Referring to our example above, it is based on the principle that the French bank would not pay the yen directly to the British bank via its clearers, but to CLS which holds the yen until the British bank has paid the corresponding dollars; CLS then releases both currency payments via the traders' respective clearers. It is a Payment versus Payment (PvP) system. If one party fails to pay in its currency, the funds are returned to the bank which has duly paid in its leg. The system effectively substitutes the settlement risk on the entire principal amount by a *replacement risk*, or risk that the exchange rate would have moved against the counterparty which paid in correctly when it trades later with another institution, which very rarely exceeds a few per cents.

Figure 10.4 shows the various parties involved in CLS.

Settlement Members (70 at the end of 2007), who are also shareholders, submit trade settlement details and payments on their behalf as well as

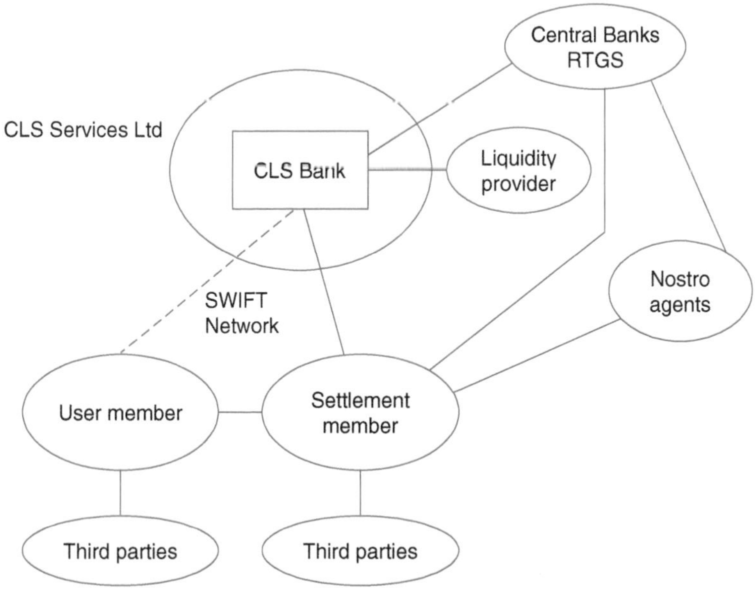

Figure 10.4 The CLS environment

on behalf of User Members and Third Parties (customers) they sponsor. They hold an account at CLS Bank International in each of the eligible currencies they choose to trade in.

User Members can submit trades to CLS Bank subject to authorization of their sponsoring Settlement Member who settles on their behalf.

Third Parties (2411 at the end of 2007) are customers of Settlement or User Members who submit trades and settlement payments on their behalf.

CLS is linked to the *RTGS system for each eligible currency* to ensure that all settlement payments received are irrevocably final.

Nostro agents or clearers are the correspondent banks through which Settlement Members submit payments in currencies for which they are not members of the relevant RTGS system.

Liquidity providers have undertaken to provide liquidity in specified currencies.

CLS Bank International is a US edge corporation incorporated in the US and regulated by the Federal Reserve Bank of New York. CLS Services Ltd is a UK registered company providing operational support and services to CLS Bank International. Both these entities are owned by CLS Group Holdings AG incorporated in Switzerland, owned by the shareholding member banks, through CLS UK Intermediate Holdings Ltd.[1] Throughout this book we will refer to all these organizations generically as CLS. The CLS system, which went live in 2002, was developed and is operated under an outsourcing contract by the IBM Corporation. To ensure the required business continuity and resilience as a SIPS, the system architecture is based on three operating centres and two command centres on both sides of the Atlantic, to mirror processes and data 24/7.

3 CLS operating procedures and timetable

Confirmations for trades to be settled through CLS are copied to CLS by SWIFT. Matched trades are netted multilaterally per currency to reduce funding requirements, resulting in each Settlement Member being either long (is owed funds) or short (owes funds) in each currency on a given settlement day. For each currency in which it is short, CLS issues a pay-in schedule breaking down the total short position in each currency into discrete pay-ins to be received with irrevocable finality, through the respective RTGS system with which CLS holds an account, by 8.00, 9.00, 10.00, 11.00 and 12.00 CET. Figure 10.5 indicates the sequence of processes throughout the day.

Initial pay-in and pay-out schedules are issued at midnight CET, up until then trades can be unilaterally rescinded. The final schedules are issued at 6.30 CET, up until then trades can only be rescinded bilaterally.

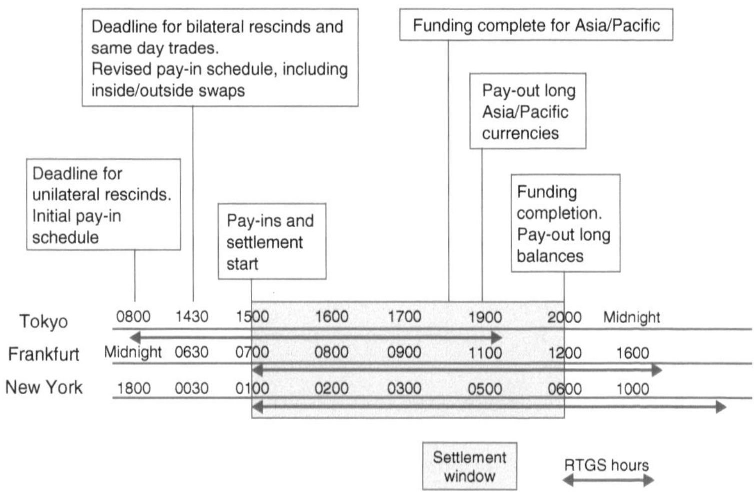

Figure 10.5 24 hours in the life of CLS

The settlement window runs from 7.00–12.00 CET, corresponding to the time at which the opening hours of the RTGS systems for the eligible currencies overlap. Short banks can start paying in from 7.00 CET; as funds are received, CLS constantly scans all trades in the queue to determine which can be settled. Pay-outs to long banks via the relevant RTGS system occur as trades settle following a Pay-in → Settlement → Pay out cycle, starting with the Asia/Pacific currencies, up until 12.00 CET. Settlement is then complete and funds paid-in for any unsettled trades are returned. Comprehensive reporting, enquiry and control facilities are available for members to monitor financial flows and the status of trades.

4 Risk and liquidity management in CLS

Risk management is based on self-collateralization as an obligation in one currency is balanced by the receipt of the equivalent amount in another, the allocation of limits, the management of the settlement queue and liquidity provision.

Limits include:

- *Short Position Limits* set for each settlement member represent its maximum net debit position in each currency. They are established based on its capital ratios and credit rating.
- The *Net Positive Value* is the algebraic sum of the member's positions across all currencies expressed in US dollars and must remain positive (no overall debit position is allowed). A *haircut* (volatility margin) is established to allow for currency fluctuations.
- The *Aggregate Short Position Limit* is the overall net debit positions for all members for each currency and is set according to the commitments of the Liquidity Providers.

CLS is probably unique as the Net Positive Value allows members to cover short positions in some currencies by long positions in the others. This allows the bank to avoid trading on the FX market which would entail transaction costs and impact the balance sheet.

The first pay-ins are calculated to ensure that each member returns within its short position limit. Trades are settled taking the above limits into account and receipts from settled trades are used to settle further transactions. Pay-outs are dissociated from settlement to ensure that the Net Value remains positive for each member.

The netting could produce imbalances between a Settlement Member's positions, for example a large short position in USD and a high long position in euro, resulting in a substantial initial pay-in in USD at 8.00 CET. CLS introduced therefore the Inside/Outside swap (also known as In/Out or I/O swap), based on two equal and opposite same day FX 'transactions', one settling inside CLS and the other outside. These operations do not modify the member's overall FX position, but balance the intraday cash flows within CLS by reducing the initial pay-in for the short currency and, of course, the pay-out in the long currency. After publication of the initial positions at midnight CET, CLS proposes swaps to settlement members based on bilateral counterparty limits they have set, minimum/maximum trade sizes and Pay-in/Pay-out Trade down limits per currency. If members choose to enter into I/O swaps, the inside leg will be taken into account during calculation of the final positions and pay-in schedule issued at 6.30 CET.

If a member defaults on its Pay-in obligations, CLS will call upon the Liquidity Providers for that currency. Trades that have already settled cannot be unwound, but CLS will halt any further pay-outs to the defaulting institution. The Liquidity Provider pays-in directly to CLS on behalf of the defaulting member and agrees a swap with the latter. Should some trades remain unsettled following the intervention of the Liquidity Providers, for instance if only part of the defaulting member's obligation could be funded, CLS will return the amounts paid-in by the counterparties for the unsettled trades.

5 Market and business impact of CLS

Settlement risk caused by time-zone differences has been virtually eliminated. The multilateral netting and the I/O swaps have reduced settlement members' pay-in requirements to approximately 3 per cent of the gross value of the trades settled through CLS.[2] On the other hand, the 'liquidity window' has shrunk from nearly 24 hours between the opening of the Asia/Pacific and the closing of the North American markets to five hours between 7.00 and 12.00 CET, forcing stronger discipline in funding and liquidity management to meet the pay-in schedule. Several RTGS systems introduced timing options for payments to ensure compliance with the pay-in hourly deadlines. Real-time monitoring of liquidity is also required as the timing of pay-outs is unpredictable. The obligation to use RTGS systems to ensure irrevocable finality required upgrading several systems (for example FXYCS to RTGS mode in Japan) and shifts between national payment systems, notably from CHIPS to Fedwire in the US. The losses however by far exceeded the gains as, for each trading institution, gross settlement payments for each trade were effectively replaced by five payments to/from CLS for netted amounts!

The introduction of CLS required a radical transformation of back-office processes and disciplines, accelerating the concentration of back-offices as the trades for global institutions are consolidated by CLS across all participating branches and/or subsidiaries. It enabled significant improvements in back-office automation and STP, substantially reducing fails and the cost of queries and investigations, but – it also meant the introduction of unsocial working hours for staff in Asia/Pacific and North America.

The User Member status has not proved successful but several major institutions, including leading investment banks, baulked at the heavy initial investments and joining fees, preferring to participate as a Third Party. Competition for third parties' business was fierce, but major settlement members have admitted publicly that the Third Party activity is not profitable on its own and should be viewed within the context of an overall relationship including credit, nostro clearing and custody.

The pay-in schedule deadlines also led to revisions and tightening-up of service level agreements (SLAs) with nostro correspondents and clearers. Competition in this area, already intense following the introduction of the euro, increased dramatically, with global banks leveraging their participation in several RTGS systems.

At end of 2007, CLS settled on average 492,000 instructions daily for a value of USD 3.8 trillion between the 15 major currencies accounting for 95 per cent of daily traded value: Australian, Canadian, Hong Kong, New Zealand, Singapore and US dollars, euro, sterling, yen, Swiss franc, Korean won, South African rand and Danish, Norwegian and Swedish Kroner. CLS has become the prime settlement vehicle for FX trades, FX option exercises, FX swaps, non-deliverable forwards and FX OTC option premiums. The volume and settlement value can double on peak days, generally after a US bank holiday.

CLS has fulfilled its objective and satisfied the regulators that settlement risk has been 'virtually'[3] eliminated. Additional currencies will add marginal traffic so its growth is linked to the evolution of the FX market driven by global commerce and financial trading.

11
Securities Settlement

On 2 August 2004, in less than two minutes, Citibank issued sell instructions on government bonds from 11 euro-zone countries for a sum of 11 billion euros. The trade involved over 200 instruments on the different electronic trading platforms of MTS, the Italian system which runs the market in euro government bonds. The purchase of government securities, mainly French, German and Italian, generated liquidity through the simultaneous sale of futures contracts, mainly German (Bunds 10 years, Bobl 5 years and Schatz 2 years). Between 20 and 30,000 futures contracts for a value of 100,000 euros each changed hands in a few seconds. This naturally pushed the price down. Half an hour later, Citibank repurchased the government bonds for 4 billion euros, making a profit of 10 million euros through this perfectly legal operation. Six of the 55 principal trading institutions on MTS are reputed to have lost around one million euros. To avoid a repetition, MTS has since imposed limits on the amounts that can be traded within a defined short period of time. Trading such high volumes in such a brief time interval, involving hundreds of diverse instruments (securities, derivatives, and cash) in different countries requires very efficient settlement infrastructures in terms of execution time, resilience and cost so as not to impact the profitability of such an operation, 0.001 per cent in this case.

As mentioned in Chapter 4 (sec. 2.5), securities trading involves two legs: the traded securities and the cash to buy them. Settlement requires communication between the payment system for cash and the securities settlement system to ensure finality over both legs, known as DVP (Delivery versus Payment): 'a link between a securities transfer system and a funds transfer system that ensures that delivery occurs if, and only if, payment occurs'.[1]

The globalization of trading, the diversification of portfolios and the launch of the euro require that the settlement costs of cross-border trades, costing up to three times more than domestic ones, be reduced without jeopardizing security and speed. If the trade involves a foreign security, or if one of the counterparties is a non-resident, access to a foreign settlement system is required either to settle the cash or to transfer ownership of the securities. International Central Securities Depositaries (ICSDs) – namely Euroclear and Clearstream – have emerged alongside national Central Securities Depositories (CSDs) to ensure the link between domestic systems. To centralize cross-border operations and streamline portfolio management, investors use the services of global custodians which carry out and monitor all activities related to a security from the moment a trade has been struck until it next changes ownership: ensure delivery and change of registration, safekeeping, collecting dividends, coupons or redemptions, tax reclamation, corporate actions, etc.

Clearing and settlement of securities trades, particularly cross-border, therefore requires communication between payment and securities settlement systems and close monitoring with attention to detail by back-office personnel to prevent costly *fails*: cash being paid without the securities being delivered or vice-versa.

1 Securities clearing and settlement systems

These are driven by financial innovation and technology throughout the entire cycle:

TRADING – CLEARING – SETTLEMENT – DELIVERY

Electronic quotation and trading drive price transparency and enable markets to absorb large trading volumes in periods of market volatility. The interlinking of real-time platforms aims to ensure STP (Straight Through Processing).

Trading in derivatives is based on the value of the underlying assets or indices and the spread between them. Derivatives offer the benefit of being recognized as off-balance sheet. Clearing and settlement must be as short as possible and costs must be kept as low as possible so as not to impact profitability measured in basis points.

Cross-border securities settlement is more complex, involves many players and requires shortening payment execution times and links between systems to increase efficiency and reduce costs. The following options are available:

- remote access to a national DVP system;
- use a local institution which has access to the national DVP system;

- use an ICSD which maintains links with the national CSD systems; or
- use the services of a global custodian with access to the CSDs and ICSDs.

The last two offer the benefit of a single access point to several countries and avoid the costs of a local intermediary. ICSDs enable 'on us' settlements if possible and also run securities lending/borrowing schemes to guard against fails.

Recent trends have highlighted concentration between Security Settlement Systems (SSS) and the quasi disappearance of vertical integration between exchanges and settlement systems to avoid cross-subsidization. Custody has also concentrated into a handful of global custodians as several players have dropped out of the business in the face of rising investments and compliance demands: The Bank of New York and Mellon merged in 2007 to create the world's largest custodian. Concentration is driven by economies of scale to reduce transaction, collateral and safe keeping costs, as investments and operating costs are largely fixed. The European Investment Services Directive of 1993 (ISD) allows price improvements if an institution can trade internally.

This concentration poses risks in terms of potential monopoly which could lead to complacency and lack of innovation. A conflict has also emerged over the past years as the ICSDs are extending their custody activities thereby competing against their members and shareholders. These are demanding separation of the two functions to ensure price transparency. In the US, trading is considered competitive between exchanges while safekeeping, clearing and settlement is recognized as a utility and managed by a neutral not-for-profit organization DTCC (see ch. 7 sec. 8).

2 Risks in securities settlement systems

Several risks can be identified during the securities settlement process:

- *Counterparty risk*: counterparty risk (credit or liquidity risk) extends over the total amount of the trade. Depending on the leg that fails, it can occur if the securities are delivered but the cash is not paid, or if the cash is irrevocably paid and the securities are not delivered.
- *Replacement risk*: extends over the cash leg. If delivery of the securities fails, or the securities are delivered but the cash leg fails, the counterparty must strike a new trade at a new quoted price which could result in a gain or loss. If the trade was financed by a loan, repayment could

be compromised if the value of the shares has dropped or a new loan might incur a higher interest rate which could wipe out the gain on the original trade.

- *Credit risk*: includes the failure of one of the counterparties or of one of the participants in the chain: custodian, cash clearing bank, etc.
- *Liquidity risk*: covers the temporary inability of a counterparty to settle the cash or deliver the securities. The other counterparty might need to borrow the cash or the securities, exposing itself to replacement risk.
- *Systemic risk*: domino effect following failure of one major participant.

3 Settlement risk management

The basic principle rests on coordinating the irrevocable settlement of both legs, minimizing the time interval during which one counterparty has handed over his asset but not the other, during which the first is exposed to the risks described above; ideally, the two irrevocable transfers should occur simultaneously.

Three possible models were identified in the Parkinson report in 1992:

Model 1: cash settled gross/securities delivered gross

Settlement of the securities leg for each individual trade is held back until the RTGS system can confirm to the CSD that the cash has been irrevocably settled before the securities are transferred in its books. There remains an exposure to liquidity risk and consequently potential replacement risk if cash settlement is delayed by liquidity shortage on the RTGS system. Nevertheless, Model 1 gross/gross remains the safest.

Model 2: cash settled net/securities delivered gross

This model obviously exposes the securities counterparty to all the risks above until the net settlement of the payment system which could occur end-of-day; this could be compounded by time zone differences (securities settled in Asia and cash end-of-day in the Americas). Risk mitigation measures must be introduced such as banking guarantees (*assured delivery*) or hedging the replacement risk.

Model 3: cash settled net/securities settled net

Readers will have hopefully guessed by now that this is the worst model as uncertainty until end-of-day persists for both legs. Delivery of the securities could be held back until cash is settled. Complex risk mitigation measures must be introduced on the cash and securities side, which would probably wipe out any gains on the original trade.

Models based on net securities settlement are not possible in practice due to the various security issues requiring human intervention to distinguish between them.

4 Consolidation of exchanges and the clearing and settlement landscape

The European markets are dominated by three systems which share the major markets while competing vigorously. The London Stock Exchange (LSE) specializes in equities, the least profitable instrument to trade in. It revamped its platform, regained competitiveness and successfully fought off several hostile bids in spite of remaining the least profitable of the three. It went on to acquire Borsa Italiana and Monte Titoli, the leading European exchange for government bonds owing to Italy's high public debt.

The Frankfurt Deutsche Börse is the most profitable, thanks to the trading in German government debt (Bunds) and its 50 per cent shareholding in Eurex, the leading European derivatives exchange. It mounted three attempts to acquire the LSE, but its approaches were rejected on the grounds of price and, to a lesser extent, incompatibilities in technology (incompatibilities of egos were not officially mentioned!). It is worth remembering the strong opposition of mainly US hedge fund activist shareholders to the LSE bid who did not wish to see the value of the share suffer, forcing a share buyback instead. One could argue that Deutsche Börse was a victim of its own success and increased share price. In March 2008 it announced its divestment of Clearstream, which contributed substantial profits, bowing to pressure from European authorities.

Euronext was created as the result of the merger between the Paris, Brussels and Amsterdam exchanges, later joined by the Lisbon exchange and the Irish government debt platform, in response to the threat of a merger between the LSE and Deutsche Börse which in the end did not materialize. It subsequently acquired LIFFE, the London derivatives exchange. Euronext also put forward a bid for the LSE, but was acquired in 2007 by the New York Stock Exchange when the prospect of a pan-European exchange had virtually disappeared, creating the first transatlantic and the world's largest exchange. It has also nearly totally divested itself of Euroclear.

In addition, we should mention smaller niche exchanges focusing on specific instruments or a geographical area like OMX, formerly known as the Stockholm exchange, which covers the Nordic and Baltic areas and had also mounted a failed bid for the LSE. Neither should we forget the trading platforms created by major institutions such as Turquoise.

Exchanges are therefore constantly seeking to expand geographically and broaden their range of instruments. As consolidation in Europe seemed to have reached its limit (only the Madrid Bolsa remained isolated by early 2008), merger mania went intercontinental. Following the NYSE-Euronext merger (strengthened by the NYSE-AMEX acquisition early 2008) Nasdaq took a 24.1 per cent stake in the LSE but was seeking to divest by 2008; it also acquired a controlling interest in the Swedish exchange OMX. Deutsche Börse tried to gain a foothold in the US through Eurex who had acquired the Clearing Corporation in Chicago. This led the Chicago Mercantile Exchange (CME) to acquire the Chicago Board of Trade (CBOT), leaving Deutsche Börse to resell its local platform after two frustrating years.

European and transatlantic exchanges are now casting their eye towards emerging markets. Deutsche Börse took steps in Eastern Europe and NYSE-Euronext took a stake in the Bombay Exchange, the second in India behind the National Exchange. Brazilian exchanges are discussing mergers to enable them to resist foreign bids and the number one exchange by new listings in 2007 was the Shanghai exchange ($60 billion, with NYSE-Euronext following at $45 billion).

The EC allowed market forces to operate unfettered during the consolidation of exchanges narrated above but, again within the vision of the Lisbon Agenda to create an efficient and dynamic Single Market, established a working group chaired by Alberto Giovannini, a deputy general manager at Banco di Roma. The group first analysed the complexities of cross-border settlement involving 11 stakeholders and close to 30 interchanges of messages, including confirmations not represented (see Figure 11.1).

In its first report published in November 2001 the group identified 15 barriers to the creation of an efficient cross-border settlement scheme, but leaving the choice of system to the market. These barriers are outlined in Box 11.1

In November 2006 the EC published an analysis of post-trade costs, concluding that 'the average excess cost of cross-border equity settlement was between €15 and €20 per transaction, making aggregate excess costs of post-trading for investors of between €2 billion and €5 billion. As it estimated the total spending of investors on trading and post-trading at €28 billion a year in Europe, the elimination of €2 million to €5 million would cut investors cost by between 7% and 18%, adding between 0.2%

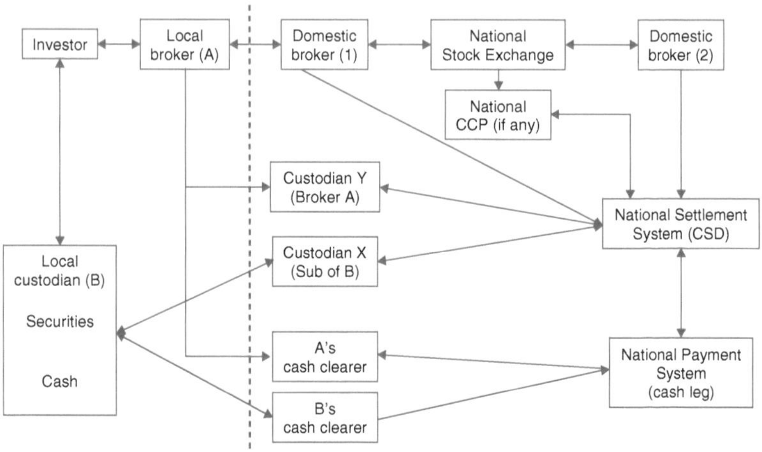

Figure 11.1 Instruction flows for cross-border equities trade
Source: Giovannini report

Box 11.1 The Giovannini barriers

Barriers related to technical requirements and/or market practice.

1. National differences in IT and computer interfaces.
2. National restrictions on location of clearing and settlement.
3. National differences for custody, corporate actions.
4. Differences/absence of intraday settlement facility.
5. Impediments to remote access of clearing and settlement systems.
6. National differences in settlement periods.
7. National differences in operating hours/deadlines.
8. National differences in securities issuance.
9. National restrictions on location of securities.
10. Restriction on primary dealers and market makers, preventing centralized cross-border settlement.

Barriers related to taxation.

11. Withholding tax rules hurting foreign intermediaries.
12. Integrated collection of taxes in local clearing and settlement systems.

Barriers relating to legal certainty.

13. National differences in legal treatment of securities.
14. Differences in legal treatment of bilateral netting.
15. Uneven application of conflict of law rules.

and 0.6% to the level of EU GDP in any given year.'[2] Like the Giovannini report, the EC also refrained from recommending a solution, preferring to publish a Code of Conduct in July 2006 which was signed the following November by the chief executives of the EU's exchanges, CCPs, CSDs and the two ICSDs mandating:

- full price transparency for each service, to include rebates and discounts;
- fair, transparent and non-discriminatory rights of access to service providers and conditions for interoperability; and
- separate accounting for the providers' main activities and unbundling of their services.

The Code of Conduct complemented the 2004 Markets in Financial Instruments Directive (MiFID) which replaced the ISD and, among many provisions it:

- allowed operators right of access to the exchanges, clearing and settlement systems of their choice, breaking the local monopolies for clearing and settlement;
- removed the need to report trades to local exchanges; and
- mandated investment firms to guarantee 'best execution' to their customers, taking into account price, speed and all costs including clearing and settlement.

The market had in fact responded within the limits imposed by fragmentation:

- dematerialization of securities enabling electronic trading and automated monitoring of orders, trades, positions and liquidity;
- Model 1 DVP gross/gross had been adopted in most major markets;
- liquidity transfer mechanisms enabled optimization, increased turnover and reduced costs; and
- the creation of a Central Counterparty (CCP) ensured final settlement in all circumstances and reduces counterparty risk.

Consolidation was also progressing in the post-trade area. Euronext acquired the London Clearing House (LCH) to be merged with Clearnet. Euroclear, following the acquisition of CRESTCo, owned clearing and settlement systems in Belgium, the Netherlands, France and the UK. As a delayed response, Clearstream announced in April 2008 that it would offer clearing and settlement services in Finland, Greece, Norway, Portugal and Spain in addition to Germany.

5 TARGET2-Securities

Progress was however not considered sufficient by the ECB which dropped a bombshell in July 2006 with the announcement of TARGET2-Securities, or T2S. 'T2S is a technical platform to support CSDs in providing core, borderless and neutral settlement services. The objective is to achieve harmonized and commoditized deliver-versus-payment settlement in central bank money in euros (and possibly other currencies) in substantially all securities in Europe. T2S thereby supports the Lisbon agenda in securities markets'.[3]

Service contracts will be with CSDs, not market participants. T2S will hold accounts for CSDs to keep all securities positions of their participants, as well as for National Central Banks with T2S dedicated cash accounts related to TARGET2 cash accounts for euro or other RTGS systems for other currencies. T2S can thus provide real-time DVP settlement in central bank money through a single integrated platform. To smoothe the settlement process and optimize liquidity needs of market participants, T2S will provide optimization and auto-collateralization procedures (see Figure 11.2).

> 'Each CSD is invited to agree to move its settlement to T2S.... CSDs will continue to operate, provide and improve efficient and safe services particularly in relation to national requirements in such areas

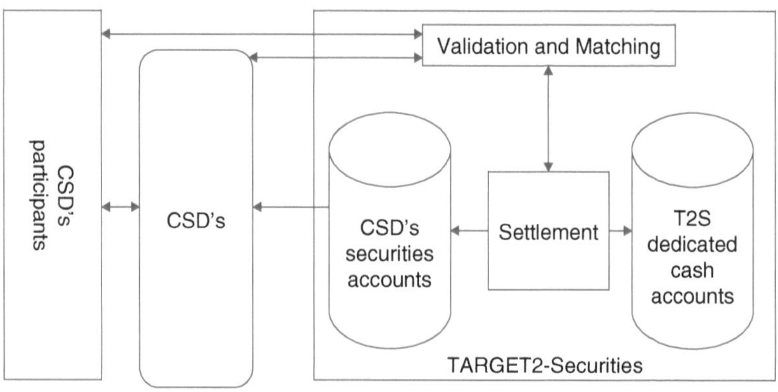

Figure 11.2 TARGET2 Securities (T2S)

> as registration, taxes, regulatory reporting and some aspects of direct holdings by retail investors, at prices which are (as required by the Code of Conduct) a transparent and fair reflection of the cost of providing each of those services ... T2S will enable direct connectivity of CSDs clients and by CCPs. They will input settlement instructions directly to the T2S platform and receive information on the results, where the relevant CSD allows this connection.'[4]

Economic feasibility studies by the ECB estimated the potential gross benefits to market participants at €145 million for the euro area and €223 million for the EU.[5]

The T2S project should be seen as the next step in the ECB's vision of integrated market infrastructures for the single currency: TARGET2, followed by SEPA, followed by T2S. It also appears to fit within a policy of not externalizing settlement in central bank money, reversing the precedent set by the Banque de France for SICOVAM, the French CSD now Euroclear France.

T2S separates the settlement into a centralized platform, benefiting from economies of scale and removing some of the Giovannini barriers, from value-added custody functions and the customer relationships remaining with the CSDs and ICSDs. The ECB stresses that participation will be voluntary, but T2S is perceived by the market as an intention to compete in a domain considered as belonging to the private sector. Market reception has been mixed, with the ICSDs maintaining a politely cool position and Euroclear half-way through the implementation of its SSE project (Single Settlement Engine for the domestic market). We should not however forget that Euroclear itself had been severely criticizsed by the 'Fair and Clear' group, led by Citibank and BNP Paribas Securities Services, for competing with the global custodians' services. T2S is planned to go live around 2013. At the time of printing, the ECB's Governing Council was expected to give its final approval for its development during the summer of 2008.

Part IV
Wholesale Payment, Cash Management and Trade Facilitation Services

12
The Requirements of Corporations

The relationship between a corporation and the banking industry is multifaceted and all major companies will maintain relationships with several institutions, depending on the capabilities and skills required, as well as the services each offers. Table 12.1 attempts to categorize the requirements of a typical corporate customer within the various financial activities:

To this we must add that most corporations operate across several lines of business in a multinational environment, through subsidiaries subject to local taxation. We should also take into account that substantial sums need to be paid between the various organizational units and countries in which a global corporation operates, for instance the Italian subsidiary of a Japanese electronics group selling high-definition TV screens produced in China. Another interesting example is the French Club Med leisure group and resort operator: the majority of customers are affluent Europeans and North Americans, while their resorts are located in emerging countries with low labour costs and requiring a mix of local and imported supplies; prices on the other hand, which must be honoured, are published in catalogues or on-line six to nine months in advance, with the resulting foreign exchange risk if we remember the slide of the US dollar and pound sterling against the euro at the beginning of 2008.

Foreign subsidiaries need therefore to maintain local banking relationships. The challenge lies in striking the right balance between centralization and local autonomy. Local subsidiaries do not necessarily possess the expertise or the 'global view' and would not normally benefit from the same credit rating as the entire group. Generally speaking, foreign subsidiaries will pay local operating costs (such as salaries, rentals and suppliers subject to approval limits) out of local revenues, while major investments and global procurement contracts are funded from

Table 12.1 Categorization of the requirements of a typical corporate customer within the various financial activities

	Credit	Capital markets	Risk intermediation	Payments and cash management
Loans	Credit, syndicated loans			
Raising capital		Securities and debt underwriting	Structured finance	
Payments	Credit lines			Effecting and receiving payments. Reporting and reconciliation
Treasury	Overdrafts Short-term credit			Balances and cashflow optimization
Working capital	Credit			Cash management
Supply chain financing	Trade finance, inventory financing, factoring.	Invoice securitisation		
Foreign exchange and money market			Trading	Settlement, cash management

head-office which would also assume responsibility for foreign exchange and interest rate management.

A global corporation effectively needs to run an internal payment system between its subsidiaries and affiliates. As numbers and amounts grow, these will be netted and balances settled at regular intervals. This can be done through a bank or internally, using external bank services only for the periodic net transfers to reduce fees. For internal purposes, fixed foreign exchange rates are determined at regular intervals: IBM, for instance, uses a 'blue dollar' between its subsidiaries.

1 The role of the treasury department

The principal objectives of a corporation's treasury department are to optimize the interest earned and/or paid by the company across the

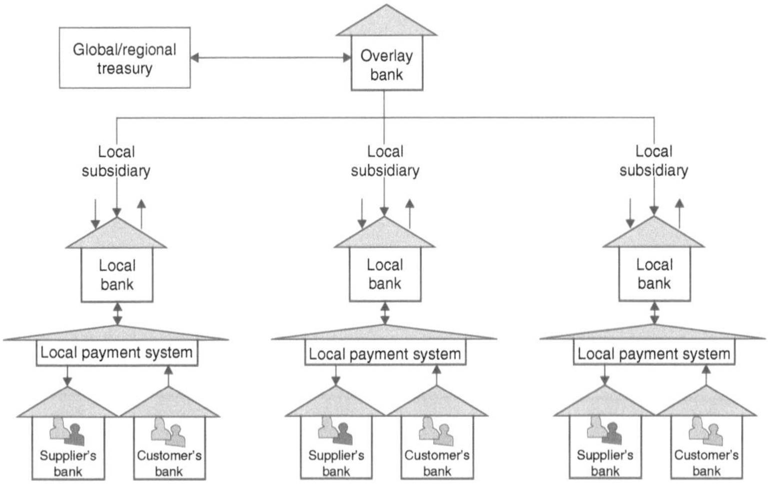

Figure 12.1 Structure of banking relationships

entire organization while ensuring adequate working capital. Treasurers are constantly seeking to accelerate inflows, control disbursements, maximize interest earned on balances and avoid overdrafts which could impact their balance sheet while keeping banking charges to a minimum.

For multinational organizations, the introduction of the euro has accelerated the concentration of the treasury function into two or three locations (Americas, Europe and Asia/Pacific). This did create some organizational and motivation problems as the local management and treasurers saw their role diminish, but the benefits in terms of interest optimization, control and negotiating position outweighed the temporary unrest.

Corporations will maintain local banking relationships to serve subsidiaries as well as regional and global relationships (see Figure 12.1).

To optimize interest on balances, they will *sweep* end-of-day balances held locally to the regional bank, known as *overlay bank* or *concentration bank* (see Figure 12.2), leaving generally a minimum *target balance* in the local accounts.

The account at the overlay bank will then accrue interest on the consolidated end-of-day balances, avoiding overdrafts.

Another technique is known as *pooling*, whereby the balances remain with the local banks but interest is calculated on the algebraic sum of the end-of-day balances (see Figure 12.3).

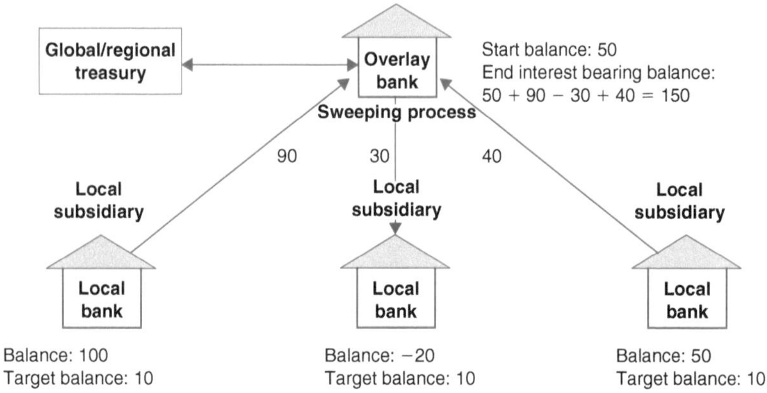

Figure 12.2 Sweeping: funds transferred to overlay bank at end-of-day

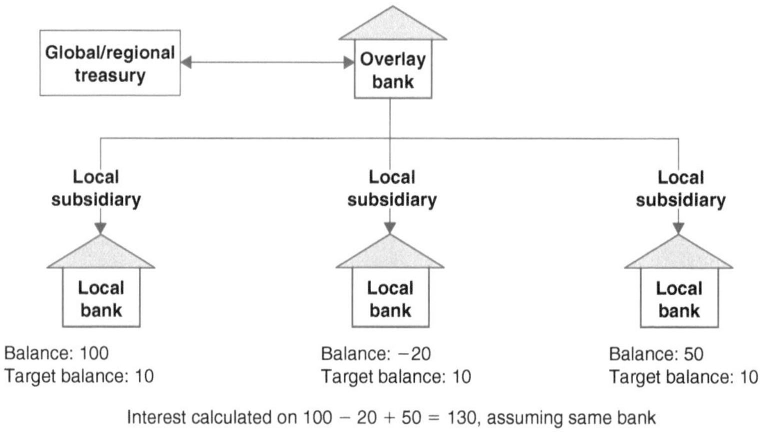

Figure 12.3 Pooling: funds remain in local banks

This service, also known as *notional offsetting*, generally only works between branches or subsidiaries of the same bank. There are also legal and tax obstacles to pooling between accounts belonging to foreign subsidiaries in different countries, even still within the EU.

These techniques give the regional treasurer better overall visibility and control: he/she can schedule disbursements, attempt to accelerate receivables and use positive balances to cover negative ones. Interest on consolidated surpluses and deposit terms can be optimized according to the yield curve. The company is also in a stronger position to

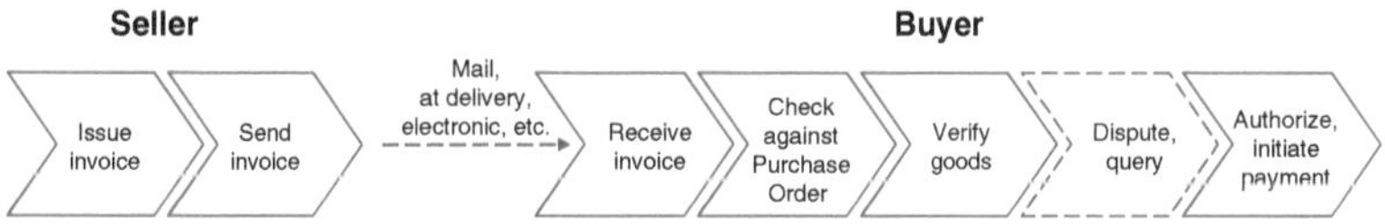

Figure 12.4 Invoice processing

negotiate terms with the banks. Some global corporations have created financial subsidiaries, without deposit-taking licences, to trade on the foreign exchange and money markets as well as manage intra-group financial flows. These should not be confused with financial service subsidiaries created to offer credit and financing facilities to customers, or even financial services to the public at large.

Corporations will be able to considerably simplify these banking relationships within the EU as SEPA (see Chapter 6) will enable payments to be effected from one payment service provider across the entire euro-zone.

2 Electronic invoicing

Form a corporation's viewpoint, initiating or receiving a payment is one process within the supply chain, whereby goods or services are ordered, delivered and invoiced; payment takes place once the goods or services have been accepted and subject to payment terms agreed between buyer and seller. The invoice is generally considered to be the link between the procurement processes and the financial settlement. As such, it is not only a commercial document, but also has a legal standing particularly regarding tax, VAT or sales tax.

The manual processing of invoices is cumbersome (see Figure 12.4), relying mainly on paper handling and fragmented processes and systems.

In Europe, the processing cost per invoice varies between €4 and €70 and the invoice-to-pay cycle is estimated to range between 30 and 100 days.[1] The working capital immobilized is enormous as some 30 billion invoices were issued in Europe during 2007, not to mention the environmental impact considering that 1 million paper invoices require approximately 400 trees![2] Efforts towards electronic invoicing, or e-invoicing have therefore been substantially increased since the turn of the century.

It is worth perhaps first clarifying some terminology. English is perhaps the only language to differentiate between a *bill* issued to a consumer, such as a utility bill, as opposed to an *invoice* issued to a corporation or a government agency. Throughout this book, we understand e-invoicing or e-billing as the creation and handling of structured data which can be processed automatically, not the transmission by e-mail of a scanned paper invoice to be printed upon receipt!

Three service models prevail:

- *Biller direct*: the seller sends the invoice electronically (push) to the buyer, or provides a portal from which customers can retrieve their invoices (pull).
- *Buyer direct*: large corporations or government agencies will require their suppliers to submit electronic invoices.
- *Consolidator*, whereby a service provider will collect and distribute invoices; consolidators also sometimes act as *aggregator* offering a single point of contact for buyers.

The first two are sometimes referred to as the bilateral model, as opposed to the 3- or 4-corner models including buyer and/or seller's consolidator or aggregator which could be a bank. These gives rise to two further models:

- *thick* consolidation whereby full details are provided by the consolidator; and
- *thin* consolidation whereby only headline details such as the biller's identity and amount are forwarded, with a link to the biller's website to obtain full details.

A key issue for billers distributing invoices through consolidators or aggregators is branding. In addition to a request for payment and a tax document, a consumer bill in particular is a marketing tool when linked to data and customer relationship management applications. A telecom operator, for instance, would wish to attract the customer to his portal where he can offer additional services such as broadband, or, based on an analysis of calls made by the customer, propose a different plan with discounted tariffs for the countries to which the subscriber makes a large number of calls. Billers therefore tend to favour biller direct or thin consolidation models.

Three fundamental prerequisites are essential for e-invoicing/billing:

- a legal framework ensuring that an electronic invoice has the same legal standing as a paper one, to include archived data;

- a security framework guaranteeing the authenticity and integrity of the e-invoice; and
- agreed standards between the parties involved.

In Europe, the legal framework is established by the EU Council Directive 2001/115/EC and security is framed by the EU Council Directive 1999/93/EC on advanced electronic signatures.

Regarding standards, the area is, if anything overcrowded. The EBA-Innopay[3] report lists over 10 initiatives in Europe alone in 2008. Some industry sectors already work with agreed standards reflecting their market practices, but fragmentation was rife at the time of publishing. Until an agreed standard emerges, the consensus is to separate the information in two:

- a structured header containing the essential elements: addressing information, identities of buyer and seller, amount and currency, tax details if applicable, references, payment details (account identifier and terms); and
- the body containing the invoice details: quantity and description of goods, discounts, etc.; this block can be structured by bilateral agreement or within an industry sector.

The logical next step is to link the invoice with the payment. Such services, known as Electronic invoice/bill presentment and payment (EBPP and EIPP), involve the buyer and the seller's banks and offer the immediate assurance that the payment will carry the correct invoice reference to automate reconciliation.

The benefits of e-invoicing/billing are undeniable and estimates of total savings across the EU range from €135 to 243 billion.[4] Reduced costs in terms of consumables, postage, processing and queries handling; increased efficiency through automation, straight through processing and faster reconciliation; improved cash flow and working capital from reductions in Days Sales Outstanding (DSO). Having concentrated their treasury and payment processing operations, some corporations are now also consolidating their invoicing and collection departments across borders.

Initiatives to date are fragmented and few countries have implemented truly national schemes (Belgium, Norway and Italy by early 2008), while a few others have achieved some success through interoperability of services provided by banks and consolidators or aggregators. At end 2007, it was estimated that 2–3 per cent of invoices had been converted to e-invoices or e-bills across Europe, with adoption by around 3–4 per cent of corporations and consumers, showing a strong increase in penetration during the last year.[5] The public sector has taken the lead in Denmark and Italy, imposing compulsory e-invoicing to any government agency. The success of e-invoicing initiatives is heavily dependent upon top-down commitment to change.

Obstacles remain for cross-border growth: legal certainty, interoperability of digital signatures of different strengths, tax regimes, data archiving requirements, lack of standards. The European Commission is driving the development of e-invoicing as a value-added service to accelerate the implementation of SEPA.

Ultimately, the success of EBPP and EIPP schemes are based on critical mass. Banks, or even a group of banks, rarely achieve this. Projects must either be initiated at national level, within industry sectors or by government.

3 Supply chain finance (SCF)

Ultimately, a payment does not exist in itself. It is created as the result of a commercial transaction to settle the purchase of goods or services. It is the penultimate step in the supply chain which includes procurement (selection of supplier), purchasing, goods reception and verification, payment and reconciliation of financial flows and inventory positions. Corporations are seeking end-to-end visibility, from 'supplier's supplier to customer's customer'. Several financial services are linked to these processes which are generically known as Supply Chain Finance (SCF) which is the funding of each step in the process: order, manufacturing, inventory, goods in transit and invoice financing as illustrated in Figure 12.5.

The essence of the banking profession is credit. Trade finance was originally based on letters of credit, through which a bank promises to pay the supplier on behalf of its customer subject to specified conditions, but international trade is moving increasingly towards open-account trading with banks losing involvement and visibility as a consequence.

For the seller, credit services also include *factoring* whereby the bank or a factoring company buys the invoice(s) at a discount, paying the creditor before the payment term negotiated with the buyer and assuming responsibility for collecting. A variation has emerged recently, known as *reverse factoring,* whereby the buyer accepts the invoice upon receipt; the factoring company then bases the discount on the credit rating of the buyer which is often higher than that of his smaller supplier.

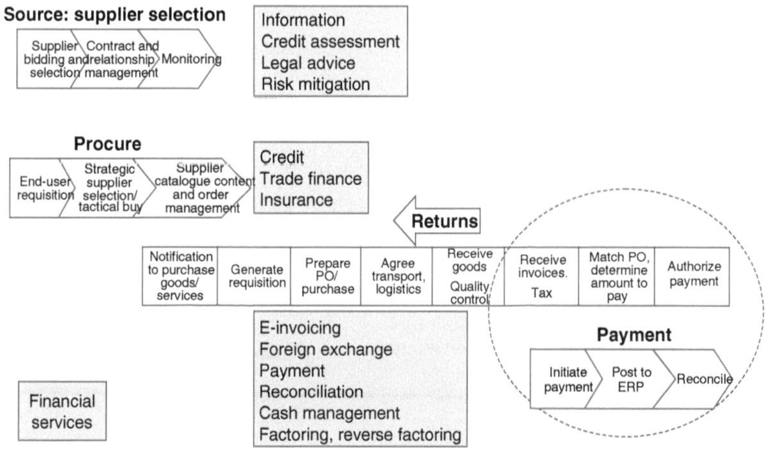

Figure 12.5 Financial services for the supply chain

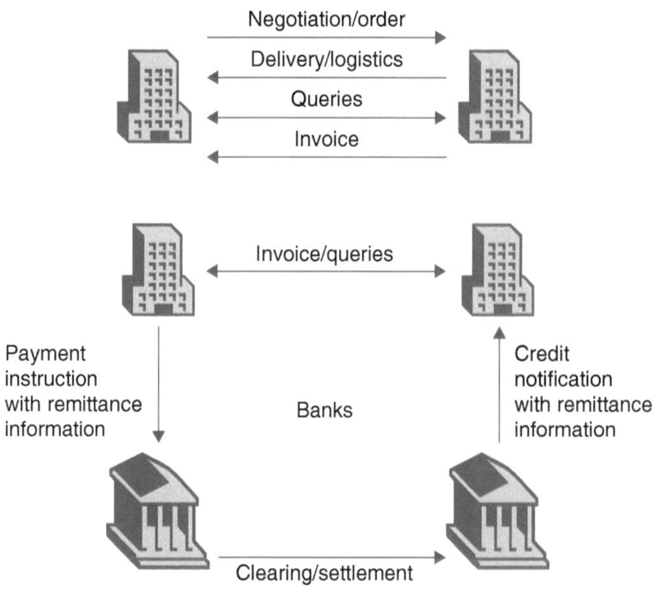

Figure 12.6 Supply and financial flows

With few exceptions, purchasing and logistics are not integrated within corporations with the financial functions (see Figure 12.6).

The invoice is commonly perceived as the link, but from the perspective of the commercial transaction the process starts with the Purchase

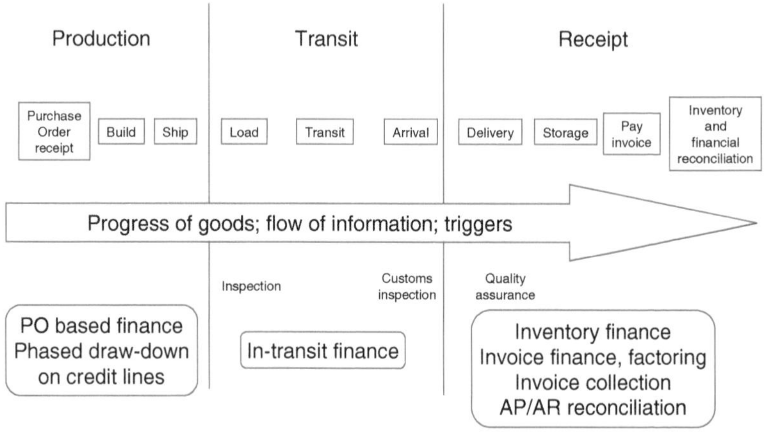

Figure 12.7 Event-driven supply chain finance (SCF)

Order (PO). This split between supply, logistics and finance commonly exists because supply chain and logistics applications are operated from one platform, normally run by the purchasing and logistics departments, as opposed to payments which are managed by the finance or treasury departments. The process is therefore error-prone due to data transfers or manual re-keying. As a result, reconciliation of accounts payable and receivable is lengthy and costly owing to:

- the invoice reference on payments is often missing, incorrect or truncated; and
- the amounts paid seldom matching the amount invoiced, due to partial payments, penalties, rejected goods, discounts, etc.

An additional complication lies in the fact that the supply and logistics applications are based on EDI standards while the payments rely upon financial industry messages, domestic or SWIFT. EDI systems are plagued by large volumes of remittance information which are currently transmitted between actors in the supply chain: buyer, logistics companies, financial institutions and seller. Each industry sector has over time developed its own standards and rules, often with national variations, while terms and conditions are generally negotiated bilaterally. Some industries have created sectorial platforms combining ordering, logistics, invoicing and payment, notably the pharmaceuticals, chemicals, automotive and electronics (RosettaNet).

Efforts today are concentrating on event-driven SCF where events, such as issuing a purchase order or an invoice can trigger financial services such as releasing credit lines or factoring, as illustrated in Figure 12.7. Sensor driven technologies such as bar codes and Radio Frequency Identification (RFID) can be used to track progress of goods in transit, in warehouses and assembly with different levels of granularity: container, palette or item.

Several standardization efforts were underway at the time of publication with little coordination; the outcome is unclear apart from the trend towards XML.

The corporate customers' key requirements remain the ability to reconcile the payment with invoices and receivables and its integration with the commercial transactions.

13
Corporate Banking Services

How do the banks respond to the corporate requirements outlined in the previous chapter? Fundamentally, the bank acts as clearing and settlement agent for all payments initiated by its customers: salaries, taxes and benefits, domestic and cross-border accounts payables, crediting of receivables, etc. If the beneficiary's account is with the same bank, settlement will take place 'on us' between the two accounts; if not, the payment will be sent to the appropriate clearing and settlement infrastructures, the bank becoming the first link in the settlement chain ending with the central bank.

To attract the business of multinational corporations who need to maintain accounts in several countries, banks will seek to match their presence and offer payment services in the same geographies. They can either achieve this through correspondent banking relationships which will entail higher costs and earlier cut-off times, or seek competitive advantage through direct participation in local clearing and settlement systems, whether through a local presence or, if permitted, remote access.

The basic payment services are becoming generic, with reducing profitability and opportunities for competitive differentiation as standardization and technology are commoditizing the business. The banks are therefore constantly striving to develop value-added services to increase revenues and profitability.

1 Electronic banking and communication channels

Today, in the corporate segment, virtually all payment initiation and notification of receipt is electronic. Large corporations will send and receive payment files and statements directly from their accounting applications and ERP systems through computer-to-computer links. Queries, status reports, cash management, payment initiation, etc are conducted through internet portals. Until the advent of the internet, electronic banking terminals were expensive to install and integrate with the customer's applications, so were only offered to large corporations. The advent of the internet has reduced the marginal technical cost of adding a customer to virtually zero, enabling access to a wider customer base. Most banks will segment their offerings between large corporations, medium-sized companies and SMEs (Small and Medium Enterprises), the latter being offered simplified portals with less sophisticated services and requiring minimal instruction. This has resulted in increased competition as, until the advent of internet banking, global banks would target only the largest corporations abroad; they are now aggressively attacking the medium and small enterprises, which are generally more profitable, and considered the preserve of the local banks.

The internet has introduced a certain element of standardization as, with the previous generation, customers would often need to operate as many terminals as banks they maintained accounts with, as banks attempted to lock customers in through proprietary standards and protocols. Large corporations can, since 2006, also connect to SWIFT to communicate with their banks if sponsored by them. This has enabled standardization of the payment initiation and reporting standards. Even though standardization and the internet have greatly facilitated the installation and education surrounding the portals, the integration of the large corporations' accounting and ERP systems is lengthy, often challenging and costly; banks will often subcontract this to IT service companies.

Some banks have also recently introduced SMS communication over mobile phones for reporting and, in some cases, selective payment initiation.

2 Reporting, cash management and treasury services

Banks offer services notifying customers in real-time of payment receipts based upon agreed selection criteria: above a specified floor limit or from a specific originator. Balances are also available on-line throughout the day, in some cases through SMS. Most banks are now developing 'track and trace' systems whereby the customer can enquire about the status of a specific payment. Efforts are focused on giving the customer as many self-service enquiry possibilities as possible to reduce calls to customer centres.

After closure, the bank will make available the end-of-day balances and statements to enable the company to reconcile their positions. Some banks will collect balance and statement information from other institutions, even abroad, to present to the customer, subject to an appropriate mandate. This can lead to protracted negotiations as the other banks lose the float and are often reluctant to pass this information to a competitor. The next step is balance optimization and cash management. This will either be done automatically, using pre-agreed guidelines and target balances for inter-company netting, sweeping and pooling as described in the previous chapter, or leaving the discretion to the corporation's treasurer who will effect transfers between accounts and place available funds according to day-to-day requirements and investment opportunities. Most banks will offer treasury forecasting models based on historic data and expenditure forecasts. Competitive differentiation lies greatly in the quality of advisory services by the bank which are based on individual or sectorial analysis and forecasts of yield curves, currency rates and volatilities. Some banks offer to manage the company's balances subject to agreed targets and objectives, the company effectively outsources its treasury function to the bank.

3 Electronic invoicing and supply chain financing services

Banks have individually, or within a consortium, attempted to offer EBPP/EIPP services but generally without success as they fail to reach a critical mass as a fair proportion of the billers' customers do not bank with a member of the consortium.

At the time of publication, several banks were focusing on Supply Chain Finance (SCF) which we described in the previous chapter. The challenge lies in integrating the various classical products and services into a coherent value-chain: trade finance; asset-backed finance; inventory finance; goods-in-transit finance; invoice financing/factoring; reverse factoring; and payables financing. As the goods progress from ordering to delivery and payment, the bank will constantly be seeking to adjust the risk profile over the total transaction. Some banks will offer to take over the entire process, assuming responsibility for logistics and quality assurance prior to shipment. A few global institutions have acquired companies specializing in this field, such as JP Morgan Chase with Vastera.

4 Fees and remuneration

Up until the 1970s, payment services were not explicitly charged for and were absorbed within the overall credit relationship, the balances on deposit and foreign exchange services. Corporations became more sophisticated and reduced balances to invest them more profitably, coinciding with falling interest rates. This was largely due to the recruitment of experienced bankers as treasurers, who often knew the business better than the younger or 'greener' relationship managers. Banks therefore moved to unbundling fees for payments and information reporting. Electronic banking terminals and portals also shifted the data capture to the customer. This entails banks charging more for payments which are not STP and require repair, for instance in the case of a formatting error or incorrect account information. One issue which is still largely unresolved is how to charge for liquidity. Banks have a very clear knowledge of the overall cost of the liquidity required for payment services, but it is very difficult to allocate it to individual payments. The treasurer of IBM, for instance, will not accept a liquidity charge for a high-value payment because his transfer happens to be queued behind a large payment by GE which dried up the bank's liquidity and forced it to call in more collateral! Banks now generally ask corporations to pre-notify them of large value payments and reserve the right to charge more in the case of an unannounced high value payment close to end-of-day when interest rates on the money market go up.

5 Selection criteria

Corporations have tended to concentrate banking relations as they have concentrated their treasury functions and this trend will accelerate in Europe with SEPA. It is unlikely that they will 'put all their eggs in one basket' and we are observing moves towards choosing separate banks for payment services and for financing. Requests for proposals from corporations are becoming more and more demanding, often written by independent consultants, requiring substantial efforts from banks to respond. Service Level Agreements (SLAs) are subject to tough negotiations to agree cut-off times per submission channel, execution times per type of payment, response time to queries and penalties for non compliance. 'Beauty contests' are hard fought, with emphasis increasingly placed on service quality, reliability, advisory services and relationship management, with pricing taking second place. Increased emphasis is likely to be placed on the bank's credit rating as a result of the write-offs revealed by major institutions during the sub-prime crisis in 2007–2008.

Most important are customer relations staff. For retail banking, it is surprising to note the ignorance of branch personnel of any payment instrument beyond plain-vanilla retail payments. The customer relations staff for corporate and institutional banking are critical and their role is multiple:

- marketing and sales to maximize revenues from each customer by cross-selling other products and services;
- education, to ensure that the customers understand the latest products, schemes, standards (for instance SEPA, BIC, IBAN, Check 21), access channels and procedures; this is particularly important for payment services to avoid fails which will disrupt STP and lead to unpleasant discussions on excess charges, penalties, etc.;
- damage limitation, when the bank (inevitably) commits errors, which will impact credibility and trust; and
- advisory – anticipating the client's demands and ensuring that the relevant expert is at hand to assist the treasurer or chief financial officer and promote the bank's expertise.

Account management teams must be mapped on to the customer's geographical presence and organization, with multiple internal reporting lines: to the senior relationship manager responsible for that customer's account worldwide; to the appropriate business line (for instance foreign exchange); and to local management. It is no surprise that banks have recently started hiring senior executives from outside the financial sector in order to develop these activities.

Part V
Banks and the Payments Business

14
The Banks' Back Offices

The level and quality of service that banks offer their customers depend on the competence of their staff, the efficiency of their processes and the quality of their IT systems. These are influenced by the role of payment services within the institution's overall strategy and the management and governance structure in place to implement it. This chapter will describe the operations that take place in a bank's back office. Chapter 15 will discuss how banks can achieve profitability in the payments business.

1 Payment processing and STP

Payment instructions will be received from customers, either directly through electronic banking channels, but also by mail, fax or even deposited at a branch. Some customer payments also originate from within the banks through corporate banking, asset management, foreign exchange or securities departments. Finally the bank will generate payments itself as a result of proprietary trading, or simply like any other enterprise to pay suppliers, salaries and other expenses.

It is generally accepted that clearing and settlement fees from payment systems represent less than 15 per cent of the overall cost of processing the payment. The bulk of the cost lies within the banks' back-offices. All efforts are therefore focused on maximizing automation to achieve Straight Through Processing or STP, ideally to process end-to-end without human intervention. Breakages or 'fails' are expensive in terms of staff costs, delayed interest charges and eventual penalties if service levels agreed with customers have not been met.

Figures 14.1 shows the processes involved for an outgoing payment, from receipt of a credit transfer instruction from the customer to final

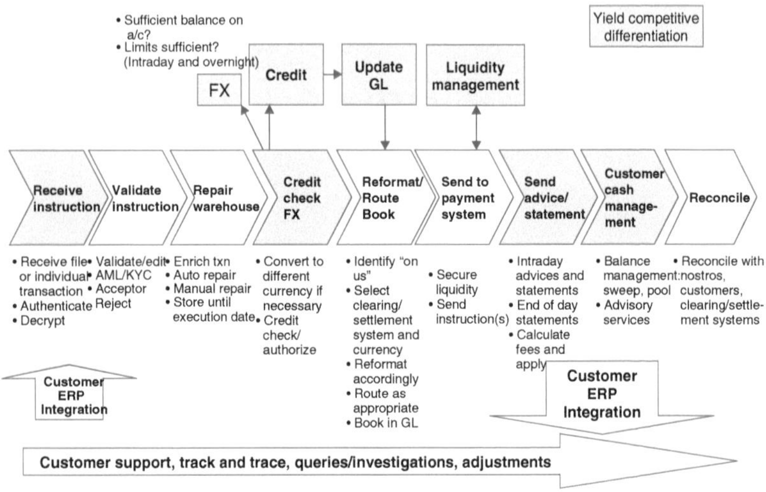

Figure 14.1 Bank processes to send a payment

reconciliation. The sequence of processes might vary from bank to bank as well as the actions undertaken during each stage, but the diagram and the following paragraphs give an overview of all tasks that need to be accomplished.

1.1 Receive

Payment instructions are received over a variety of channels: internet banking; mobile; telephone call centre; direct file submission from corporations' ERP and accounting systems; ATM or banking kiosk; letter; branch instruction; etc. If required, the data will be decrypted and the identity of the customer authenticated (signature, password, PIN or more sophisticated).

1.2 Validate

The payment will first be validated in terms of completeness of information, adherence to standards and formats, including if possible checking the account numbers. If validation fails, it will be passed to repair. The names and account numbers of the initiating customer will be checked for identity verification against the bank's own files and security procedures: Know your Customer (KYC). Sender and beneficiary will also be checked against stop lists of criminals, terrorists, blacklisted organizations, etc.; official files issued by law enforcement agencies are available on a country by country basis, the one most used on an international basis being the US OFAC list (Office of Foreign Asset Control).

1.3 Enrich and repair

Payments which did not pass validation must be repaired. Automated repair applications are available, many relying on Artificial Intelligence and past history to propose changes. Manual repair is costly, therefore many banks will penalize the customer by charging him a repair fee. Some payments will need to be enriched, such as cross-currency payments when the name of the nostro correspondent will be added if it is different from the beneficiary's bank. In this case, the bank's back office system will automatically issue the cover note from SSI (Standard Settlement Instructions) and routing files. If the payment is not for immediate execution, it will be stored.

1.4 Credit check and foreign exchange

If the payment involves a different currency, the conversion must be effected. The bank will have set up a daily file of rates for the most usual currencies, valid up to a certain amount and for customers with whom special rates have not been negotiated. For higher amounts a quote will be requested from the bank's FX department and the appropriate discount will be applied for negotiated rates. The amount will then be checked against the customer's balance or credit/overdraft line. If negative, the payment will be rejected for retail and SME customers. For large corporations or high-net-worth individuals, the relationship manager will be alerted who will contact the customer and agree a course of action.

1.5 Routing and reformatting

A decision must now be made as to which payment system to use. 'On us' payments, for customers of the same bank are immediately separated. External routing is straightforward if the payment is a domestic ACH transfer, or a cross-currency payment which would be sent over SWIFT. Low-value cross-border transfers in euro will be sent over the CSM selected by the bank (PE-ACH, SEPA, scheme-compliant ACH or bilateral file exchange). Options exist however for high-value payments (CHIPS or Fedwire in the US, or EURO1 or TARGET2 for payments in euro). The choice will depend on the service level agreed with the customer, the time of day and the liquidity position of the bank vis-à-vis the RTGS system. Most banks have implemented liquidity management systems which schedule payments according to the available liquidity. Some banks have developed automated routing systems which select the payment system according to the criteria above. Once a payment system has been selected, the format of the message will be appropriately converted. The payment will be booked against the customer's account at this stage. If appropriate, the nostro correspondent's account will also be updated.

1.6 Send to payment system

The payment is sent to the selected payment system, after securing liquidity in case of an RTGS system.

1.7 Send advice/statement

The majority of customers will obtain confirmation that the payment has been effected from their statement. . . . or sense that a problem might have occurred when receiving a reminder form the creditor. In corporate banking, the customer will have negotiated receiving real-time notifications for large amounts throughout the day. The fees will be booked accordingly.

1.8 Corporate customer cash management

At end-of-day, the bank or the corporate customer's treasurer will optimize the balances across its various accounts as described in Chapters 12 and 13.

1.9 Reconciliation

Finally, the bank must reconcile with all parties involved – customers, payment systems, clearing house(s), RTGS systems, SWIFT, nostro correspondents and internal departments.

The processes for an incoming payment are shown in Figure 14.2.

They are similar to the above except for *internal routing* which transmits the payment information after validation and repair to the appropriate department in the bank: retail banking; corporate banking; FX; or securities trading.

As mentioned in previous chapters, many banks cannot afford the high investments required to upgrade their payment processing systems to achieve economically sustainable costs or comply with continuous regulation, and are considering outsourcing. They must however identify carefully the processes that yield competitive differentiation as opposed to those which are generic and driven by economies of scale. The processes highlighted in the above figures are those which, in the opinion of the authors, yield competitive differentiation and should be retained in-house.

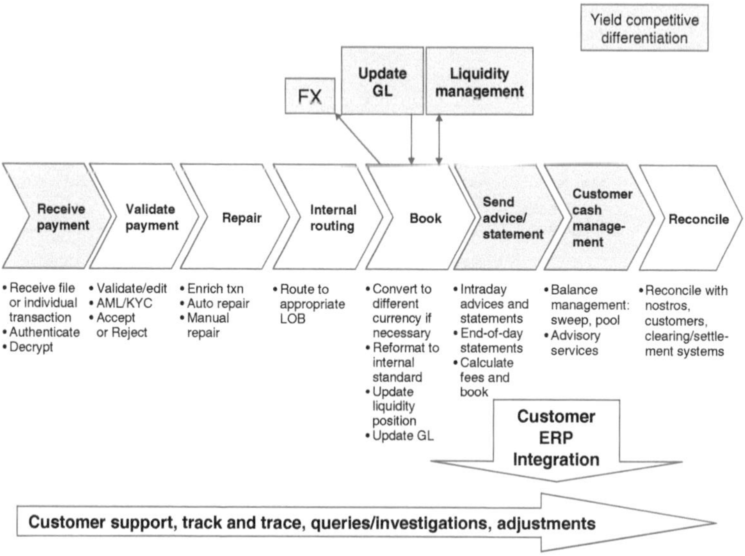

Figure 14.2 Bank processes to receive a payment

2 Departments involved

Outside the payment processing and operations departments, the bank's treasury plays an important role. It is their responsibility to manage the liquidity on RTGS and high-value systems and ensure appropriate funding for timed payments such as CLS pay-ins or when the balances from netting systems, such as ACHs, are submitted to the RTGS for final settlement. Treasury must also ensure that foreign nostro correspondent and clearing accounts are adequately funded for cross-currency transfers and settlement of FX or foreign securities trading. It is also their responsibility to manage excess balances on those accounts. Treasury must be seen as a profit centre and act proactively, leveraging customer demands for FX and cash management in terms of exchange and interest rate spreads.

3 Operations

In most banks payment processing is fragmented across different departments in different lines of business, between retail, cards, corporate, international payments, settlement of FX and securities trading, with duplication of several functions such as customer identity

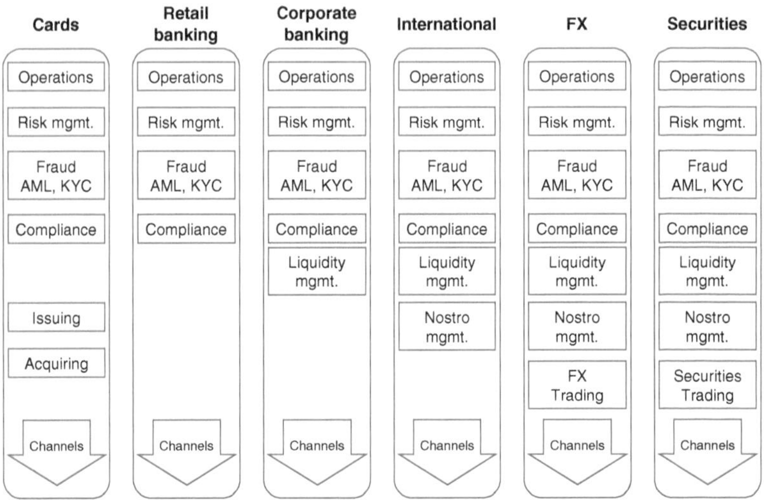

Figure 14.3 From silos . . .

verification, AML (Anti Money Laundering), liquidity management, etc. (see Figure 14.3).

Banks are now beginning to concentrate all payment processes and related staff and IT systems in 'payment factories', re-using common components and systems across instruments and business lines as illustrated in Figure 14.4. In addition to cost savings, centralization enables more efficient liquidity management and better overall monitoring and control.

This trend is accelerating thanks to standardization schemes, such as SEPA across Europe. In addition to cost savings and improvements in operational efficiency, concentration greatly assists fraud detection and AML as criminals will tend to break-up large sums and pay or receive them through multiple channels: international payments, cheques, ACH, cards, etc. Centralization of databases is also invaluable in terms of Customer Relationship Management (CRM), enabling overall analysis of customer behaviour for marketing purposes.

Several banks have, or are considering, relocating these payment shared service centres to low-cost countries such as India or Eastern Europe.

4 IT systems

IT systems and applications for payments demand a business-oriented enterprise-wide view of payment processing that is standards-based, with

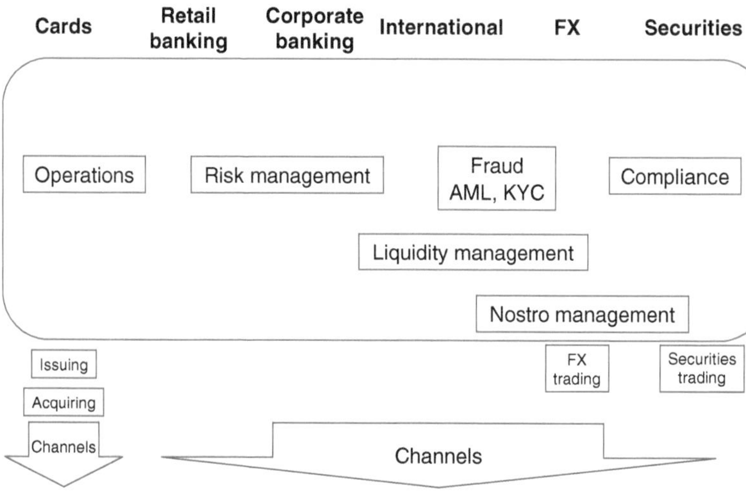

Figure 14.4 ... to shared services

a flexible architecture using defined common data and process models. Business continuity is essential as regulators insist that guidelines for Systemically Important Payment Systems (SIPS) extend to 'critical participants' which contribute a significant share of volume and/or value. A resilient architecture must therefore be implemented with remote back-up sites. Agility to adapt to new opportunities has become a survival issue, not a nice-to-have, so the architecture must allow for rapid development, testing and launch of new products and services. Finally, in spite of SEPA and other harmonization efforts, customization to comply with national practices, or to satisfy important customers, remains an essential requirement.

However, the IT systems most often encountered reflect the siloed organization we discussed in the previous paragraph. These systems were built on different standards, featuring duplicated applications, interfaces and point-to-point interconnections with the business logic imbedded in the applications. The recent spate of mergers and acquisitions also contributed to the fossilization of these silos. Maintenance was costly and upgrades to comply with new regulations or to develop a new product difficult and even dangerous. In the words of one expert: 'You touch one application and everything moves!'. This resulted in parallel applications being developed for virtually every new product.

These shortfalls are not unique to the financial services sector and the same problems are encountered across all industries as well as the public sector. The IT industry's response was the development of the Services Oriented Architecture (SOA) concept:

> 'Service-oriented architecture (SOA) is a style of developing and integrating software. It involves breaking an application down into common, repeatable "services" that can be used by other applications, both internal and external, in an organization independent of the applications and computing platforms on which the business and its partners rely. Using this approach, enterprises can assemble and reassemble these open, standards based services to extend and improve integration among existing applications, support collaboration, build new capabilities, and drive innovation at every point in the value chain. SOA is an IT architectural style that separates an organization's applications into their elemental parts, called service components (common business commands like "check credit" or "calculate interest rate"). These can then be rearranged with unprecedented speed to create new applications (meaning, among other things, that banks can extend the life of existing IT assets almost indefinitely, and conserve on the purchase of new assets). Think of the Lego toy, or the atomic elements, from a few basic parts, banks can create a virtually unlimited number of combinations, of any size or shape. This modular concept is at the heart of SOA. Now, due to open business and technology standards, service components from an institution's applications can be combined with those of its partners, suppliers and even its customers to create new "super applications" – composites of functionality that can span companies and industries. Through this kind of integration and collaboration, SOA can spark innovation, and lead to entirely new business opportunities. In essence, SOA makes IT adapt to the needs of business in a way never before possible. Before SOA, to have this level of flexibility, an institution might have compelled to deploy – and integrate – 20 different software applications. With SOA, an enterprise has to build only one – which, comparatively fast, it can reconfigure 20 different ways to meet the imperatives of changing business and market conditions.'[1]

Modern 'payment hub' architectures rely on the SOA components linked by an enterprise platform which routes the payments between the applications according to a choreography adapted to each payment type, as illustrated in Figure 14.5. A key requirement for any contemporary system is the ability to accept and convert any standard: EDI, NACHA, SWIFT, UNIFI ISO 20022 XML, etc. Conversion routines must

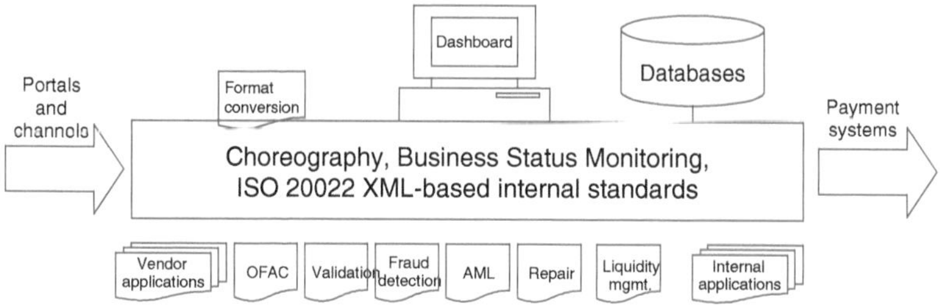

Figure 14.5 Payments platform architecture

therefore be implemented between the various standards or even older proprietary formats. They must also convert into and from the standard internal format used by the bank, most modern developments being based on ISO 20022 XML.

SOA enables users to retain legacy systems and gradually replace them by components developed in-house or sourced externally. Benefits can be delivered gradually as new features are launched or legacy systems replaced by more efficient applications. Project risk is therefore significantly reduced by this progressive transformation approach, in contrast to a 'big bang, rip and replace' implementation.

15
Payments as a Business for Banks

1 Payments within banks' overall strategy

No commercial bank can operate without offering payment services to its customers, but different banks place differing emphasis on payment services. To most medium and small banks, payments are a necessary service to offer to their customers which are generally retail or SMEs. For larger institutions however, payment services are a strategic offensive vector to capture and retain corporate banking business, cross-sell other financial and advisory services, attract retail customers with innovative products such as mobile banking and increase profitability.

This distinction based on size is somewhat arbitrary: service quality is in no way linked to size and some 'medium-sized' banks maintain extremely profitable payments businesses based on innovative value-added services, while many 'large' institutions display complacency. In this respect we should remember that payment services, which are largely fee based, do not significantly affect the balance sheet and the various ratios under scrutiny by the regulators. Large banks are therefore less advantaged by their capital base than by the financial and staff resources they can muster to sustain the necessary investments. Smaller institutions however often benefit from a leaner and more reactive organization with fewer internal obstacles to the launch of new projects.

2 The economics and profitability of payments services

As mentioned in the Introduction, the payments business constitutes up to 35 per cent of revenues and 40 per cent of costs for banks.[1] It is estimated to account for 30–50 per cent of revenues among the top 15 US banks[2] and about a quarter of banking revenues and more than one third of operating costs in Europe.[3]

Revenues from payment services originate from:

- fees explicitly charged for processing various payment instruments, to the originator as well as to the beneficiary;
- interest on revolving credit cards, alongside merchant and interchange fees;
- float between the value date at which the originator is debited and the beneficiary is credited;
- balances, principally on non-interest (or very low interest) current accounts; and
- foreign exchange spreads for cross-currency payments.

Cross-subsidization between payment instruments and customer segments is rife. Payments services in the UK are only profitable overall thanks to the interest collected from revolving credit card holders.[4] Revenues per instrument in Europe vary from country to country: for instance the revenue from a credit transfer varies between €0.32 in France and €1.47 in Italy.[5] The revenue split between corporate and retail customers also varies: 66 per cent corporate and 44 per cent retail in Germany as opposed to 33 per cent corporate and 67 per cent retail in Spain, excluding cash.[6] Thus revenues between banks in the same country will also differ depending on their customer mix.

Costs will also differ, depending on the instrument mix. Countries where cash and cheques are still heavily used will have a higher cost base than those where electronic transfers and cards dominate. Even then, the cost of processing a credit transfer was €0.20 in Belgium as opposed to €0.60 in Germany according to a study published in 2005, probably due to fact that Belgian banks had steered their customers to cheaper channels such as internet banking and ATMs while German customers prefer the paper credit transfer slips.[7]

We can see that the profitability of payment services depends on a large number of factors: pricing philosophy, instrument and customer mix and even initiation channel.

These profits are also vulnerable. Interest on credit card revolving credit is at risk from large-scale monoline issuers such as Capital One, while revenues in Europe are particularly at risk from SEPA. In addition to the disappearance of float, mandated by the PSD, banks in countries heavily dependent on fees will see profitability erode as pan-European competition will force them down. As mentioned in Chapter 6, revenues are expected to decline by 30–60 per cent below non-SEPA levels by 2010.[8]

Above all, these discrepancies show the need for banks to conduct a serious review of the profitability of their payment services across all instruments, customer segments and countries in which they operate.

3 Organization and governance

Payments have always posed an organizational headache as they pervade all lines of business. Large institutions, particularly those specializing in payments, clearing and custody services have regrouped their operations and IT for payments and securities processing into Transaction Banking Divisions ('Banque de Flux' in France), led by a senior executive, generally one level below the Executive Board.

This, however, was generally limited to operations while the strategy and product management remained in the lines of business (retail and corporate banking, custody, FX, cards). This also implied that different representatives of the bank sat on the various industry bodies or Boards, preventing the bank from gaining an overall view and often leading its representatives to act in contradiction. We have seen the importance of gaining an enterprise-wide view of payments across all instruments to elaborate successful product management and development within the bank's overall strategy. This has led several institutions to create a Payments Council (or Board) and to appoint a Payments Czar (or Supremo).

The Payments Council should regroup senior representatives, preferably the heads of all concerned lines of business, including operations and IT. Its role should be to review and approve the bank's overall strategy for payments as well as all major product development proposals. The payments czar (or czarina) should obviously be part of the Payments Council but not necessarily the chair. The role includes keeping abreast of industry trends, competitive threats and relevant regulation, participating in industry groups and Boards (or consolidate their outcome), elaborating an overall payments strategy and product/services development plan and monitoring execution of the projects across the lines of business.

4 Development of an enterprise-wide payments strategy

The first step would be to construct a payments revenue and cost model across all instruments, customer segments and countries in which the bank operates. This incidentally implies that the enterprise has a solid understanding of its costs which is seldom the case.... The model will highlight the profitable and loss-making instruments and customer segments within each geography. It can then be used to evaluate the exposure to competition, shifts in customer behaviour, regulation such as SEPA and technology changes such as cheque electronification.

The model should then assist with the elaboration of an enterprise-wide payments strategy to support the banks overall strategy. For instance, in which customer segments is it seeking most growth: retail, high-net value individuals, SMEs or large corporations? Would issuing cards in a new country provide a stepping stone for further activities? Would mobile payments reduce costs and/or attract new customers? Should the bank join an e-invoicing scheme? Should they offer Supply Chain Finance services?

Based on the strategy, a review of the product and services portfolio should be conducted to identify products and services to be discontinued, improved or developed. It should be noted however that, with the exception of credit cards, a bank cannot choose to withdraw payment instruments unilaterally like cheques in the countries where they are still used, even if they drain profitability. It is worth repeating that developments should focus on value-added services around the payment as the margins on commoditized instruments will reduce to virtually zero. A comprehensive product/services management and development plan should emerge from this review, identifying eventual partnerships for certain products. A segmented sample of customers should be associated with the elaboration of the user requirement specifications for new products.

The bank will then need to define their operational and IT architecture and appraise its own capabilities and identify the processes and systems driving effective competitive differentiation. Some activities are dependent on large volumes and economies of scale to reduce costs, but offer little competitive opportunity. These are clearly prime targets for outsourcing to other institutions or shared service centres operated by bank consortia or third parties. So, too, are those processes for which the bank is unwilling to invest in the re-engineering, technology and skills required to achieve the relevant critical success factors. For processes yielding competitive value and retained in-house, the bank should examine whether they can be re-used across other payment instruments, lines of business and geographies as outlined in the previous chapter. It is perfectly conceivable to centralize operations and IT while retaining sales, advisory services and first-line customer support locally. Process modelling and simulation enables optimization from a cost and/or execution time standpoint.

Finally the bank will need to define an enterprise-wide IT architecture for payments as described in Chapter 14 (sec. 5).

Last but not least, a detailed roll-out and marketing plan must be defined, including staff training and external communication. Securing representative customers as pilots should precede full launch.

Only a comprehensive review of payments strategy will enable banks to retain profitability in the face of customer demands, competition from new entrants and regulation.

Above all banks must remember that people are key to retaining customers: branch and call centre staff, corporate relationship managers, advisors, operations and IT personnel, etc. Savings on operations and IT should be reinvested in increasing and training personnel in contact with clients.

Part VI
The Future

16
Where is the Payments Industry Going?

We have examined the fundamentals of the payments business, its instruments, participants, their relationship, the components and trends in various regions and the services offered to retail and wholesale customers. As a conclusion, it is now time to look ahead and attempt to anticipate what further changes can be expected, the future drivers of this business and how each of the various players can run a successful and profitable business.

1 Instruments

Cash is king and is unlikely to lose its crown for low-value retail transactions, barely declining in number of payments and slightly in share of wallet, but remaining dominant. The number of annual payments in cash is estimated to remain virtually constant in the US, hovering around 50 billion until 2010.[1] In the EU, cash payments are expected to continue to grow, from a base of 390 billion payments in 2007, by 25 billion annually until 2011.[2] Dreams of a cashless society are, in the view of the authors, utopian and unlikely to materialize, certainly not within their lifetime and most probably not within that of the readers of this book.

Cards will continue to gain market share, particularly debit cards as we can foresee a squeeze on revolving credit in a period of economic uncertainty and amid concerns about the high level of personal debt. Technology will evolve towards contactless cards, or payments initiated via mobile devices, but we are ultimately talking about the same principles upon which the card instrument operates, be it prepaid, debit or credit.

Direct debits will continue to grow as billers will increase incentives for customers to move to them, particularly from cheques. Credit transfers might experience a moderate growth as e-invoicing/billing develops.

Table 16.1 Viable alternatives to cheques

	Face-to-face	Remote
Occasional	Cash Debit card Credit card Prepaid card Contactless card Mobile payment	Debit card (paper, telephone or internet) Credit card (paper, telephone or internet) Direct credit (paper, telephone or internet) One-time direct debit (paper, telephone or internet) RTGS or other high-value Mobile payment
Regular	Not truly relevant, but as above.	Direct credit (for salaries, pensions, benefits) Standing order Direct debit Debit card Credit card RTGS or other high-value Mobile payment

Cheque usage will continue to decline. Cheque processing is inherently based on fixed costs, so the unit cost of cheques will rise as volume declines until it becomes unsustainable. Countries must seize the bull by the horns and develop a plan to proactively manage the decline, leading to the withdrawal of cheques over a defined time horizon. Experience in countries where cheques have already been replaced (e.g. Sweden, the Netherlands and Belgium) shows that:

- a cooperative approach is required, taking into account the needs and habits of all stakeholders: consumers, large and small retailers, SMEs, corporations, government and banks;
- efficient and user friendly alternatives must be provided for all payment types across all customer segments, including vulnerable individuals;
- pricing differentiation should be used to further discourage the use of cheques; and that
- rationing can also be introduced to encourage the use of alternative instruments: for example, Belgian banks gradually brought the number of cheques down to 8 per new book/wallet issued.

Existing alternatives are shown in Table 16.1.

As mentioned above, a national plan achieving consensus between all interested parties should be elaborated around the following actions:

- introduce the obligation to mention account identifiers and/or the BIC and IBAN on every invoice and request for charity to encourage migration from cheque to credit transfer;

- introduce compulsory payment of salaries, benefits, pensions by credit transfer;
- encourage the possibility to pay invoices, donations, etc. remotely by debit/credit card;
- subsidize POS terminals at small merchants to achieve critical mass;
- promote e-invoicing;
- ensure that the government sector gradually discontinues effecting and accepting payments by cheque and adopts compulsory e-invoicing;
- re-examine pricing, across all instruments and customer segments, to discourage the use of cheques in favour of more efficient alternatives;
- gradually reduce the number of cheques issued in cheque books;
- conduct a review of any potential legal implications alongside the elaboration of the withdrawal plan; and
- develop a segmented and targeted communication plan focusing on:
  - the costs of cheques to all stakeholders, highlighting the savings offered by alternative instruments; and the
  - benefits of moving away from paper: earlier availability of funds, reduced fraud and errors, faster queries handling, reduced economic and environmental waste.

It is important to define a deadline for withdrawal (6–7 years seems realistic) to create the necessary momentum and stimulate the development of innovative alternatives.

It is worth remembering that several emerging countries, as well as transition economies in Eastern Europe, chose to leapfrog the cheque.

Finally, e-money which is already the preferred instrument in Singapore. Credible schemes for decentralized real-time e-settlement, whereby the central bank cover is attached to the payment, were being proposed at the time of publication.[3] They are certainly feasible from a technology standpoint, but do however face serious challenges in terms of consumer and stakeholder inertia, as well as lack of international standardization in terms of messaging formats and identification security.

2 Payment system architectures, schemes, standards and operators

RTGS will maintain its role as settlement platform for high-value and systemic payments such as high-priority movements between central and commercial banks to implement monetary policy and settlement of ancillary systems: DVP for securities settlement, CLS and foreign exchange, DNS systems and ACHs. Those countries which have not already done so will transfer to the next generation of hybrid systems, similar to TARGET2, to improve liquidity management. Participants will increasingly focus on liquidity efficiency which is likely to become the top criteria as turbulent markets will impact availability and the cost of collateral. It is also likely that the SWIFT standards will become universally adopted for RTGS systems even though SWIFT might not be retained as the access network. Central banks will maintain ownership and control of these RTGS systems, albeit if its operation is outsourced to a third party as has already happened in a Nordic country. Owners of systemically important systems, such as CLS and the EBA-Clearing, have outsourced the operation of their platforms to non-financial entities since the 1980s.

For low-value ACH type payments such as credit transfers and direct debits, we can hope that the SEPA schemes will become universally adopted in the long term. The expression 'long term' has been used purposely: payment systems evolve through 'generations' lasting 8 to 10 years on account of the effort to transform not only the central system but also each participant's applications and processes. Countries beyond the EU should however seriously consider changing to the SEPA schemes when planning their next generation of ACHs. It is worth stressing that a monetary union is not required to achieve standardization through adoption of the SEPA schemes and formats, which can be used with the appropriate currency code. Legal harmonization will however need to be voluntary, as no supranational institution such as the European Parliament exists outside the EU to mandate changes in national legislation through directives. The Bank for International Settlements could act as catalyser. The World Bank or the EU, which fund the implementation of payment systems in emerging economies through aid programmes, could impose adoption of the SEPA schemes as a condition. The EU will hopefully have abandoned their national schemes for the SEPA schemes by 2012 at the latest and, realistically, most countries could move to the SEPA schemes by 2020.

Similarly the move towards UNIFI ISO 20022 XML standards will generalize over time, enabling payment service providers and their customers to interoperate end-to-end. Increased processing speeds and growing storage density will largely overcome the overheads created by XML. The same applies for conversion routines to provide temporary assistance during transition. This uniformity of schemes and standards will reduce costs for all stakeholders, as the same applications and vendor solutions will be reusable on a much wider scale and operations can be concentrated into a small number of shared service centres. Technological progress points towards optimized payment routing: routing payments to the most appropriate clearing and settlement mechanism according to amount; time of day; service level agreement with customer; and available liquidity.

Once this nirvana of global standardization has been reached, we can envision, subject to protectionist regulation or access rules, banks connecting cross-border to major payment systems in Europe, US, Asia/Pacific, the Middle East and Latin America. An International Payments Framework was established in 2007 to achieve interoperability between domestic and international ACHs and the ability to exchange transactions in multiple currencies. This will lead to a reduction of the correspondent banking business among major institutions and consolidation of ACHs on a worldwide scale following the trend already in evidence in Europe. The same pattern will develop for card processors as cross-border acquiring will generalize and global retail chains will concentrate their business with one or two global acquirers and processors, squeezing fees during the selection process.

This consolidation will lead to ACHs and payment processors enlarging their activities as volumes cleared through them are likely to decline. We discussed earlier (ch. 5 sec. 3) how their revenues are concentrated among a small number of major participants and how vulnerable they would be to these deciding to operate bilaterally, remembering that the Clearing and Settlement Mechanisms referred to in the SEPA schemes specifically mention bilateral netting (see ch. 6 sec. 4). We must also bear in mind the impact of mergers and acquisitions. It would be preposterous to pretend that payments are at the forefront of the strategic criteria driving merger mania, but each one removes volumes from ACHs and processors as payments become 'on us' which is already estimated at 22 per cent of ACH transactions on average in the US and higher for the major banks.

As the fees and profits for the core clearing will reduce under competitive pressure, ACHs and processors will seek to differentiate through value-added services: e-invoicing/billing, format conversion, security, AML and OFAC screening, etc. Above all they will offer to take over the back-office tasks of banks, payment service providers and corporations: payment and card processing, reconciliations, customer support, claims handling, invoice collection, etc.

Finally, the international remittance volumes are growing as workforce becomes increasingly mobile. As mentioned previously (ch. 3 Sec. 4), these services have operated, until now, through specialized service providers and parallel circuits mainly outside the conventional banking circuits. Some banks have belatedly stepped in to this market, leveraging their presence at both extremities of selected corridors, such as US-Mexico, Europe-North Africa and Turkey, Gulf-Asia. They are however likely to find it difficult to gain significant market share through the lack of a capillary distribution network and also because they are prevented by law from offering the anonymity of the parallel systems which are mainly based on cash.

3 Risk and fraud management

Concern about risk is likely to increase and more and more safeguards imposed. We have mentioned above the concerns about liquidity for RTGS systems. We have observed during the sub-prime crisis a trend to lower the quality of the eligible collateral required by the central banks when making liquidity available to the markets, which will hopefully be corrected as calm returns. In the meantime, 'haircuts' and margin calls are likely to increase.

Technology can be expected to improve the resilience of market infrastructures to ensure business continuity, such as increasing the distance at which synchronous data-mirroring can be achieved, as well as advances in auto-diagnostics and self-healing systems. We are also likely to see a more coordinated approach to crisis management across major financial centres, as the market turbulences and rescue operations of institutions not generally considered as 'too big to fail' at the end of 2007 and early 2008 highlighted the interdependencies between instruments, institutions and markets globally. By all accounts, the 'moral hazard' dogma has been severely challenged.

Fraud detection anti money laundering and countering terrorism finance will remain major challenges. Technology is however likely to be again of assistance as progresses in high-speed data analysis across distributed databases will help with suspicious pattern analysis, anti-money laundering and customer identification. Biometric identification based on voice, face and fingerprint recognition will also spread. The arbitrage between risk management, technology, data privacy and cost will continue.

4 Governance and oversight

Central banks will continue to exercise oversight over payment systems, including those belonging to and operated by the private sector. The separation of schemes and infrastructure, as already implemented in the US and the EU with SEPA, is likely to become more widespread to stimulate competition. Under pressure from customers and competition authorities, scheme management will be broadened to include a representative sample of customers. It can also be hoped that more countries will follow the example of the UK in publishing a National Payments Plan to enable all stakeholders, including service providers and technology vendors, to plan and manage their activities and investments within an agreed strategic vision and time horizon.

Finally, increased research and attention will be devoted to the impact of payment systems on the overall economy, a subject largely ignored until recently, to encourage progress towards more efficiency. Valuable contributions can be expected from academia and research centres.

Ultimately, the industry will evolve until the right balance is established between regulation, cooperation between providers on standards and security, competition and consumer protection.

5 Settlement of financial markets trading

Few fundamental changes are foreseen in settling foreign exchange trades, CLS being expected to gradually expand the eligible currencies. It will however hit the law of diminishing returns as the volume contribution from additional currencies is likely to be marginal.

The landscape for securities trading will however evolve more dramatically. Consolidation of exchanges and CSDs is likely to continue. ECNs have been launched and disappeared, or retreated to niche markets as they failed to dent the dominance of the major stock exchanges which reduced their fees.

The big unknown lies with TARGET2 Securities. Will it see the light of day or is the ECB raising a scarecrow to force the CSDs and ICSDs to reduce settlement charges? The jury was out at the time of publication as seven European private sector securities settlement providers 'said post-trade costs in the region's capital markets could be slashed by 80 per cent by a new joint venture' and announced the 'Link Up Markets' project, spearheaded by Clearstream, which 'also appears to be an effort by central securities depositories (CSDs) to establish their own system in advance of a separate plan by the European Central Bank due for completion in 2013'.[4]

Will Euroclear and Clearstream merge following the latter's separation from Deutsche Börse? The authors consider this unlikely, as the large institutions controlling each will wish to maintain competition and preserve their zone of influence.

6 Regional developments

SEPA will dominate the European scene until the national schemes have finally been abandoned to the benefit of the SEPA schemes. These are however likely to evolve in the light of operational experience. The authorities will continue to press for closer integration of securities settlement schemes to achieve levels of efficiency comparable to the US. However, does the announcement of TARGET2 Securities indicate a move towards the US model, featuring competition between the private and public sectors?

The US will continue to focus on driving cheque usage down, but the authors do not foresee a withdrawal before 2020. In the meantime, there are hopes that NACHA standards could evolve towards UNIFI ISO 20022 XML and that Fedwire moves to SWIFT standards.

In Asia, the interesting issue will be to observe which city emerges as the dominant financial centre. Contenders (in alphabetical order!) are Hong Kong, Shanghai, Singapore and Tokyo. We can also hope that they will adopt internationally recognized standards and schemes as anticipated in Japan.

7 Corporate banking

Global corporates will apply increasing pressure for standardization around ISO 20022 XML and account portability. The concentration of treasury functions, banking relationships and payment processing towards Head Office or regional centres will accelerate. The emphasis will shift to intraday cash management and value-added services around the payment, such as event-driven SCF as discussed in Chapters 12 and 13. E-invoicing and e-billing will develop in spite of the fragmented standardization efforts, hoping that at least interoperability will be guaranteed. Banks will hopefully start to leverage the customer data they possess. Analysis should enable them to identify the supply chain clusters in which their customers are most closely involved to develop tailor-made solutions. To lock customers in, banks will offer to take over their clients payment processing applications, treasury, invoice collection and reconciliation and accounts receivable, which they will probably outsource to specialized service companies.

Banks are however suffering from regulatory overload: Basel II, MIFID, SEPA, changes to domestic infrastructures, etc. These 'must dos' leave little resources, financial or personnel, for new developments.

A new disintermediation threat arises in the EU as some global corporations could decide to create an independent payments subsidiary and register it as a Payment Institution under the PSD to effect payments, thus bypassing the banks.

8 New entrants

Innovation will continue to originate from outside the banking sector, and by definition it is difficult to anticipate from who or where. We can certainly foresee the development of new PayPals or Earthports. Mobile phone operators are likely to dominate the market for very low-value transactions. Other competitors could be the ACHs and payment processors as they develop value-added services.

In spite of the uncertainty surrounding the implementation of the PSD and particularly the status of the new Payment Institutions and their supervisory regime, it will be interesting to see whether the concept will be adopted in other regions.

Partnerships would appear to offer the best route to leverage different skills and technology assuming that satisfactory agreements can be reached on revenue sharing and branding.

9 Operations

No bank can operate without offering payment services. The heavy technological investments to comply with SEPA, the PSD and other regulatory changes will force many small to medium institutions to outsource payment processing to large banks or payment processors keen to gain volume to achieve economies of scale. Neither party should however underestimate the difficulty in carving out applications and processes, airlifting them to the new processor and reintegrating them with those retained.

10 Revenue shifts and shrinkage

Float will disappear; illegal in the EU under the PSD, the trend is likely to spread under consumer pressure and major corporations.

Merchant and interchange fees in the card business will shrink under pressure from regulators, anti-trust legislators, consumer groups and major corporations who will also demand increased transparency over charges.

Banks and payment service providers will move to explicit fees for retail customers but charges will continue to be negotiated in the corporate sector. The revenues for the basic payment services will in any case be driven down by competition and regulation such as SEPA. Reducing costs by improving operational efficiency will not be enough. A comprehensive study showed that profits per transaction between 2001 and 2011 will reduce by half to an average maximum of $0.15 in the US and by two thirds to $0.12 in Europe.[5]

As mentioned several times, the profitability of payment services varies from one service provider to another. Each bank should undertake a comprehensive profit and loss review of its payment operations across all instruments and customer segments before finalizing their business, product and operational strategies. All service providers will be attempting to make up revenues from value-added services which will become the weapons for competitive differentiation.

Conclusion

For our readers who have had the patience to remain with us until the last page, the authors would like to end with their personal conclusions and some thoughts on the future.

Like writing, money is an instrument that liberates us from the constraints of space and time. Through writing, we can transmit information, ideas, knowledge and feelings such as love to a distant person, or leave them for posterity. Money also allows us to pay a remote person immediately or in the future. Already in the Middle Ages, when certain city states forbade usury, bills of exchange issued in Venice were fictitiously drawn on Torcello, a small island off Venice, while adjusting the date. But the spatial constraints of money are fast disappearing: few spots on earth are unreachable by a credit transfer and the execution time has, from a technological viewpoint, shrunk to milliseconds. The same can be said for writing, transmitted by e-mail to mobile devices anywhere. Money and securities are dematerialized and now reduced to a string of bits or an electronic impulse on a computer. Has the payment system substituted itself to money? Are banks losing their financial role to become information processing companies?

It has become a cliché to say that competition will increase, but the financial services industry will face a multilayered competitive environment between banks, payment instruments, payment clearing and settlement systems, exchanges and securities settlement systems, with several feeling free to compete on all levels. This will be exacerbated by competition from new entrants, freed from regulatory barriers to entry. Central banks would appear to be the only stakeholders likely to remain immune from competition.

This sharpened competitive environment and the increasing commoditization of most aspects of the business, requiring economies of scale and a broader capital base, will lead to further consolidation across and between layers: we are likely to see the re-emergence of vertical silos.

Corporations will dramatically reduce the number of banks and financial institutions with whom they maintain relationships. This trend, accelerated by SEPA in Europe will spread, particularly as schemes and standards enable interoperability.

The volume of high-value payments processed by RTGS systems will reduce. Schemes such as Faster Payments in the UK and payment systems such as CHIPS in the US and EURO1 which guarantee real-time finality will increase market share. As mentioned in the previous chapter, RTGS systems will be left with monetary policy and systemic payments, reducing their volumes to levels which could be handled by a laptop, subject to business continuity considerations of course!

Based on the experience of the early twenty first century, innovative services and solutions are most likely to originate from outside the financial sector. New entrants and payment service providers will cherry-pick the most profitable activities and become increasingly trusted brands.

In June 2007, well before the Northern Rock failure and the global subprime crisis, a survey in the UK showed that 71 per cent of customers did not trust their banks.[1] Approval ratings are unlikely to have risen since then. Banking is based on trust: 'Credit' comes from the Latin 'credere' which means trust. The Bank Manager was a respected individual whose advice often extended beyond financial matters and banks were, until now, protected by a legal/regulatory framework that gave them a near monopoly on financial services and payments in particular. This is fast disappearing, so if banks lose the trust of their customers, what will they be left with to defend their shrinking franchise?

Appendix

Comparison between large-value payment systems: daily averages 2007

System	Volume (000 payments)	Value in local currency (billion)		Value (USD billion)*
TARGET	366	EUR	2,400	3,503
EURO1	211	EUR	228	333
CHAPS	141	GBP	274	543
BOJ-NET	23	JPY	100,000	897
FXYCS	32	JPY	730	7
Fedwire	534	USD	2,800	2,800
CHIPS	348	USD	1,900	1,900

* Indicative figures based on exchange rates at 31 December 2007: USD 1 = EUR 0.6852 = GBP 0.5043 = JPY 111.46

Notes

Introduction

1. Boston Consulting Group. *Global Payments*, 2002.

1 The Architecture of Payment Systems

1. BIS, CPSS: *A glossary of terms used in payments and settlement systems*, March 2003.
2. Ibid.
3. Ibid.
4. Payments Council: *National payments plan, Consultation on change in UK payments*, November 2007.
5. BIS, CPSS: *Core principles for systemically important payment systems*, January 2001; CPSS 43.
6. BIS, CPSS: *A glossary of terms used in payments and settlement systems.*

2 Payment Instruments

1. BIS, CPSS: *A glossary of terms used in payments and settlement systems*, March 2003.
2. Payments Council: *National payments plan, Consultation on change in UK payments*, November 2007.
3. PSE Consulting: *Europe set to lose its war on cash*, March 2008.
4. NACHA: *A strategic plan for the ACH network and NACHA 2006–2010*, available from: www.nacha.org.
5. Payments Council, *National payments plan.*
6. Rustin I Carpenter and Ward H Gailey, Jr: 'How will payments electronification and convergence change the payments business model? How do you retain competitive advantage?' *Journal of Payments Strategy and Systems*, 2(1) October 2007, pp 48–59.
7. www.visaeurope.com, April 2008.
8. www.mastercard.com. *Corporate overview*, April 2008.
9. The *Financial Times*, 19 March 2008.
10. The *Financial Times*, 8 January 2008.

3 Cross-Currency Payments and SWIFT

1. See www.swift.com.
2. Nancy Todor: 'Remittances – Can the Industry meet the demands of consumers and regulators?' *Journal of Payments Strategy and Systems*, 1(2), January 2007, pp 116–24.

3. David Seddon: *Informal money transfers: Economic links between UK diaspora groups and recipients 'back home'*, Centre for Study of Financial Innovation (CSFI), 2007.
4. Ibid.
5. BIS, CPSS: General principles for international remittance services. January 2007.

4 Risks in Payment Systems, Oversight and Security

1. BIS, CPSS: *Core principles for systemically important payment systems*, January 2001; CPSS 43.
2. Directive 98/26/EC of the European Parliament and the Council of 19 May 1998 on settlement finality in payments and securities settlement systems – *Official Journal L 166*, 11/06/1998, pp. 45–50.
3. ECB: *Business continuity oversight expectations for systemically important payment systems (SIPS)*, 31 May 2006.
4. Ibid.
5. BIS, CPSS: *Core principles for systemically important payment systems*, January 2001; CPSS 43.
6. ECB: *Oversight standards for euro retail payment systems*, June 2003.
7. BIS: *Policy issues for central banks in retail payments*, 2003.
8. BIS, CPSS: *Central bank oversight of payment and settlement systems*, May 2005.
9. Ibid.

5 The Role of Payment Systems in the Economy

1. BIS, CPSS: *Statistics on payment and settlement systems in selected countries*. March 2008.

6 European Payments and SEPA

1. European Payments Council: *Making SEPA a Reality*, 2006.
2. Ibid.
3. http://ec.europa.eu/internal_market/payments/framework/index_en.htm
4. ECB: TARGET2 Single *shared platform – user detailed functional specifications-core services – 1st book – Version 2.3.*
5. www.ecb.int/stats/payments.
6. European Payments Council: *Framework for the Evolution of the Clearing and Settlement of payments in SEPA – including the principles for SEPA scheme compliance and re-statement of the PE-ACH concept (PE-ACH/CSM Framework)*, 5 January 2007.
7. www.abe-eba.eu.
8. www.ebaclearing.eu, February 2008.
9. Ibid.
10. Ibid.
11. Ibid.

12. EBA Clearing: *STEP2 platform and services*, December 2007.
13. www.ebaclearing.e, February 2008.
14. www.europeanpaymentscouncil.eu.
15. Capgemini, ABN AMRO, EFMA: *World payments report 2005*.
16. Boston Consulting Group. *Preparing for the endgame – global payments 2004*.
17. Christian Westerhaus, Deutsche Bank: *A step in the right direction*, Financial i, Q4, December 2007.
18. Cheque and Credit Clearing Company, www.chequeandcredit.co.uk, March 2008.
19. APACS: *Annual summary of clearing statistics 2007*, www.apacs.org.uk.
20. Payments Council, *National Payments Plan, Consultation on change in UK payments*, November 2007.
21. Ibid.
22. Cheque and Credit Clearing Company, www.chequeandcredit.co.uk, March 2008.
23. Payments Council, *National payments plan, consultation on change in UK payments*, November 2007.
24. APACS: *Payment trends, facts and figures 1998–2005*, www.apacs.org.uk.
25. Payments Council, *National Payments Plan – Setting the strategic vision for UK payments,* May 2008.

7 The US Payment Systems

1. Data source: www.federalreserve.gov, March 2008.
2. Data source: www.chips.org, March 2008.
3. Federal Reserve Financial Services: *FedACH International Services*, ref: 041507RP00336.
4. Data source: www.nacha.org, March 2008.
5. Federal Reserve System: *The 2007 Federal Reserve Payments Study*, December 2007.
6. Ibid.
7. Data source: www.nacha.org, March 2008.
8. Rustin I Carpenter and Ward H Gailey, Jr: 'How will payments electronification and convergence change the payments business model? How do you retain competitive advantage?' *Journal of Payments Strategy and Systems*, 2(1), October 2007, pp 48–59.
9. See www.svpco.com, March 2008.
10. Federal Reserve Financial Services: *FedACH international services*, ref: 041507RP00336.
11. Data source: www.federalreserve.gov, March 2008.
12. Nasreen Quibria, Federal Reserve Bank of Boston: 'Understanding emerging payments – moving towards a cashless society?' Presentation at Regional Cash Services Advisory Group, 8 May 2007.
13. Federal Reserve Financial Services: 'Federal Reserve studies confirm electronic payments exceed check payments for the first time,' press release, 6 December 2004.
14. Rustin I Carpenter and Ward H Gailey, Jr: *How will payments electronification and convergence change the payments business model?*

15. NACHA: *A Strategic Plan for the ACH Network and NACHA 2006-2010* available from: www.nacha.org.
16. www.dtcc.com, April 2008.

8 Major Asian Payment Systems

1. Statistics from www.boj.or.jp/en, March 2008.
2. Ibid.
3. Ibid.
4. Takashi Kimori: 'The Japanese payments landscape and its future', *Journal of Payments Strategy and Systems*, 2(1), October 2007, pp. 81–7.
5. Bank of Japan: *Payment and settlement systems report 2006*, English version, July 2007.
6. Bank of Japan: *RTGS-XG project phase 1 implementation guide*, October 2007, from www.boj.or.jp/en
7. Takashi Kimori: 'The Japanese payments landscape and its future'.
8. Ibid.
9. Bank of Japan: *Payment and Settlement Systems Report 2006.*
10. Tower Group: *The year of the pig: Chinese interbank payment systems in 2007*, August 2007, reference # V52:21P.
11. Ibid.

9 New Entrants

1. Sophie Tacchi: 'Mobile payments challenges and opportunities in retail banking', *Journal of Payments Strategy and Systems*, 2(2), January 2008, pp 159–66.
2. Presentation by Vipul Shah, Senior Director of Global Financial Services, PayPal. International Payments Summit conference, London 23 April 2008.
3. The *Financial Times*, 18 April 2008.
4. www.earthport.com, March 2008.
5. Ibid.

10 The Settlement of Trading Activities

1. www.cls-group.com.
2. Ibid.
3. BIS, CPSS: *Progress in reducing foreign exchange settlement risk*, May 2008.

11 Securities Settlement

1. BIS, CPSS: *A glossary of terms used in payments and settlement systems*, March 2003.
2. Peter Norman: *Plumbers and Visionaries – Securities settlement and Europe's financial markets*, Chichester: John Wiley, 2007.
3. ECB: *T2S User requirements – management summary*, ref T2S-07-0373. 12 December 2007.

4. Ibid.
5. ECB, Directorate General Payments and Market Infrastructure: *T2S Economic Impact Assessment*. 21 May 2008.

12 The Requirements of Corporations

1. EBA and Innopay: *E-invoicing 2008*, February 2008.
2. Ibid.
3. Ibid.
4. Ibid.
5. Ibid.

14 The Banks' Back Offices

1. IBM: *Service oriented architectures – revolutionizing today's banking business*, 2008, GBE03015-USEN-00.

15 Payments as a Business for Banks

1. Boston Consulting Group: Global Payments 2002.
2. Raymond M Mulhern: 'What can banks do to manage their enterprise payments strategy better?' *Journal of Payments Strategy and Systems*, 1(3), April 2007, pp. 200–5.
3. McKinsey & Company: *European payment profit pool analysis: Casting light in murky waters*, June 2005.
4. Ibid.
5. Capgemini, ABN AMRO, EFMA: *World payments report 2005.*
6. Ibid.
7. McKinsey & Company: *European Payment Profit Pool Analysis: Casting Light in Murky Waters*. June 2005.
8. Capgemini, ABN AMRO, EFMA: *World payments report 2005.*

16 Where is the Payments Business Going?

1. Nasreen Quibria, Federal Reserve Bank of Boston: 'Understanding emerging payments – moving towards a cashless society?' Presentation at Regional Cash Services Advisory Group, 8 May 2007.
2. PSE Consulting: *Europe set to lose its war on cash*, March 2008.
3. Harry Leinonen: *Payments habits and trends in the changing e-landscape 2010+*. Bank of Finland Expository studies. A:111, 2008.
4. The Financial Times, 3 April 2008.
5. Boston Consulting Group. *Preparing for the endgame – global payments 2004.*

Conclusion

1. Finextra daily news, 22 June 2007. www.finextra.com/fullstory.asp?id=17078.

Bibliography and Useful Websites

Bibliography

Andries M. and Hervo F. (2006) *La surveillance des moyens de paiement et des systèmes d'échange*, Bulletin de la Banque de France, No. 156, December.

Bank for International Settlements (BIS) (1990) *Report of the committee on interbank netting schemes of the central banks of the Group of Ten countries*, Lamfalussy Report, November, Basel: BIS.

Bank for International Settlements Committee on Payment and Settlement Systems (BIS, CPSS) (1992) *Delivery versus payment in securities settlement systems*, September, Basel: BIS.

Bank for International Settlements, Committee on Payment and Settlement Systems (BIS, CPSS) (1996) *Settlement risk in foreign exchange transactions*, Allsopp Report, Basel: BIS.

Bank for International Settlements, Committee on Payment and Settlement Systems (BIS, CPSS) (1998) *Reducing foreign exchange settlement risk*, Basel: BIS.

Bank for International Settlements, Committee on Payment and Settlement Systems (BIS, CPSS) (2001) *Core principles for systemically important payments systems*, January, Basel: BIS.

Bank for International Settlements, Committee on Payment and Settlement Systems (BIS, CPSS) (2003a) *A glossary of terms used in payments and settlement systems*, March, Basel: BIS.

Bank for International Settlements, Committee on Payment and Settlement Systems (BIS, CPSS) (2003b) *The role of central bank money in payment systems*, August, Basel: BIS.

Bank for International Settlements, Committee on Payment and Settlement Systems (BIS, CPSS) (2005a) *Central bank oversight of payment and settlement systems*, May, Basel: BIS.

Bank for International Settlements, Committee on Payment and Settlement Systems (BIS, CPSS) (2005b) *New developments in large-value payment systems*, May.

Bank for International Settlements, Committee on Payment and Settlement Systems (BIS, CPSS) (2006) *General guidance for national payment systems development*, January, Basel: BIS.

Bank for International Settlements, Committee on Payment and Settlement Systems (BIS, CPSS) (2007) *General principles for international remittances*, January, Basel: BIS.

Bank for International Settlements, Committee on Payment and Settlement Systems (BIS, CPSS) (2008a) *Statistics on payment and settlement systems in selected countries*, March, Basel: BIS.

Bank for International Settlements, Committee on Payment and Settlement Systems (BIS, CPSS) (2008b) *Progress in reducing foreign exchange settlement risk*, May, Basel: BIS.

Bank for International Settlements, Committee on Payment and Settlement Systems (BIS, CPSS) (2008c) *The interdependencies of payment and settlement systems*, June, Basel: BIS.

Beau D. and Woefel G. (2004) *The resilience of post market infrastructures and payment systems*, Banque de France, Financial Stability Review, No. 5, November.

Bernard H. and Bisignano J. (2000) *Information, Liquidity and Risk in the Interbank Market: Implicit Guarantee and Private Credit Market Failure*, BIS Working Papers Nr 86, March.

Bonnier V. (2008): *Supplementing settlement functions with a decision-support system in TARGET2*, Banque de France Bulletin Digest, No. 172, April.

Boston Consulting Group (BCG) (2002) *Global payments 2002*, Boston, MA: Boston Consulting Group.

Boston Consulting Group (BCG) (2004) *Global payments 2004*, Boston, MA: Boston Consulting Group.

Capgemini, ABN, AMRO and EFMA (2005) *World payments report*: Capgemini.

Decressin J., Faruqee H. and Fonteyne W. (Eds) (2007) *Integrating Europe's financial markets*, Washington, DC: International Monetary Fund.

De Seze N. (2006): *TARGET2: from concept to reality*, Banque de France Bulletin Digest, No. 144, May.

DiVanna J.A. (2002) *Redefining financial services*, Basingstoke/ New York: Palgrave.

Euro Banking Association (EBA) and Innopay (2008) *E-invoicing 2008*, February, Paris: EBA.

European Central Bank (ECB) (2007) *Blue book: Payment and securities settlement systems in the EU*, vols 1–2. August, Frankfurt: ECB.

European Commission (EC) (2001) *Cross-border clearing and settlement arrangements in the European Union*, Giovannini Report 1, November, Brussels: EC.

European Commission (EC) (2003) *Second report on EU clearing and settlement systems*, Giovannini Report 2, April, Brussels: EC.

Foss B. and Stone M. (2001) *Successful customer relationship marketing*, London: Kogan Page.

Garvy G. and Byn M. (1969) *The velocity of money*, New York: Federal Reserve Bank.

Goodhart C.A.E. (1975) *Money, information and uncertainty*, Basingstoke: Macmillan (now Palgrave Macmillan).

Jackson Eric M. (2006) *The PayPal wars*, Los Angeles: World Ahead Publishing, Inc.

Leinonen H. (2008) *Payments habits and trends in the changing e-landscape 2010+*, Helsinki: Bank of Finland Expository studies. A:111.

Lietaer B. (2001) *The future of money*, London: Century.

Lucas Y. (2008): *TARGET2 and European financial integration*, Banque de France Bulletin Digest, No. 172, April.

Mazars E. and Woelfel G. (2005): *Analysis, by simulation, of the impact of a technical default of a payment system participant*, Banque de France, Financial Stability Review, No. 6, June.

McKinsey & Company (2005) *European payment profit pool analysis: Casting light in murky waters*, June, USA: McKinsey & Company.

Mesonnier J.S. (2001) *Monnaie électronique et politique monétaire*, Bulletin de la Banque de France, 91, juillet, Paris: Banque de France.

Norman P. (2007) *Plumbers and visionaries – securities settlement and Europe's financial markets*, Chichester: John Wiley & Sons.

Organisation for Economic Cooperation and Development (OECD) (2002) *The Future of Money*.

Payments Council (2008) *National Payments Plan – Setting the strategic vision for UK Payments*, May.

Seddon D. (2007) *Informal money transfers: Economic links between UK diaspora groups and recipients 'back home'*, London: Centre for Study of Financial Innovation (CSFI).

Wicksell K. (1935) *Lectures on Political Economy, Vol 2, Money*, Routledge and Keegan Paul Ltd.

Useful websites

APACS	www.apacs.org.uk
Banque de France	www.banque-france.fr
Bank for International Settlements	www.bis.org
Bank of Japan	www.boj.or.jp
Cheque and Credit Clearing Company (UK)	www.chequeandcredit.co.uk
CHIPS	www.chips.org
CLS	www.cls-group.com
EBA	www.abe-eba.eu
EPC	www.europeanpaymentscouncil.eu
European Central Bank	www.ecb.int
European Commission	http://ec.europa.eu
FATF	www.fatf-gafi.org
Federal Reserve	www.federalreserve.gov
NACHA	www.nacha.org
Payments Council (UK)	www.paymentscouncil.org.uk
PCI	www.pcisecuritystandards.org
SWIFT	www.swift.com

Glossary

We are grateful to the Bank for International Settlements who have kindly allowed us to reproduce selected terms from their publication: *Committee on Payment and Settlement Systems: A Glossary of terms used in payment and settlement systems*. March 2003.
The full document, like all BIS publications, can be downloaded free of charge from their website www.bis.org.

Acquirer The entity or entities that hold(s) deposit accounts for card acceptors (merchants) and to which the card acceptor transmits the data relating to the transaction. The acquirer is responsible for the collection of transaction information and settlement with the acceptors.
Authentication The methods used to verify the origin of a message or to verify the identity of a participant connected to a system and to confirm that a message has not been modified or replaced in transit.
Automated clearing house An electronic clearing system in which payment orders are exchanged among financial institutions, primarily via magnetic media or telecommunications networks, and handled by a data processing centre. See also clearing/clearance.
Automated teller machine An electromechanical device that permits authorized users, typically using machine-readable plastic cards, to withdraw cash from their accounts and/or access other services, such as balance enquiries, transfer of funds or acceptance of deposits. ATMs may be operated either online with real-time access to an authorization database or offline.

Bank draft In Europe, the term generally refers to a draft drawn by a bank on itself. The draft is purchased by the payer and sent to the payee, who presents it to his bank for payment. That bank presents it to the payer's bank for reimbursement. In the United States, the term generally refers to a draft or cheque drawn by a bank on itself or on funds deposited with another bank. In the case of a cashier's cheque, the bank is both the drawer and drawee. In the case of a teller's cheque, one bank is the drawer and a second bank is the drawee. Bank drafts may be written by a bank for its own purposes or may be purchased by a customer and sent to a payee to discharge an obligation. See also draft.
Bank reserves Deposits held by banks with the central bank.

Bilateral net settlement system A settlement system in which participants' bilateral net settlement positions are settled between every bilateral combination of participants. See also net credit (or debit) position.
Bilateral netting An arrangement between two parties to net their bilateral obligations. The obligations covered by the arrangement may arise from financial contracts, transfers or both. See also multilateral netting, netting, net settlement.
Bill of exchange A written order from one party (the drawer) to another (the drawee) to pay a specified sum on demand or on a specified date to the drawer or to a third party specified by the drawer. Widely used to finance trade and, when discounted with a financial institution, to obtain credit. See also draft.
Book-entry system An accounting system that permits the transfer of claims (e.g., electronic transfer of securities) without the physical movement of paper documents or certificates. See also dematerialization, immobilization.
Business continuity A payment system's arrangements which aim to ensure that it meets agreed service levels even if one or more components of the system fail or if it is affected by an abnormal external event. Include both preventative measures and arrangements to deal with contingencies.

Call money A loan contract which is automatically renewed every day unless the lender or the borrower indicates that it wishes the funds to be returned within a short period of time.
Caps Quantitative limits on the funds transfer activity of individual participants in a system; limits may be set by each individual participant or may be imposed by the body managing the system; limits can be placed on the net debit position or net credit position of participants in the system.
Cash settlement agent The entity whose assets are used to settle the ultimate payment obligations arising from securities transfers within the CSD. Accounts with the cash settlement agent are held by settlement banks which act on their own behalf and may also offer payment services to participants that do not have accounts with the settlement agent. See also settlement agent.
Central bank credit (liquidity) facility A standing credit facility that can be drawn upon by certain designated account holders (e.g., banks) at the central bank. In some cases, the facility can be used automatically at the initiative of the account holder, while in other cases the central bank may retain some degree of discretion. The loans typically

take the form either of advances or overdrafts on an account holder's current account which may be secured by a pledge of securities (also known as lombard loans in some European countries), or of traditional rediscounting of bills.

Central counterparty An entity that is the buyer to every seller and seller to every buyer of a specified set of contracts, e.g., those executed on a particular exchange or exchanges.

Central securities depository A facility (or an institution) for holding securities, which enables securities transactions to be processed by book entry. Physical securities may be immobilized by the depository or securities may be dematerialized (i.e., so that they exist only as electronic records). In addition to safekeeping, a central securities depository may incorporate comparison, clearing and settlement functions.

Cheque A written order from one party (the drawer) to another (the drawee, normally a bank) requiring the drawee to pay a specified sum on demand to the drawer or to a third party specified by the drawer. Cheques may be used for settling debts and withdrawing money from banks. See also bill of exchange.

Chip card Also known as an IC (integrated circuit) card. A card containing one or more computer chips or integrated circuits for identification, data storage or special purpose processing used to validate personal identification numbers (PINs), authorize purchases, verify account balances and store personal records. In some cases, the memory in the card is updated every time the card is used (e.g., an account balance is updated).

Clearing and settling institution An institution which transmits information and funds through a payment system network. It may operate as an agent or a principal.

Clearing/clearance The process of transmitting, reconciling and, in some cases, confirming payment orders or security transfer instructions prior to settlement, possibly including the netting of instructions and the establishment of final positions for settlement. Sometimes the term is used (imprecisely) to include settlement.

Clearing house A central location or central processing mechanism through which financial institutions agree to exchange payment instructions or other financial obligations (e.g., securities). The institutions settle for items exchanged at a designated time based on the rules and procedures of the clearing house. In some cases, the clearing house may assume significant counterparty, financial or risk management responsibilities for the clearing system. See also clearing/clearance, clearing system.

Clearing member A member of a clearing house. All trades must be settled through a clearing member. A direct clearing member is able to settle only its own obligations. A general clearing member is able to settle its own obligations as well as those of clients. Variations of these two types of clearing member may also exist.

Clearing system A set of procedures whereby financial institutions present and exchange data and/or documents relating to funds or securities transfers to other financial institutions at a single location (clearing house). The procedures often also include a mechanism for the calculation of participants' bilateral and/or multilateral net positions with a view to facilitating the settlement of their obligations on a net or net net basis. See also netting.

Collateral pool Assets owned by members of a payment system that are collectively available to the system as collateral to enable it to obtain funds in circumstances specified in its rules.

Correspondent banking An arrangement under which one bank (correspondent) holds deposits owned by other banks (respondents) and provides payment and other services to those respondent banks. Such arrangements may also be known as agency relationships in some domestic contexts. In international banking, balances held for a foreign respondent bank may be used to settle foreign exchange transactions. Reciprocal correspondent banking relationships may involve the use of so-called nostro and vostro accounts to settle foreign exchange transactions.

Counterparty The opposite party to a financial transaction such as a securities trade or swap agreement.

Credit limit The limit on the credit exposure a payment system participant incurs vis-à-vis another participant (bilateral credit limit) or vis-à-vis all other participants (multilateral credit limit) as a result of receiving payments that have not yet been settled.

Credit risk/exposure The risk that a counterparty will not settle an obligation for full value, either when due or at any time thereafter. In exchange-for value systems, the risk is generally defined to include replacement cost risk and principal risk.

Credit transfer A payment order or possibly a sequence of payment orders made for the purpose of placing funds at the disposal of the beneficiary. Both the payment instructions and the funds described therein move from the bank of the payer/originator to the bank of the beneficiary, possibly via several other banks as intermediaries and/or more than one credit transfer system.

Day of value The day on which a payment is due to be credited to the receiving participant in the payment system. The day of value for the receiving participant's customer (that is, the day on which the receiving participant credits the customer in its books) may or may not be the same day, depending on specific arrangements or local practice.

Daylight credit Credit extended for a period of less than one business day; in a credit transfer system with end-of-day final settlement, daylight credit is tacitly extended by a receiving institution if it accepts and acts on a payment order even though it will not receive final funds until the end of the business day. Also called daylight overdraft, daylight exposure and intraday credit.

Deferred net settlement system A system that effects the settlement of obligations or transfers between or among counterparties on a net basis at some later time.

Delivery Final transfer of a security or financial instrument.

Delivery versus payment A link between a securities transfer system and a funds transfer system that ensures that delivery occurs if, and only if, payment occurs.

Delivery versus payment system A mechanism in an exchange-for-value settlement system that ensures that the final transfer of one asset occurs if and only if the final transfer of (an) other asset(s) occurs. Assets could include monetary assets (such as foreign exchange), securities or other financial instruments. See also exchange for value settlement system, final transfer.

Dematerialization The elimination of physical certificates or documents of title which represent ownership of securities so that securities exist only as accounting records.

Depository An agent with the primary role of recording securities either physically or electronically and keeping records of the ownership of these securities.

Direct debit Preauthorized debit on the payer's bank account initiated by the payee.

Direct participant A participant in an interbank funds transfer system (IFTS) who is responsible to the settlement agent (or to all other direct participants) for the settlement of its own payments, those of its customers and those of the indirect participants on whose behalf it is settling.

Draft A written order from one party (the drawer) to another (the drawee) to pay a party identified on the order (payee) or to the bearer a specified sum, either on demand (sight draft) or on a specified date (time draft). See also bank draft, bill of exchange, cheque.

Electronic money Value stored electronically in a device such as a chip card or a hard drive in a personal computer.

Final settlement A settlement which is irrevocable and unconditional.
Foreign exchange settlement risk The risk that one party in a foreign exchange transaction will pay the currency it sold but not receive the currency it bought. This is also called cross-currency settlement risk or principal risk; it is also referred to as Herstatt risk, although this is an inappropriate term given the differing circumstances in which this risk has materialized.

Gross settlement system A transfer system in which the settlement of funds or securities transfer instructions occurs individually (on an instruction by instruction basis).

Haircut The difference between the market value of a security and its collateral value. Haircuts are taken by a lender of funds in order to protect the lender, should the need arise to liquidate the collateral, from losses owing to declines in the market value of the security. See also margin.
Herstatt risk See principal risk.
Hybrid system A payment system that combines characteristics of RTGS systems and netting systems.

Immobilization The placement of physical certificates for securities and financial instruments in a central securities depository so that subsequent transfers can be made by book entry, that is, by debits from, and credits to, holders' accounts at the depository.
Imprinter A mechanical device to reproduce the name and account number of a cardholder on a paper sales slip. See also imprinter voucher.
Imprinter voucher In card transactions, a sales slip that is to be signed by the customer on which the name and card number of the customer are imprinted. See also imprinter.
Indirect participant/member Refers to a funds or securities transfer system in which there is a tiering arrangement. Indirect participants are distinguished from direct participants by their inability to perform some of the system activities (e.g., input of transfer orders, settlement) performed by direct participants. Indirect participants, therefore, require the services of direct participants to perform those activities on their behalf. In the EC context, the term refers more specifically to participants in a transfer system which are responsible only to their direct participants for settling the payments input to the system. See also direct participant/member, settling participant/member, tiering arrangement.

Interchange fee Transaction fee payable in the context of a payment card network by one participating financial institution to another, for example by an acquirer to a card issuer in respect of a card payment by the cardholder to the card acceptor (merchant).
International central securities depository A central securities depository which clears and settles international securities or cross-border transactions in domestic securities. At the moment there are two ICSDs located in EU countries, Clearstream and Euroclear.
Intraday credit See daylight credit.
Intraday liquidity Funds which can be accessed during the business day, usually to enable financial institutions to make payments in real time. See also intraday credit.
Irrevocable and unconditional transfer A transfer which cannot be revoked by the transferor and is unconditional.

Legal risk The risk of loss because of the unexpected application of a law or regulation or because a contract cannot be enforced.
Letter of credit A promise by a bank or other issuer to a third party to make payment on behalf of a customer in accordance with specified conditions. Frequently used in international trade to make funds available in a foreign location.
Liquidity risk The risk that a counterparty (or participant in a settlement system) will not settle an obligation for full value when due. Liquidity risk does not imply that a counterparty or participant is insolvent since it may be able to settle the required debit obligations at some unspecified time thereafter.
Loss-sharing agreement An agreement among participants in a clearing or settlement system regarding the allocation of any losses arising from the default of a participant in the system or of the system itself.
Loss-sharing pools Cash, securities or possibly other assets that are provided by the participants in advance and are held by the system to ensure that commitments arising from loss-sharing agreements can be met.

Margin Generally, the term for collateral used to secure an obligation, either realized or potential. In securities markets, it is the collateral deposited by a customer to secure a loan from a broker to purchase shares. In organizations with a central counterparty, the deposit of collateral to guarantee performance on an obligation or cover potential market movements on unsettled transactions is sometimes referred to as margin.
Margin call A demand for additional funds or collateral, following the marking to market of a securities lending transaction, if the market

value of underlying collateral falls below a certain level relative to the loaned asset. Similarly, if the value of the underlying collateral assets, following their revaluation, were to exceed the agreed margin, the return of collateral might be required.

Multilateral net settlement position The sum of the value of all the transfers a participant in a net settlement system has received during a certain period of time less the value of the transfers made by the participant to all other participants. If the sum is positive, the participant is in a multilateral net credit position; if the sum is negative, the participant is in a multilateral net debit position.

Multilateral net settlement system A settlement system in which each settling participant settles (typically by means of a single payment or receipt) the multilateral net settlement position which results from the transfers made and received by it, for its own account and on behalf of its customers or non-settling participants for which it is acting. See also direct participant, multilateral net settlement position, multilateral netting, settling participant/member.

Multilateral netting An arrangement among three or more parties to net their obligations. The obligations covered by the arrangement may arise from financial contracts, transfers or both. The multilateral netting of payment obligations normally takes place in the context of a multilateral net settlement system. See also bilateral netting, multilateral net settlement position, multilateral net settlement system.

Net credit (or debit) position A participant's net credit or net debit position in a netting system is the sum of the value of all the transfers it has received up to a particular point in time less the value of all transfers it has sent. If the difference is positive, the participant is in a net credit position; if the difference is negative, the participant is in a net debit position. The net credit or net debit position at settlement time is called the net settlement position. These net positions may be calculated on a bilateral or multilateral basis.

Net settlement The settlement of a number of obligations or transfers between or among counterparties on a net basis. See also netting.

Net settlement system A funds transfer system whose settlement operations are completed on a bilateral or multilateral net basis.

Netting An agreed offsetting of positions or obligations by trading partners or participants. The netting reduces a large number of individual positions or obligations to a smaller number of obligations or positions. Netting may take several forms which have varying degrees of legal enforceability in the event of default of one of the parties. See also bilateral netting, multilateral netting, novation, position netting, substitution.

Novation Satisfaction and discharge of existing contractual obligations by means of their replacement by new obligations (whose effect, for example, is to replace gross with net payment obligations). The parties to the new obligations may be the same as those to the existing obligations or, in the context of some clearing house arrangements, there may additionally be substitution of parties. See also substitution.

Operational risk The risk that deficiencies in information systems or internal controls could result in unexpected losses.

Overnight money A loan with a maturity of one business day. Also called day-to-day money.

Oversight of payment systems A central bank task, principally intended to promote the smooth functioning of payment systems and to protect the financial system from possible 'domino effects' which may occur when one or more participants in the payment system incur credit or liquidity problems. Payment systems oversight aims at a given system (e.g., a funds transfer system) rather than individual participants.

Participant/member A party who participates in a transfer system. This generic term refers to an institution which is identified by a transfer system (e.g., by a bank identification number) and is allowed to send payment orders directly to the system or which is directly bound by the rules governing the transfer system. See also direct participant/ member, indirect participant/member.

Payment The payer's transfer of a monetary claim on a party acceptable to the payee. Typically, claims take the form of banknotes or deposit balances held at a financial institution or at a central bank.

Payment order An order or message requesting the transfer of funds (in the form of a monetary claim on a party) to the order of the payee. The order may relate either to a credit transfer or to a debit transfer. Also called payment instruction.

Payment system A payment system consists of a set of instruments, banking procedures and, typically, interbank funds transfer systems that ensure the circulation of money.

Payment versus payment A mechanism in a foreign exchange settlement system which ensures that a final transfer of one currency occurs if and only if a final transfer of the other currency or currencies takes place.

Position netting The netting of instructions in respect of obligations between two or more parties which neither satisfies nor discharges those original individual obligations. Also referred to as payment netting, in the case of payment instructions, and advisory netting.

Principal risk The credit risk that a party will lose the full value involved in a transaction. In the settlement process, this term is typically associated with exchange-for-value transactions when there is a lag between the final settlement of the various legs of a transaction (i.e., the absence of delivery versus payment). Principal risk that arises from the settlement of foreign exchange transactions is sometimes called cross-currency settlement risk or Herstatt risk. See also credit risk/exposure.

Real-time gross settlement The continuous (real-time) settlement of funds or securities transfers individually on an order by order basis (without netting).

Remote participant A participant in a transfer system which has neither its head office nor any of its branches located in the country where the transfer system is based.

Replacement cost risk The risk that a counterparty to an outstanding transaction for completion at a future date will fail to perform on the settlement date. This failure may leave the solvent party with an unhedged or open market position or deny the solvent party unrealized gains on the position. The resulting exposure is the cost of replacing, at current market prices, the original transaction. Also called market risk, price risk. See also credit risk/exposure.

Repurchase agreement A contract to sell and subsequently repurchase securities at a specified date and price. Also known as an RP or buyback agreement.

Reserve requirement The obligation for banks to maintain balances (bank reserves) at the central bank in respect of certain types of liabilities (in some cases vault cash can be counted towards this).

Same day funds Money balances that the recipient has a right to transfer or withdraw from an account on the day of receipt.

Securities settlement system A system which permits the transfer of securities: either free of payment (free delivery), for example in the case of pledge; or against payment. Settlement of securities occurs on securities deposit accounts held with the CSD (both private CSDs or a national central bank acting as a CSD) or with the central bank (safe custody operational accounts). In the latter case, the central bank acts as the intermediate custodian of the securities. The final custodian is normally a CSD. Settlement of cash occurs in an interbank funds transfer system (IFTS), through a settlement agent.

Seigniorage In a historical context, the term seigniorage was used to refer to the share, fee or tax which the seignior, or sovereign, took to cover the expenses of coinage and for profit. With the introduction of paper money, larger profits could be made because banknotes cost much less to produce than their face value. When central banks came to be monopoly suppliers of banknotes, seigniorage came to be reflected in the profits made by them and ultimately their major or only shareholder, the government. Seigniorage can be estimated by multiplying notes and coin outstanding (non-interest bearing central bank liabilities) by the long-term rate of interest on government securities (a proxy for the return on central bank assets).
Settlement An act that discharges obligations in respect of funds or securities transfers between two or more parties. See also final settlement, gross settlement system, net settlement, net settlement system.
Settlement agent An institution that manages the settlement process (e.g., the determination of settlement positions, monitoring of the exchange of payments, etc.) for transfer systems or other arrangements that require settlement. See also cash settlement agent, final settlement, multilateral net settlement system, settlement, settlement institution.
Settlement bank Either a central bank or private bank used to effect money settlements.
Settlement interval The amount of time that elapses between the trade date (T) and the settlement date (S). Typically measured relative to the trade date, e.g., if three days elapse, the settlement interval is T+3.
Settlement risk General term used to designate the risk that settlement in a transfer system will not take place as expected. This risk may comprise both credit and liquidity risk.
Settlement system A system used to facilitate the settlement of transfers of funds or financial instruments.
Settling participant/member In some countries, a settling participant in a funds or securities transfer system delivers and receives funds or securities to/from other settling participants through one or more accounts at the settlement institution for the purpose of settling funds or securities transfers for the system. Other participants require the services of a settling participant in order to settle their positions. Currently, in the EC direct participants are by definition also settling participants. See also direct participant/member, tiering arrangement.
Substitution The substitution of one party for another in respect of an obligation. In a netting and settlement context, the term typically refers to the process of amending a contract between two parties so that a third party is interposed as counterparty to each of the two parties and

the original contract between the two parties is satisfied and discharged. See also novation.

Supervision of financial institutions The assessment and enforcement of compliance by financial institutions with laws, regulations or other rules intended to ensure that they operate in a safe and sound manner and that they hold capital and reserves sufficient to support the risks that arise in their business.

Systemically important payment system A payment system is systemically important where, if the system were insufficiently protected against risk, disruption within it could trigger or transmit further disruptions among participants or systemic disruptions in the financial area more widely.

Systemic risk The risk that failure of one participant in a transfer system, or in financial markets generally, to meet its required obligations will cause other participants or financial institutions to be unable to meet their obligations (including settlement obligations in a transfer system) when due. Such a failure may cause significant liquidity or credit problems and, as a result, might threaten the stability of financial markets.

Tiering arrangement An arrangement which may exist in a funds or securities transfer system whereby participants in one category require the services of participants in another category to exchange and/or settle their transactions. See also direct participant/member, indirect participant/member, settling participant/member.

Trade netting A legally enforceable consolidation and offsetting of individual trades into net amounts of securities and money due between trading partners or among members of a clearing system. A netting of trades which is not legally enforceable is a position netting.

Unwinding A procedure followed in certain clearing and settlement systems in which transfers of securities or funds are settled on a net basis, at the end of the processing cycle, with all transfers provisional until all participants have discharged their settlement obligations. If a participant fails to settle, some or all of the provisional transfers involving that participant are deleted from the system and the settlement obligations from the remaining transfers are then recalculated. Such a procedure has the effect of transferring liquidity pressures and possibly losses from the failure to settle to other participants, and may, in an extreme case, result in significant and unpredictable systemic risks. Also called settlement unwind.

Value-at-risk An estimate of the upper bound on losses an institution would expect to incur during a given period (e.g., one day) for a given confidence level (e.g., 95%).
Velocity The average number of times a measure of money (as captured, for instance, by a monetary aggregate) turns over within a specified period of time. The income velocity of circulation is typically calculated as the ratio of a monetary aggregate to nominal GDP.

Zero hour rule A provision in the insolvency law of some countries whereby the transactions of a closed institution that have taken place after midnight on the date the institution is ordered closed may be retroactively rendered ineffective.

Index

GPSR Compliance
The European Union's (EU) General Product Safety Regulation (GPSR) is a set of rules that requires consumer products to be safe and our obligations to ensure this.

If you have any concerns about our products, you can contact us on

ProductSafety@springernature.com

In case Publisher is established outside the EU, the EU authorized representative is:

Springer Nature Customer Service Center GmbH
Europaplatz 3
69115 Heidelberg, Germany

www.ingramcontent.com/pod-product-compliance
Ingram Content Group UK Ltd.
Pitfield, Milton Keynes, MK11 3LW, UK
UKHW040231290926
15471UKWH00002B/133
9781349300556